Play
by
Play

25 Years
of Royals
on Radio

by Denny Matthews
and Fred White
with Matt Fulks

Foreword by
George Brett

Nelson Elliott
Managing Editor

Bob Mead
Editor

Randy Breeden
Art Direction/Design

Cover design by Jerry Hirt

Cover Photo by Chris Vleisides

Insert Section Photos courtesy Denny Matthews and Fred White

Published by Addax Publishing Group, Inc.

For information address:
Addax Publishing Group, Inc.
8643 Hauser Drive, Suite 235, Lenexa, KS 66215

ISBN: 1-886110-78-6

Printed in the U.S.A.

Distributed to the trade by Andrews McMeel Publishing
4520 Main Street
Kansas City, MO 64111

1 3 5 7 9 10 8 6 4 2

Library of Congress Cataloging-in-Publication Data

Play by Play : 25 years of Royals on radio / by Denny Matthews and Fred White with Matt Fulks.
p. cm.
ISBN 1-886110-78-6
1. Matthews, Denny, 1942- . 2. White, Fred, 1936-
3. Sportscasters—United States—Biography. 4. Kansas City Royals (Baseball team)—History. I. White, Fred, 1936- . II. Fulks, Matt. III. Title.
GV742.4.M38 1999
070.4'49796'0922778411—dc21
[b] 99-19435
CIP

Dedication

To my parents, George and Eileen Matthews, who developed my interest in sports and supported it all the way. To my three brothers, Steve, Doug and Mike, who gave me plenty of competition while we were growing up. To my grandmother, Gert Dohm, who found time to take me to St. Louis once a summer to see the Cardinals.
-Denny Matthews

To my parents, Mary and Eddie, who worked so hard for us. To my brother, Jack, the best friend I've ever had. To my sister, Marilyn, who finished my paper route for me on winter evenings so I could practice basketball. And, of course, to Barb and the kids, Stacy, John and Joe.
-Fred White

To my grandma, Betty Koger, for letting me borrow your transistor radio and ear plug so I could listen to the Royals' day games when I was in school. To Helen Pace Fulks, who waited until six days after the completion of this project to be born; may you one day reach all of your goals and have all of your dreams in life fulfilled.
-Matt Fulks

Contents

Acknowledgments

Thank you...to Jack Horenberger, athletic director and baseball coach at Illinois Wesleyan, who somehow thought I might enjoy sports announcing. To Illinois Wesleyan football coach Don "Swede" Larson, who convinced me that someone who had never played high school football could catch passes in college. To Don Newberg and Don Munson, who thought I might be okay on the air at WJBC in Bloomington. To Charlie Brannan, who drove me to St. Louis to tape a Cardinals-Cubs game for my resume tape. To Glen McCullough, who advised me to market my resume tape. To Jack Brickhouse and Jack Rosenberg of WGN in Chicago, who encouraged me to be a big league announcer. To Bud Blattner, who somehow thought I could be a big league announcer for more than a couple of years.

–Denny Matthews

I would like to thank Dave Divan and Elzer Marx, the two people who got me started at WITY in Danville, Illinois. To John Powell, who hired me at KHAS in Hastings, Nebraska. To Jerry Holley, who did the same at WIBW in Topeka. To Bill Glidden, who gave me my first shot with the Royals. To Bob Fromme, our first network manager, the guy who really put it all together. To Bob Stiegler and Nadine Woods, of Royals Radio. To Tom Cheatham, successor to Bob Fromme. To Sue Rayson, successor to Tom Cheatham. To the late Joe Burke, for wise counsel so many times. To Ed Shepherd and Don Free, two terrific producer/engineers. To Buddy Blattner and Denny Matthews, who welcomed me to the booth. To all the guys in uniform, for doing all the things we talked about every night. And, to all the listeners for all the input, through all the years.

–Fred White

Singling out people who helped this dream is nearly impossible, but I do need to personally thank the following (If you're not named, don't take it personally): most importantly, Jesus Christ, through whom all things are possible; Denny and Fred (and Barb) for opening up your incredible memories. I'm truly a better person for knowing you; Kevin and Sarah, thanks for putting up with me; Rhonda Hale, the best travel agent; huge influences, Ken Samelson, Wiss, MoJo, Tom, Gig, Jonathan and Rudy, the Royals family, especially Bob Davis, Steve Fink and Don Free; George Brett for writing the foreword; Bob Snodgrass, Nelson Elliott and everyone at Addax; my favorite in-laws, Todd and Pat Burwell; my parents, Fred and Sharon, my life is not possible without you guys; my brother Josh; and my best friend, Libby, for making sure our first kid (eh, "miracle") wasn't born before January…you've got your husband again. Thank you, all.

–Matt Fulks

Foreword

by George Brett

One of the things I am most proud of from my Major League Baseball career is the fact that all 20 years were spent with the Kansas City Royals. I probably could have gone to other clubs, but why?

Kansas City is a great place to live, and as I am learning now, a perfect place to raise a family. In essence, I have grown up with the Royals family, having joined them in 1971, two years after their inaugural season. I am still with the club, serving as Vice President-Baseball Operations. One motivation for staying in the organization for 28 years is the people. Two of the people who have been a part of that family and history are radio broadcasters Denny Matthews and Fred White.

I grew up in Southern California in the 1960 mainly listening to Vin Scully and Jerry Doggett with the Los Angeles Dodgers in baseball, and Chick Hearn with the Lakers in basketball. Vin is in a special class of broadcasters and is as good as it gets.

Vin Scully had a lot of different partners, whereas Fred and Denny were together as partners for 25 years. When I came up with the Royals in 1973, it was Buddy Blattner and Denny mainly doing the games with a little bit of Fred; then Buddy left shortly after that and it was just Denny and Fred. So I came up as a player with Fred and Denny. Fortunately and unfortunately for me I never got a chance to listen to them while I was playing. It was fortunate in the sense that it meant I was playing, but unfortunate because I rarely got a chance to listen to their broadcast. Playing in the major leagues for 20 years, I got a chance to play in front of a ton of announcers but never really got the chance to listen to any of them for more than a couple minutes. Every once in awhile, a player might go to the clubhouse in the middle of a game to change his sweaty shirt, or change his spikes, or he might break a bat and need to go to the bat supply and find the bat with the best wood in it. At those times he might hear the game for a minute, and that's all. Because of that, it's awfully hard for me to try to compare Denny and Fred to other people because I never really heard any other announcers. There are some other announcers I would enjoy hearing for more than a minute. Bob Uecker in Milwaukee, for instance, would be great to listen to for an entire game. Listening to Fred and Denny since my retirement, I can't imagine many announcers who would be better. They were great as a team.

Probably the most important thing about them was that they knew they worked for the Kansas City Royals - but were not "cheerleaders" for the home team. They were not "homers" like Tom Paciorek and Ken "Hawk" Harrelson with the Chicago White Sox, or Harry Caray and Steve Stone with the Chicago Cubs, but rather Denny and Fred just broadcast the games. Fans could always tell by listening to them if the Royals were winning or losing.

With Denny and Fred it was never "we need a hit" or "we need to strike this guy out if we're going to win" or other comments like those. Some announcers in their gravel-sounding, yet somewhat distressed, voices will say, "Oh no, we gotta strike this guy out or we're going to lose!"

Fred and Denny worked well together but went their separate ways off the field. They both love to play golf, they're both very competitive, but for the most part that may be where the similarities end. Denny is kind of a quiet guy that people don't see much of at all. We didn't see him on the Royals Caravans very often during the off-season. When the team was on the road, we never saw him in the hotel bar late at night, or in restaurants during the day. Even though we hardly ever saw Denny, we knew where he was. Denny would go to his room and watch hockey films or Cubs games. That's how he occupied his time on the road and at home. Denny is always the master of ceremonies at the Royals Awards Dinner, so everyone does get to see him at least once a year.

It was not uncommon to walk into a hotel bar, or a restaurant, or someplace on the road and the next thing we knew there was a drink at our table. When asked who the drink was from, the server would reply, "That gentleman over there," indicating Fred. (I'm sure Denny would have done the same thing, but he was never there.) Fred was everywhere.

Living in Palm Springs one winter, I turned on the television and saw a bowling match, and there was Fred doing the play-by-play for it. He was talking about someone getting a 7-10 split and how that's the toughest in bowling. I thought, "What in the world does this guy know about bowling?!" In the "old days" of the Big 8 Conference, we could turn on our TV to the basketball game of the week and see Fred doing the play-by-play. In early 1999 I turned on a basketball game and there was Fred. Fred has always been out doing broadcasts and has always been in front of the public.

Denny always has great one-liners. My dream growing up was to become a professional athlete; Denny's dream may have to become a comedian. He and Fred worked so well together and were so compatible. In fact, at times they were extremely funny. They could make light of a lot of different situations. Sometimes, when a game is a blow-out, humor is important to keep the audience tuned in...Denny and Fred consistently provided that humor.

For me it was fun reading through *Play by Play* and reliving some of the great times in Royals history, plus remembering some good times that I've shared with Denny and Fred. For instance, Denny and I have had some fun times on the ice rink, even though he usually kicks my tail. Growing up in

Southern California, we didn't skate a lot, obviously, but one of my brothers, Bobby, and I are involved in the ownership of the Spokane Chiefs, a minor league team in Washington. On the other side, Denny is a wannabe hockey player who plays in all sorts of adult leagues. One day he told me that he and some guys had the ice at Kemper Arena and asked if I skated. I told him that I had once or twice in high school but that was about all.

At the time he asked me to play, I had a shoe contract with Hyde Athletic Footwear, which make Spotbilt shoes, but they also make great ice skates. So I told Denny, "You know, I've got my own skates from this company and I'd love to go skating."

I can skate forward pretty well, but I can't stop, turn sharp, or skate backwards. I can skate a long, narrow river pretty well, but if someone tells me to skate around an arena, I have to be sure to slow down to turn, or be ready to fall down, slide on my back, brace my legs and crash into the boards.

All of the guys who play hockey with Denny are really good skaters. They aren't National Hockey League quality, but they're good. Regardless, those guys were skating circles around me. At the end of the day we were all kind of horsing around, when Denny and I squared off into a fake fight. Within 30 seconds, Denny had pulled my long-sleeved baseball undershirt over my head, like those bad fighters in the NHL. My arms were trapped and useless. The next thing I knew, my bare back was on the ice. After skating around for an hour, we were sweating which made the ice even colder. It was pretty embarrassing to have the baseball radio announcer kick my butt on the ice!

After we had gone skating a few times, even though I could only skate straight, I offered to race Denny for five dollars. Ahh...competition. Did I win? I don't remember for sure, but if I lost, I paid him. If I won, gee...let me see...did I ever collect on that?

Fred joined the Royals broadcasts the same year I joined the club in Kansas City - 1973. Since then he has been a great friend to me. A story about Fred that immediately comes to my mind happened one year when the New York Yankees were in Kansas City. Charley Lau, who was the hitting coach for the Yankees at that time, Yogi Berra, and some of the coaches went over to Fred's house after a day game for a barbecue. I was invited to go but had plans earlier in the evening, and got to Fred's at 9:00. By that time they were just starting to put the steaks on the grill (they had about 20 steaks for 10 people). So they put 15 of the steaks on the grill and left the rest in the kitchen.

The steaks had come from the butcher, so they didn't have any type of wrap on them. I took the remaining steaks and put them in one of the cabinets. As the night grew longer, everyone continued to have wine with dinner, and then after-dinner drinks. We had a great time...Charley Lau and I were talking about hitting, while Yogi and Fred held court about something else. We all forgot about the remaining steaks and went our separate ways.

Fred had a black lab retriever named Boo. For the next three or four days, Boo apparently just stood and stared at that cabinet; he would not leave it alone because he could smell the steaks. Finally Fred's wife, Barb, opened the cabinet and there were these steaks that were half-rotten. Fred called me and said, "George, you wouldn't believe what happened. Someone must have put some steaks in our cabinet. Barb opened the cabinet door, and Boo nearly had a heart attack before chowing down on those steaks." Fred, did I ever tell you, that someone was me?

That was an unbelievable night.

Since my retirement I have visited the radio booth to watch a game, sat in between Denny and Fred and talked to the one who was not on the air at the time. During the 1998 season, they let my oldest son Jackson, who was five-years-old then, do an inning of a game. The game was a boring blow-out, so Denny asked Jackson if he wanted to talk on the air. When Jackson got on the air, Denny explained to the audience how they had a guest in the booth, Jackson Brett, and started to ask him a few questions. It was great. At the end of the half-inning, Denny said, "Well, Jackson, thanks, we really appreciate you coming by for half an inning and helping us." Jackson replied, "Are we done?"

"Yeah, we're done."

Jackson exclaimed, "I'll do another inning!"

Denny said, "No, we can't afford you."

"That's okay, I'll do it for free." That may have been the greatest line. Fred almost fell off his chair he was laughing so hard. Sure enough, Jackson got to do another half-inning.

I have had some great times with Denny and Fred, but there have also been some not-so great experiences. During the off-season following the 1998 campaign when Fred was fired. In fact, there were other things going on in the Royals organization during that period that I didn't understand or like. For instance, long-time groundskeeper George Toma was also released from his duties. When George got fired, that really hurt me. He has been like a father to me ever since I came to Kansas City. What made Fred's firing even tougher to swallow was here was the guy who seemed to be at the microphone for every great play in my career. We also had some great times off the field.

A few days after the decision, I called Royals general manager Herk Robinson and told him that we needed to talk. When we met, I said to him, "You don't have to tell me why this happened to Fred White, but I'm curious." I told him that I am still the biggest Royals fan in town, and as a fan, some of the decisions that were being made concerned me. He told me why Fred was fired. Do I agree with the decision? NO! Does Herk have the right to fire Fred? Yes, and that's what he did.

Fred's being fired was almost like a player transaction. A lot of times as a player, a friend would be traded, and we always wondered why our guy got traded for some stiff. A player, though, does not have the luxury of talking to the general manager or telling him that it was a bad trade. Talking to Herk about Fred was my way of letting him know that the decision hurt me as a person. In my Hall of Fame announcement speech on January 5, 1999, I mentioned that meeting with Herk. I really wanted my feelings on Fred's firing to be on the record.

The timing of bringing that forth publicly may have surprised some people, but it was important to me because Fred may have been on the microphone for half of my career of 3,154 hits. Ours was and is a special kind of relationship.

Play by Play has one chapter that talks about my career with the Royals. First of all, I was shocked when I saw the chapter, but I am extremely grateful. One of the topics in the chapter is my respect for the game of baseball, which hopefully is apparent to fans, not only of the Royals, but of baseball. Well, Denny and Fred have that same type of respect for the game, and it showed on every broadcast they ever did together in 25 years. Having that love of the game and their longevity together says so much in professional sports nowadays.

I go to about 20 home games a year, and listen to our broadcasts when I can't be there. Not to take anything away from our TV announcers Bob Davis and Paul Splittorff because they are very good, but I think lots of times people probably turned down the volume on the television and listened to Fred and Denny's radio broadcast. Denny and Fred took an incredible broadcasting trip for a quarter-century, and brought the games home to fans across the Midwest like very few could. Get set as they take you on that journey, behind the scenes, to relive some of the highs and lows of the Royals organization and the broadcasting business. What Denny Matthews, Fred White and Matt Fulks have done with *Play by Play* is provide the reader with these memories in a unique two-person autobiography...I guess one of them without the other just wouldn't seem right.

Introduction

"**Fred, do you** still like the DH (designated hitter)?"

"Yeah, I do. Here's where I've always been on the DH...whether I like it or don't like it, doesn't matter, but I think it needs to be the same in both leagues. What I don't like is the inference that American League baseball is not good baseball because of the DH. American League baseball is fine. Baseball is good with or without it."

"Where I'm going with that question, and I know I'm sawing on an old piece of wood, is to the idea that the balance in baseball has been tipped way too much now in favor of offense. The pitchers are going to have to get a little something back."

"I agree, but you know I really get tired of people saying, 'Well, the DH, that's American League baseball'. That's an inference that the American League is not good baseball. That's patently false."

"The DH is just a small part of the problems that pitchers have. I think the caliber of pitching in the big leagues is made to look a little worse than it really is because of the small strike zone, the DH, and things like that. They're just going to have to do something to get out of that mindset that all people want to do is see offense. That is not true. A good baseball game is not all offense...it never has been and never will be. Unfortunately that's the direction the 'leadership' of baseball has taken this game in the last 10 to 15 years."

"The DH is far from being the biggest problem in the equation."

"I agree with that. The biggest problem is the strike zone."

"I think it's a good game either way. I don't care if they have the DH or not; I wish it was standard in both leagues."

"I really wasn't talking about the DH, I just threw that out there to get the discussion going."

This sounds like a debate between a Chicago Cubs fan and a Chicago White Sox fan, right? Or between a sports radio talk show host and one of his callers? Actually, it was an on-air discussion between Denny Matthews and Fred White, the long-time radio broadcasters for the Kansas City Royals, during a game on April 26, 1998, as the Royals hosted the Texas Rangers.

The phrase "long-time" may not be fair, or entirely accurate; the 1998 season marked the 25th year Matthews and White were on the air together, making them, at that time, the longest-running broadcast crew in the American League. In the National League, they were surpassed only by Jack Buck and Mike Shannon (and by only two years) of the St. Louis Cardinals.

Marty Brennaman and Joe Nuxhall also celebrated their 25th anniversary together in 1998 with the Cincinnati Reds.

If a calculator were put to task, it could be said that Matthews and White did approximately 4,050 games together; or, based on an average three hour game in the American League (although lately they've been more like three-and-a-half hours), the two logged-in about 12,150 hours of play-by-play together. That's almost one-and-a-half years.

To someone hearing that on-air conversation about the DH, someone not familiar with Matthews and White, it might appear that the two were going in opposite directions, or were being curt with each other; actually, it was just an average discussion between two people who worked together for so long.

Can you imagine working with the same person, day-in and day-out in a small office for 25 years? Not many of us can.

The 1998 season also marked their final season together, because Fred White's "handshake contract" was not renewed after the season. The news of White's dismissal sent shock waves to Royals' fans, and nearly incited a listener riot. Many Royals fans have known only Denny and Fred as the team's broadcasters. Many people were not around at the beginning, or had forgotten that legendary announcer Buddy Blattner was the team's original play-by-play man.

The news came as a shock to others, because in a business that tends to breed egos the size of the Truman Sports Complex, White and Matthews have everything *but* big egos. A friend told me a story about seeing one of the broadcasters out one evening sums up Denny and Fred. He saw one of the announcers eating dinner with some friends and family. As the Royals' announcer was leaving, this friend of mine introduced himself and described how he was a big fan of the Royals broadcasts and told of how much he appreciated the broadcasters. He said the broadcaster stopped and talked to him and his wife and baby for a few minutes, before leaving. That's Fred White. That's Denny Matthews.

Away from the microphone Denny and Fred are very similar to Felix and Oscar of *Odd Couple* fame. Denny is somewhat reserved, but Fred enjoys crowds. Denny records, often out of necessity, a sporting event, and knows in advance when he is going to watch it. Fred, by his own account, isn't very mechanical, but he likes to cook. You want to know the funny thing about them? The persona they emit on the air is very much the way they are away from the stadium.

For more than 75 years, from April through early October, Americans have been inviting baseball broadcasters into their homes. Baseball broadcasters who could feed our imaginations better than anyone else could. Many people who grew up without television have said that when they listened to a good baseball announcer, they could almost smell the freshly cut grass. Baseball is a sport that deserves to be on the radio; it may be best-served on the radio. The flow of a baseball game, the length of the game, dictates that we will form a relationship with these announcers. They become a part of our family.

Think, for a second, about some of the pioneers in broadcasting, or some of the broadcasting names and voices we have heard most often. Mel Allen. Red Barber. Harry Caray. Vin Scully. Jack Brickhouse. Curt Gowdy. Ernie Harwell. Sure, most of them have broadcast other sports, but they are remembered, mostly, for what they did behind the microphone in such storied places as Yankee Stadium, or the Polo Grounds, or Wrigley Field, or Sportsman's Park.

Baseball announcers are a special brand of broadcasters. In this day and age of cable television, it takes a unique person to become a good radio broadcaster, let alone become a great one. To many of us, Denny and Fred are great.

I am one of those fans who grew up with White and Matthews; I lived and died Kansas City Royals baseball. They, along with Max Falkenstien doing Kansas Jayhawk games, provided the perceptions of "my" teams.

Because of an incredible family, I was able to go to a ton of Royals' games while I was growing up, but when I couldn't, Pop and I were listening to the radio. I have a cornucopia of incredible memories. My biggest, is 1985. The World Series.That was the year that Royals fever struck and struck hard. We had two tickets to Game 7, but my dad couldn't go, so I called a friend, Jim Wissel. I honestly think that before we hung up the phone he was at my house ready to go. Royals Fever.

As did all of those fans, Wiss and I felt that the Royals were *our* team, and Denny and Fred were *our* broadcasters. For me, they helped form my early impressions of baseball and baseball broadcasters. I would sometimes take my grandma's transistor radio and ear plug to school, hide them in my coat, and then listen to see how the Royals were doing in the playoffs during classtime.

This is a project I started because of that nostalgic love of radio, and especially sports on radio.

The first time I met Denny and Fred was in the summer of 1991, when I was a junior at Lipscomb University, just beginning to break into the sportscasting business. Fred and Denny invited me up to the booth before a game. Immediately, I realized how lucky we were to have these guys as our announcers.

Radio is a wonderful medium and a wonderful art form. The famed architect Frank Lloyd Wright once said, "Television is chewing gum for the eyes." If that is true, then radio must be chewing gum for the mind...for the imagination, with good announcers providing the flavor. For fans of the Kansas City Royals, Denny Matthews and Fred White have been those announcers. Have a listen...

1 25 Years: From Acquaintances to Partners

Denny Matthews

I'm lucky to be in this business. There were over 200 applicants for the number-two job with the Kansas City Royals when I applied in 1968. I basically had no experience, but that ultimately worked in my favor. Branch Rickey said, "Luck is the residue of design." So I'm lucky in the sense that I'm the one who was picked; I got the resume in; had the tape; did the groundwork for it to put myself in that position; I evidently had the ability to do it; it was supposed to be. If all of that is luck, then yes, I'm lucky. The element of luck, or fate, or whatever word you want to attach, was there...it has to be for anything like that to happen. Over those 30 years I've had an opportunity to work with a great organization, and I've had a great partner for 25 of those years, Fred White.

Between the two of us, in our booth over the last 25 years, I think there was an excellent blend of humor, other scores, things going on in baseball as a whole, evaluation of the Royals, evaluation of the Royals versus evaluation of the other teams, respect for the players and ability to describe the difficult job that managers and coaches have. We also had an excellent blend of loyalty to the team. Those things are important for a broadcast team. Play-by-play, what's going on down on the field, is the basic, that's why you're there as a broadcaster, but there needs to be the ability to mix in the other things as well.

The one thing that stands out to me most about Fred is his sense of humor. He's not a particularly moody guy, you pretty much know what you're going to get with him. He's very upbeat, with a great sense of humor. He normally looks for the fun, and human, side of things, which is apparent in his broadcasts, whether it is with the Royals, or when he does college basketball.

I think my assets include real good concentration; a good feel for the game; a good feel for how a pitcher is doing early in a game; anticipation for what might happen in different situations; ability to take two or three plays early in a game and figure out how they fit in now, and then how they impacted things in the 8th inning; and an ability to reflect in my voice if a play was exciting or not, so the listeners can decide if they want to scream. Colorful I'm probably not, because broadcasters in the late 1960s and early 1970s, my generation, essentially, were suppressed from being "characters." I did not intern at ESPN.

With the strengths that each of us brought to the booth, our broadcasts, I felt, were very good, with a good mix of personalities. There were times when fans thought Fred White and I didn't get along because we had our differences on the air. Those differences are normal. Things worked out extremely well; I think duration and tenure tend to prove that. We still get along great. It's been a fine relationship.

AS GOMER WOULD SAY, "SURPRISE, SURPRISE, SURPRISE!"

1973 brought the move to the new stadium, prospects for a successful season, and television. So, Fred joined our broadcast team that year. Before joining the Royals, Fred had been working in Topeka, Kansas, at WIBW, and would come over to Kansas City periodically, so I vaguely knew him. I had never heard any of his work, so I can't say I knew him in that regard, but I knew who he was.

When he joined us, it was a little awkward at first because there really wasn't a lot for him to do; there weren't a lot of games for him to do since not all of the games were televised. My partner, Buddy Blattner, did his six innings, I did my three, then Fred did some fill-in stuff, especially when we were on TV. It was just one of those things where there wasn't much for him to do. It was somewhat awkward, for obvious reasons.

When I began doing the Royals shortly out of college, I was Buddy's protégé, so when he left after the 1975 season, it was just Fred and myself. Fred had never done baseball at a professional level before joining the Royals, and I hadn't been doing games for very long, so it was really kind of an interesting situation when we began working alone together.

When Bud retired, and I took over the number one play-by-play job, I had to be concerned about carrying the game. Bud had carried the game because he had the beginning and the end with some innings mixed in the middle, which is also how the broadcasts were structured with Fred and myself. At that time, Fred took over my spot as the number two man. At the very outset I told him that, for his three innings, I was not going to crowd him.

My philosophy, as a result of working with Bud, was that if one of us had something to say while the other was on the air, then we would say it. I never wanted either of us to feel like we couldn't jump in and say something. On the other hand, don't feel like you have to keep talking, because if you do, then it's going to sound forced and it's going to sound phony. We've all heard broadcasts where the guy who isn't doing the play-by-play thinks he has to keep saying things, and it sounds awful. You just want to tell him to shut up.

If Fred or I wanted to make a comment, or if all of a sudden something occurred to one of us and we thought something needed to be said, then we would say it. Chances are it would be a good and timely comment. That is the way Fred and I always worked. When he would say something, it was meaningful. He didn't just sit over there on-line and babble, nor did I when he was on the air.

Even though Fred and I started working together on the brink of the team's break-out season, I don't necessarily think it helped us blend together any better.

Personally, how the team does has no effect on me as a broadcaster. In fact, if the team is bad, I think I have to bump it up a notch and be better. If the Royals are losing, as a broadcaster I don't take it personally, and I don't let it drag me down. If the team is doing well, then you are perceived as being better because the message is better. That automatically makes you better in the eyes of the fans.

By the same token, when we say something on the air about a Royals player, or the team, it's fair and you don't need to dwell on it, whether it's good or bad. A good play is a good play. Okay, forget about it and go on to the next pitch. A bad play is a bad play. If it costs you the game, it costs you game. An announcer has got to say it, because it's a fact. I, as a broadcaster, didn't have anything to do with it; I'm just telling you what happened. I didn't make the play or not make the play. Yes, there are times I am critical on the air. A good play is a good play, and a bad play is a bad play; and there's no difference in saying it.

Overall, I doubt the team's success helped us blend together any better, although it may have helped to make the experience more pleasant, overall. When the team is winning, everyone around the team and everyone in the front office is in a better mood. The key was that we established our style right from the get-go. It seemed to work pretty well, and it got us off and running as a team.

THE GAMES ARE FUN, BUT OH, TO BE BACK IN THE GOOD OLD DAYS...

There are several things I really enjoy about this business. First and foremost, I enjoy the people who I get to meet, because those relationships endure. And there are some memorable games, but eventually the memories of those fade, in a sense. They're still exciting to think about, but they fade over time. Friendships and relationships, hopefully, endure.

I love doing the games. To sit down and do a game is fun, for the most part. Sometimes there are games that are just crappy, and no fun to do. Unfortunately, there are more and more games that are over three hours in length, and it's not the length of those as much as it is the brutal pace when nothing is happening. The hardest thing to do is to keep talking, and in some of those games, there is really virtually nothing to talk about. That bothers me. That has kind of soured me over the last 10 years - the way the games have begun to lengthen out. It was a piece of cake 25 years ago because most of the games lasted between 2:15 and 2:40.

When we were in Cleveland in 1998 there was an interesting feature in their newspaper that we were eventually laughing about. In the *Cleveland Plain Dealer* they ran a box score every day of how the 1948 Indian team did on that particular day. The paper did a tiny story, and included the box score. On our last road series in 1998, we noticed that the 1948 Indians had played a game that encompassed two hours and 10 minutes. The next game was

2:08. Then they had a double-header against the Washington Senators in which the first game lasted one hour and 30 minutes, and the second game took two hours and 16 minutes. They played two games in the amount of time, now, that it takes to play a lot of single games. All the team's games were being broadcast by 1948. It would have been a snap, a piece of cake, to broadcast a game at that time.

Nine innings in 90 minutes? An announcer's brain would never get into that lull period where we're just fried, and racking our brains for new things to say. To talk extemporaneously for 1:30, or for 2:10, or 2:16, versus 3:23, on an average - I would love to go back to the 1940s and 1950s and broadcast under those conditions. Granted, the 90-minute game was an exception, but the two hour games were not the exception, those were the rule. If they had a game lasting 3:45 back then, it was probably a 16 or 17 inning game, instead of nine, like today.

IN THE ZONE

A comfort zone has kept me with the Royals all of these years. The organization, under owner Ewing Kauffman, was excellent. The people, for the most part, have kept me here; the people I've worked with and the people I've worked for. The city. The livability of the town.

I thought when I came to the Royals in 1969 that I would work in Kansas City for five or six years, then try to go to Chicago or St. Louis, since I grew up in Bloomington, Illinois, which is right between the two cities. I had grown up a St. Louis fan, so to me at that time the ideal job, the dream job, was doing Cardinals baseball. When I was in high school, then college, before I began to formulate ideas about broadcasting baseball, I had been shooting toward becoming a player.

When the broadcasting thing popped up in college, I had a chance to do three years of high school and college basketball and some high school football while I was a student at Illinois Wesleyan. I started to kick the broadcasting idea around in the back of my mind as a possible career. With that, I figured the dream jobs would be doing either the Cardinals or the Cubs, or something else in Chicago. I guess if you're unhappy in a job, you try to get a different job or you try to move. If you're not unhappy, you feel comfortable, and even if a new opportunity comes along, you don't really pursue it. There have been other opportunities (interestingly enough, in Chicago and in St. Louis with the Cardinals), but I'm happy in Kansas City. After all, I've had some great times in this organization, ranging from the great moments on the field, to the good friends I've made, to even watching the veterans show the ropes to the rookies on road trips.

Most of the pranks toward the rookies, things that have probably been going on as long as baseball has been played were pretty harmless, but they were funny. For instance, a lot of times the veterans will charge a couple of room service bills to a rookie's room and see how he handles it. Or, they'll take a rookie out for dinner and some drinks, including tequila shots. Then, unbeknownst to the rookie, he's getting tequila shots while everyone else is getting water in their shot glasses. He starts to wobble and he can't figure out why the veterans aren't. Before things get out of hand, the veterans take the rookie back to his hotel room, and everyone calls it a night.

We have had a couple interesting flights. One that sticks out was a flight to Chicago. We had an "abort" going into O'Hare for a landing. We were about 1000 feet off the deck on the long final approach when the pilot did a full throttle on the engines and we went almost straight up. I knew what was going on, and it really wasn't that scary; a plane that had just landed hadn't cleared the runway yet, so the controller in the tower told our captain to make another pass. Some people on board were startled by it but I was pretty sure what was happening, so it really didn't bother me. I guess if you don't know what's happening you might be scared, but you didn't have to be Einstein to figure it out. That was memorable.

SHEP AND DON...A BROADCASTER'S DREAM

Maybe the most important person in the booth is the producer/engineer. He basically gets us on the air, and helps us stay on. We've been pretty lucky because in the 30-year history of our broadcasts, we've only had two producers/engineers, Ed Shepherd and Don Free. When you work with someone for that long, you don't have to be concerned with them doing their job, and that's great. If we're wondering about how competent our partner is, or how competent the engineer is, then it's detracting from our concentration. That hasn't been something we've had to worry about. Having that comfort zone, that comfort level, has been a great asset.

It was tremendous when I first started, having an experienced producer, Ed Shepherd. The Royals family lost a great friend when he died in 1992. He was a real easy going veteran of both radio and television engineering. Before joining the Royals, he had worked for the Kansas City Athletics. Ed was a real pleasure to work with because he was so easy going. Since he was a low key guy, there was no pressure on us. He just let us do our thing, he stayed out of the way, and did his thing. And, I might add, he did his job very, very well.

He was also very knowledgeable; he knew a lot, about a lot. To talk to him, you wouldn't think that he knew a lot about baseball, but every once in a while he'd blow his cover and say something that would make us realize that he knew a lot more than he let on. Shep was unconventional - he didn't care about cars, he didn't care about clothes, he just cared about people; that was his thing.

His health partially played into his leaving after the 1985 season, but he was also just ready to shut it down. He had traveled enough, seen all the piano bars in America, and was tired of it, just like everybody else in this business. I think 95% of the people who have left baseball would say they did it because of the traveling. When Ed left, Don Free took his spot.

Don is extremely dedicated to his job; he's very meticulous, he's a perfectionist. He knows baseball, and he knows engineering. He and Ed – both wizards with wires and electronics. People bring things to them that don't work, and five minutes later they work. Don is always the first to get to the booth, and the last to leave.

We depend a ton on these guys. On the rare occasion when one of the two hasn't been around, someone else has filled in, and it's a little bit awkward. We realize then how comfortable we are and how skillful they are. It's one of those things taken for granted because they're always there. All of a sudden they are gone for a couple of days and we think, "Wow, it isn't as easy as they've been making it look!" It's not as easy on you as a result of that. Yes, we've been lucky with Shep and Don.

CLOSING A QUARTER CENTURY

It was obviously 25 great years working with Fred. People, almost without exception, really enjoyed what we did, or at least what we tried to do. Fred works hard, he has a great sense of humor, and he's easy to be around. It's a pretty small booth, and when you work that closely with someone every night or day for six or seven months, there might be a tendency for friction. Fred and I always got along and seldom had a cross word. We would argue and debate things, which was normal, but we never crossed swords. We disagreed about some things, but that happens to everybody. We got along great.

I think we certainly had an influence on people. From time to time I think about what we've meant to people. We get letters from people explaining how, for instance, their mother can't move around much and is confined to the house, but, as the highlight of her day, she religiously turns on her radio every night at 6:45 to listen to the Royals. Ironically things like that have an impact on us, too. Those letters show us that we've made a difference for people.

When I heard that Fred's contract had not been renewed at the end of the 1998 season, it was disappointing in the sense that for the most part our broadcasts have been well-received for 25 years. I have said it before: I will put our broadcasts up against any in baseball, and I think we're going to finish in the top five. That is the disappointing aspect of it. Fred was fired because some people felt there was a need for change, but I think there might have been a little better way of doing that, like bringing in a young guy to work with us. Then the perception would be that Denny and Fred have accepted this guy, so he must be okay. Then the listening public is willing to give him a chance.

But with the way they did it, some people are left unhappy and confused, and they don't understand why. Now the new guy gets raked over the coals, not giving him the best of it either, in a sense. It could have been done in a much more orderly fashion; one that made a little more sense.

It is going to be quite a transition as I break in the new guy. Buddy broke me in when I started, so it might be a similar situation for me now, breaking in someone else. It is hard to imagine working 25 years in close quarters with one person who is better or easier to get along with than Fred.

Fred White

I first heard Denny broadcast Royals games while I was the sports director with WIBW-TV in Topeka, Kansas. Out of necessity I listened to every game as much as I could while waiting for the 10:00 sports, so I would know what was happening. I was stunned at how good he was. He was better than I thought he would be, after hearing the team had hired a young guy to work with Buddy Blattner. He was an outstanding play-by-play guy the first time I heard him. I had expected to hear a young, inexperienced guy who they were going to try to cultivate. I was mistaken.

FROM ACQUAINTANCES TO PARTNERS

When I first started with the Royals, there was a cushion of a couple years, 1973 and 1975, when Buddy, Denny and I were all there. When you are working with someone, as Denny and I did with each other, working relationships just kind of develop into whatever they're going to eventually become. Personally, I've always been comfortable working with other people; it has never been a problem for me. Our relationship just grew from the first day on. When Buddy left, there we were, the two of us together, Denny and Fred. I've always had a lot of respect for his abilities as a play-by-play guy, and joining him was an easy thing for me to do.

The only thing I didn't really like in the beginning was the format, which to me was strange, because the announcers did not really work together. Denny was trained to be on the air by himself, and leave Buddy alone. But when I was doing play-by-play I would ask them questions to try to draw them into conversations. It was different than I was used to, but it was still very easy. Because of that style, and the fact that we weren't alone for the first couple seasons, the formation of a close relationship may have been slowed somewhat. It's funny, though, because people used to comment about how Denny and I sounded alike on the air. We don't really think we did, but if enough people say it, we've got to think that it may be true. I don't know if that happened over the course of time, or if we just picked up on certain ways each of us said things. Either way, we were doing something right in order to stay together for 25 years.

Denny was always easy to get along with. We are different, yet we come from the same part of the country with somewhat similar backgrounds. The important similarity is that we were both young guys who loved baseball. We loved what we were doing, so it was very easy to get along.

Our relationship is very easy. Denny and I both grew up in similar towns in Illinois. One thing about growing up as baseball fans in the state of Illinois when we did is that we grew up listening to the same baseball announcers. We grew up with Jack Brickhouse, Bob Elston and Harry Caray. They had as big an influence on Denny and me as anybody did. Those are three pretty good broadcasting role models.

Denny is a confirmed bachelor, and I'm a married guy who enjoys being that. (That creates different lifestyles right off the bat.) Denny loves hockey, I love college basketball.

Socially, we have never done a lot together. In the early days we went out and had a beer after the game, and various things like that. We used to play golf together once in a while, and still do. We were together 162 games a year, and in the booth together for four or five hours a day, for seven months a year, for 25 years, so we didn't need to go out and have dinner to get to know each other.

One thing we have in common is that neither of us ever felt the need to go out and do things together. That is the way it should be; Denny has his friends and I have mine. Four or five hours a day is plenty of time to get to know someone. Since Denny is very much a live-and-let-live kind of person, we have a very easy relationship. I enjoyed working on the air with him.

When it all came down to it, we both wanted the same things. We wanted a good broadcast, and we wanted to be happy doing what we were doing. We just approached it differently. We probably have different theories on what a good broadcast should be, regardless of the sport, but I think that actually helped our broadcasts through the years.

This might sound strange, but we weren't fast friends. We certainly weren't enemies; we were just two guys who worked together and got along together. Things grew out of that. That was always good enough for us.

DENNY

Denny is very thorough. That is the first thing that comes to mind when I think about him. He is a creature of habit; Denny does everything today exactly the way he did it when he began. Denny is not a guy who likes change; he likes everything to stay the same and he keeps everything the same in his life. Denny probably still likes the same things he liked when he was 15 years old. He's still a hockey fan. He's still a baseball fan. He just hasn't changed much down through the years. Denny would probably make a great hermit if he chose to do that.

He is very deliberate. Once he gets a routine set, he's going to keep that routine because it works well for him.

Denny, I think, is a terrific baseball announcer. He is as accurate and as fair as anyone I have ever seen or heard. I sat next to him for 25 years and watched each game, listening to him do the play-by-play, and I have complete confidence in his ability to paint you an accurate word picture of what's going on at the ballpark. I don't think I can pay him a bigger compliment than that.

THEY KEEP US GOING...AND GOING...

We were lucky with the Royals in that we had only two engineers/producers. Some clubs experience a much higher turnover, but I worked with two great ones in Ed Shepherd and Don Free.

Ed Shepherd was a very bright man. He knew a little bit about a little bit of everything. He read a lot. He was very interested in every city he visited, and he did interesting things in each city. For instance, once during an off-day in Boston he signed up as a spear-carrier in the opera *Aida.* He often did things like that. He was a very curious human being, always learning.

After the 1985 season, he decided he had been doing it long enough, and left the business. I guess it was kind of a good way to go out for him. He went out the year we won the World Series. That was appropriate for Shep.

When Ed left, he was replaced by Don Free, who is still the producer. He is a very hard working bulldog-kind of a guy who is very thorough in everything he does. He's quite different from Ed. Yeah, each of them is unique and very bright in his own way. I guess all engineers are kind of unique, but I was lucky to work with two great ones.

IMPACTING A REGION

It makes me feel terrific when fans express outrage toward the Royals and Entertainment Communications, Inc. (Entercom) about the decision to not bring me back after the 1998 season. I never realized how much people cared about me. It gives me a great feeling to know that they will take the time to let it be known, and stand up for me. The reaction has come from all kinds of people.

I don't think so much about the impact I've had on them, as I do about the impact they've had on me. I've really appreciated a lot of people who do watch and listen, people involved in the stations, as well as Royals listeners. It really is meaningful when I see someone, or get a letter from someone who's a shut-in, and they tell me how much the broadcasts mean to them.

When I really feel like we are important to our listeners is when a letter comes from a guy who writes, "You wouldn't understand this, but I ride a tractor all day, and listen to the Royals on radio, and it gives me great pleasure." I always write them back explaining, "Yes, I do understand, because that's exactly what I did when I was a young guy." Growing up in a farm community, as I did, there were a lot of days when we were out there working, with a ballgame on the radio.

I told my wife, Barb, after we found out that I wouldn't be back after the

1998 season, that we lost a good job, but we also found out that we're rich in a lot of ways. When you find out that many people care that much about you, it gives you a whale of a warm feeling. I will forever feel indebted to the people who did that.

FRED ON FRED

Describing myself, I would say that I'm simply a play-by-play guy who has been pretty lucky and has had a lot of fun. That's probably my best self-description. I'm a guy who worked to earn what I got, and then had a great appreciation for it. I'm not flashy, and not spectacular. I bring a work ethic to the job. I'm as accurate as possible, which is all I ever wanted to be. My feeling is that when a game ends, if the listeners know what happened and they don't know my name, then I did a pretty good job that day. Notoriety and being a big name announcer have never meant anything to me.

Beyond that, I'm a guy who greatly values his family and friends, loves life and likes having a good time. I liked to go out after a Sunday game, and play golf with my wife and son. I love to meet with friends and go to Stroud's. I don't have a large number of friends, but the friends I do have are really good ones and I enjoy their time. Hopefully I'm a good friend to other people. I like people, and always have. I've enjoyed people and enjoyed being around them.

There are no regrets for me. I can honestly say that if I could go back and choose my profession again, or choose my wife and family, I would choose the same ones I have now. I wouldn't change a thing.

I just see myself as a small-town guy who happened to pop up with a pretty good job and found a pretty good life somewhere along the line, had three great kids, and a great wife, Barb. It just doesn't get any better than that. I don't know what I would change, why I would want to change, or what I could ask for that's any better than this.

THIS ISN'T HOW I EXPECTED IT TO END

I was shocked when I first found out that the Royals and the broadcast rights holder, Entercom, were not going to bring me back to broadcast games after the 1998 season. A lot of emotions played into it from my side; I was shocked and hurt, and it made no sense to me. It still doesn't, and it probably never will. The reaction in Kansas City after it happened was amazing. People still ask me about it, but I don't have an answer for them. All I was ever told was that the "powers that be" wanted to "go in a different direction; a younger, fresher sound."

My basic feeling is that it should never have happened. I'm a more knowledgeable person about the combination of baseball and broadcasting than the four people are who made the decision. People whose opinions I respect, such as scouts, who watched our games and listened at the same time; other broadcasters; and guys we worked with like Paul "Split" Splittorff and John "Duke"

Wathan, thought we had one of the best broadcasts in baseball. These guys know the game and baseball broadcasts far better than do the people who made the decision to fire me.

The decision to end the three man booth, with Duke and Split working with us, was a mistake. That was a good baseball broadcast, but these same people decided to do away with that after the 1997 season. We realized then that we were working for people who didn't really appreciate or understand a good baseball broadcast.

After all the public reaction to my firing, the Royals and Entercom tried to put different spins on it. At one point, they were quoted as saying that there really wasn't much reaction, and what there was was split 50-50. SIMPLY NOT TRUE!

The truth is this: they would not listen to their fans, our listeners. At the end of November, 1998, about a month after it happened, I found out there were 800 messages to the *Kansas City Star,* 500 messages to KMBZ radio, and probably as many to the Royals and to me (2,000 in all), as well as countless calls to the talk shows. And that is just in Kansas City; it doesn't count places like Topeka, Wichita, Omaha and all the other places where it's going on around the network. The reaction in almost every case was, "What are they doing?!"

The answer to that question is that they didn't care what the fans wanted. They had what they wanted, whatever that was (is). Sadly, an organization built by Ewing Kauffman, who prided himself on loyalty and rewarded others for theirs, wound up in the hands of people who have none.

The people who really count in my life are on my side, it seems to me. There really are only four people who aren't on my side, and they happen to be the four guys who made the decision.

As a matter of fact, during George Brett's press conference at Kauffman Stadium on January 5, 1999, to announce his induction into the Baseball Hall of Fame, he mentioned my firing by telling about a conversation he had with General Manager Herk Robinson. George recounted, "I asked him [Herk] some questions and he was very, very honest with me about some things that were going on. One thing in particular, I'll be very honest with you, the Fred White firing, because Fred's a very dear friend of mine. I wanted to know why he got fired, and I said, 'You don't have to tell me if you don't want to, Herk.' And he gave me his answer of why."

George, in one of his finest moments, was taking time to care about somebody else. It makes me feel good to know that people like George are standing behind me. When George was talking about that conversation, Herk turned really red.

Personally, I'm disappointed that Herk didn't prevent my firing. He had nothing close to a good reason for doing it. He could have stood up and saved my job, but he didn't; and then he could never give me a good reason why it happened. The closest he ever came to giving me a reason was to say that Denny and I sounded too much alike; yet he thinks Denny is a great baseball announcer - so where is the problem with us sounding alike?

In all fairness to Herk, my firing wasn't all his responsibility, but he probably listened to the wrong people. Who knows, maybe he is completely responsible for everything that happened. Regardless of who had the initial idea, I do hold Herk accountable because he had the ability to stop it.

Herk's comment to the press was that the ratings had dropped. My answer to that is that attendance is down by a million people from its peak and so is interest in the team. If he could put a winning team on the field, creating more fan interest, then I could probably bring his ratings up. (I wouldn't be responsible for the increase, but the ratings would naturally go up if the team were better.) Call me naive, but I don't think I'm personally responsible for the drop in ratings; it was a group effort.

On the other side of the coin, I have no ill-feelings at all toward the people who applied for the job. I would have done it myself. In fact, they would've been crazy if they didn't apply. It's a helluva job, and they should want it.

In fact, I would take the job back, given the opportunity. I would like to come back because I feel like I should, and I would feel vindicated. Mostly, I would want to come back because I love what I have done and I love Kansas City. If I did come back, I probably would be working for different people, and that would be okay.

I don't know what I'll end up doing, but it would be great to stay in this area. My wife is from Kansas. My two older kids are in Kansas. One is in Topeka, one is in Manhattan. The quality of life in Kansas City is better than it is in most places. The Royals were a terrific organization for a long time, and the games were fun. Travel is easier from here in the middle of the country, and that's an important consideration during basketball season. Basically, Kansas City has become home after all these years. I grew up in a small town where people were very close, and because of that I've always liked the sense of community that we get in Kansas City.

If I never do another Royals game after the 1998 season, when it's all said and done, you remember people more than you remember things or moments. I've met a lot of really great people, and I will always remember those friends that I made in the game and the experiences we had.

Obviously there were great baseball moments in the 25 years; the playoffs, the World Series, the George Brett highlights, Dennis Leonard's comeback, and I could go on and on about different moments. But the moments really fade compared to the memories of the guys and the fans I met along the way.

I would like to thank my family for helping me pursue my dream. You know I love you for that, and so much more. Thank you to the fans for letting me into your homes, and for sharing your summer evenings with me; I hope it was half as much fun for you as it was for me. All the guys who wore the Royals uniform and made the memories possible, especially George, Jamie, Duke, and Split...great friends, and great pros every one. Every one of them is everything a Kansas City Royal and a friend should be.

Finally, I want you to know that I close this with no bitterness. I had 25 great years in the booth and cherished every one of them. If someday, somehow, I can do something to help give the fans back the kind of Royals they want, and deserve, I'm ready.

2 The 1990s: Rebuilding Faith

Fred White

The infamous strike of 1994 will forever blemish baseball in the 90s. No playoffs. No World Series. I'm still startled at how dumb the people who ran baseball and the players were. They had a season going that was even better than the 1998 season, with so many things happening - from guys trying to hit .400, to guys putting up huge home run numbers, to teams accomplishing great things.

It is just absolutely incredible to me that (no matter what the differences were between the owners and players) they could pull a plug on a season like that. Fans were in love with baseball. The game, in that regard, was healthy and thriving. The 1994 baseball strike may have been the greatest public relations mistake in the history of sports. My feeling was that differences should have been put off until the end of the season. Finish the season, it's too good. Fight in the winter time, and let the fans have this season. Obviously they weren't listening to me.

Eventually most of the fans will come back. The 1998 season certainly was helped with the home run race of Mark McGwire and Sammy Sosa. As long as you can give the fans something to really get into they are going to be interested. Baseball has always been a great game, and it always will be. The game hasn't changed, and the people in it haven't changed, but some of the issues have changed.

Fans want no more than to be able to afford to come to the ballpark and to watch a good ballgame and to watch good ballplayers perform. I don't think people care about all the other stuff. Quite frankly, I don't either. I'm still a fan and that's what I want to see, too; the game on the field. I don't want to hear about 70-million dollar payrolls, or about the differences between the players union and the owners. I don't want to hear about any of that stuff. Just get me to the ballpark and show me a ballgame. That's all the fans really want.

If baseball will keep the labor problems out of the news and let the fans enjoy the game on the field, the game will be fine. There is still a little hangover effect from that strike, and there probably always will be in some fan's minds. Some of the fans really felt jilted over that and I think they had a right. I felt that way myself.

As we approached a possible strike that season, I was worried, because we knew that a lot of people were going to be hurt. Unfortunately, most of the people who wound up being hurt were people who had no voice in the thing. Many were people who worked at baseball stadiums around the country and used the income to put their kids through school, or pay off medical bills. The same situation prevails today. Some of those people don't have much disposable income and they depend on what they get from working at the stadium. We worry about them.

Stauffer Publications (Royals radio rights holder in 1994) lost a ton of revenue on the broadcasts. Advertising revenue was simply lost. It was a major blow to the company, and it bothered me because of all the people who had no voice in the matter. They had to take the hit and there was nothing they could do about it.

On a personal level, the strike didn't affect the broadcasters' incomes, but if there is another one, it will be a different story. We went through two strikes and a mini-strike, and our company was good enough, each time, to continue providing our salaries - conceding that we had agreed to broadcast all the games in the season, whether, in essence, there were any games or not. Since that was the agreement, we were paid for the season. But that won't happen again. Henceforth, we were told, a strike would void our agreements. At the very least, we would have to re-negotiate, based on whatever was being salvaged of the season.

My argument was that we had set aside that block of time and we at least deserved something in the way of a retainer to keep that block of time open. During the time off, for instance, we couldn't go out and get another job somewhere, because if the season were to resume, we had to go back to work. We didn't know. The strike certainly wasn't our fault.

As we went through the early part of the season, obviously we kept hoping the strike wouldn't happen. If there had been better leadership from both the owners and the players, and maybe a little more common sense, then it never would have happened. Egos were involved. Leaders on both sides were in the mode of "I'm going to show you." The owners always say, "We're going to break them this time." Well, they are not going to do that. The players never buckle. Then the owners look around at the end of the season and say, "My God, we are losing a lot of money. We better get the game back on the field." The players think the same thing. Sounds like your garden-variety strike to me!

Since it's pretty obvious at the beginning what is going to happen - why not prevent it? We need to reach the point where we have the kind of leadership on both sides capable of saying, "Hey, we are not going to let this happen again." And there is a better labor climate now - better than we've had in a long time.

But in 1994, instead of watching what began as a promising season, I sat at home and watched television. Even though we had a feeling that the strike could last a few days, I really didn't do anything extravagant. Basically, I spent time with my family and sat around. Every time CNN's *Headline News* made that little tone signaling the sports headlines, I ran to the TV. I sat around every day hoping it would end.

And I felt guilty. I don't know why, because I didn't have anything to do with it, but a lot of people involved in the game felt some guilt. It was just no fun to talk with people about the labor issues, instead of talking about what a great game it is, and about the pennant race, and all the other things.

I look back at it to this day and wonder how the baseball "powers" could have done it, and ask myself how could they have been so selfish and so petty, to pull a plug on a season like that? They aren't over it yet. It cost them so much. Whatever they gained from it didn't make up for what it cost them.

THE 1990s: DID YOU SAY PROGRESS OR REGRESS?

Watching the Royal's progress, or lack thereof, during the 90s has been difficult, because of what happens to the people we want to do well. Strictly from a broadcast standpoint, the team's development never really bothered me because obviously, we would do the games in good times and bad. But when the team is doing poorly, broadcasting games is not as easy as it was when the team is doing well. We hate to see what has happened to the franchise and we hate it for the fans.

There are a few reasons I think things have gone the way they have during this decade: the 1985 team winning the World Series (I'll explain in a minute); the illnesses of Dick Howser, Mr. Kauffman and Joe Burke; and John Schuerholz leaving.

Because the 1985 team won the World Series, I think the front office decided to keep the team together for a year longer than normally would have been the case. (Remember, that wasn't an unbeatable team.) Some changes were made at the end of that season, but I think the front office would have made a lot of changes, and probably would have retooled the team more, had they not won.

Then there was the sickness of manager Dick Howser. During the 1986 season, he was diagnosed with a brain tumor. When he became ill, the Royals did a very humane thing with him. In an effort to give Dick hope when he had to stop managing, they didn't replace him. They could have gone out and tried to hire someone like, say, a Tony LaRussa (who was available) to manage the team, but they didn't. They left Dick in there as manager (in name only) and brought in Billy Gardner to run the team in the interim. Unfortunately, that didn't work out.

The Royals wanted Dick to have that carrot out in front of him; the hope that he could be back and manage the team again some day. I think they did the right thing, and it was something that I really admired them for at that time, but it may have cost them a couple of years. I think they did it knowing it would cost them a little bit, but it also showcased what the organization under owner Ewing Kauffman was all about. Family. Compassion. Loyalty.

Shortly after Dick passed away in 1987, the front office decided John Wathan should take over as manager, whether he was ready or not. He was rushed along, but he eventually became a good manager.

Then as Mr. Kauffman began getting along in years, management felt some urgency to win one more for him, so a couple of guys were signed who maybe shouldn't have been; and there were a couple of trades that mortgaged a little bit of the future of the ballclub - trying to win one more for Mr. K. Unfortunately that didn't work out either.

I think it was a combination of things that started the team on the downhill slide. Things snowballed on them and it's like a lot of things - no one in the organization could stop the slide after it reached a certain point. Things are probably going to hit rock bottom, but when the team gets the new owner here, perhaps things will begin to turn around.

It's a thrill to sit in Kauffman Stadium, look up on the hill and see all those flags up there. It's like running newsreels backward through my mind to see Splittorff and George Brett and Frank White and Hal McRae and Dennis Leonard and Freddie Patek — all those guys who we watched play. As we look back now we realize how good those teams really were. They worked hard, they played hard — they were just champions. I think they made the city very proud; the city really adopted them. And many of them became lifelong Kansas Citians.

That says something pretty special about their relationship and about this city and about what kind of people live here. I think we'll see all that again, I really do. I firmly that believe this is just a great place and that the right owner is going to put the organization back on its feet.

BUILDING THE MINOR LEAGUES TO SURVIVE

For a small market team like the Kansas City Royals to survive in baseball's economics today, a solid minor league system needs to be built, similar to what the Royals had in the 1970s and into the 80s. That is possible, and it's the only thing the team can do if it hopes to compete and win. The Royals certainly can't go out and compete for free agents with the dollars they have now. Unless the rules change dramatically, the Royals won't even be able to compete for their own players, after the guys reach free agent status. Cases in point include recent players like Jay Bell, Dean Palmer and Jose Offerman.

The first thing they should do is change arbitration. In fact, just get rid of it. Current baseball arbitration really isn't arbitration anyway.

The screwed up thing about arbitration for a club like the Royals, is this: If the New York Yankees have a guy who hit .260 with two home runs and 23 runs batted in, but they still want him on the roster, they might pay him 2.5-million dollars. If the Royals have a guy who does the same thing and they don't think he's worth $2.5-million, and he goes to arbitration, the arbitrator simply looks and says this guy with the Yankees did this and he made this much, so this guy with the Royals gets it, too. There are arbitrators who really aren't baseball guys. If they had an arbitration panel made up of baseball guys, they might look at that example and say, "No, that guy doesn't deserve that kind of money for that kind of performance. Here's what we think he should get." That would help. But that's the first thing I would get rid of, because I see that as a bigger issue than free agency.

It is possible to develop good players and to have a good minor league system. Theoretically it should be easier because the team is drafting at a better position than it used to, when it was a good ball club. Then, if a player gets to the big leagues, the team has control of him for a period of time before free agency becomes a factor. In turn, the parent club can keep a fresh supply of talent coming out of that minor league system, and maintain a reasonably competitive team.

It is very possible for smaller market teams to develop such a minor league system, and we'll see the day when the Royals do it again. After all, a strong minor league system is precisely how the team got to the top in the first place.

LOSING A LEADER, LOSING FOCUS

One of the most dramatic events ever to affect this organization occurred in August of 1993, with the death of Ewing Kauffman. It hardly needs saying that what he did for this franchise and this city is immeasurable; not only with his baseball involvement, but also his civic work.

The overall philosophy in the Royals organization may have changed after that, but some of that should be attributed to the simple lack of ownership. Since that time I think general manager Herk Robinson has had to decide what the new owners "may" want, without knowing who the new owners are. There hasn't been a Ewing Kauffman or a Joe Burke there to say this is what we want out of this thing; here's how much money you have to run with; let's get it done this way. Herk has had to take all of that upon himself, plus be the general manager, and he has had to try to make trades and do all of those kinds of things. How has he done? History will decide how the Royals fared on Herk's watch. I will leave my opinion out of it.

At some point, however, things changed from "This is our philosophy," to "What is our philosophy?" It's still a work in progress. They are still trying to figure it out, and I'm not sure it's going to be clarified until the new owner is in place and they can all sit down and say, "Okay, here is where we are going and this is how we are going to get there."

MAKING THE PERFECT STADIUM EVEN MORE PERFECT

When I joined the Royals in 1973, I thought Royals Stadium was the best place to work in America. This is the perfect baseball stadium. Well, throughout the 1990s it has undergone some dramatic changes which, actually, did nothing but help the overall makeup of the place.

The most significant, and best, change made to Kauffman Stadium was the switch to natural grass in 1995. The new feature changed it from a baseball stadium to a ballpark - and what a beautiful ballpark! That same year, the fences were shortened and brought in. The front office felt that without the artificial turf, the park had to be shortened a little bit to make the home run more viable. When the field was turf, it was a huge park at 385 feet to the alleys and 410 to center with 12 foot high fences. Royals Stadium was a big, big ballpark. With the change, fences were brought in 10 feet; so it is now 400 to center with 9-foot high fences.

On grass, obviously, the ball wasn't going to play as fast, the ball wasn't going to get to the gaps as quickly as it used to, so there was no need for such a huge park. The field has been changed from a billiards table to a real baseball park. Now guys can jump to the top of the fence and bring the ball back, and that happens on occasion.

The change in playing surfaces has changed the organization's philosophy about the type of player it has brought in over the years. With the turf in the 1970s, the emphasis was on speedy ballplayers. The Royals at one time, were probably the fastest team in baseball, and they used their speed and they used the artificial turf to great advantage. They just ran teams silly in what was then Royals Stadium.

When you look at the farm system now, you don't see the speed that was there at one time. A different kind of a player has developed now. In previous decades, they brought up kids with great arms. They drafted a lot of pitchers who had terrific arms, and they turned a lot of them into terrific pitchers. Somewhere along the line that changed. The ballpark probably dictates a little bit different kind of a player right now, because of the grass and because the fences were brought in a few feet.

The most appropriate change to the stadium was in 1993, when it went from being called Royals Stadium to being re-named Kauffman Stadium. Mr. Kauffman was opposed to the change for a long, long time, because he thought Royals Stadium was perfect. He specifically didn't want his name used. He certainly deserved to have his name on the stadium since he was responsible for this franchise being in Kansas City. Let's hope the name of this stadium won't be an issue - that is, subject to change - under new ownership.

There is one change this stadium has seen that bugs me, and that is the advertising signs around the outfield. I understand why those signs are there. One word – REVENUE. We are operating in a different day and age and the club needs the revenue - all it can get through every source conceivable. The stadium was as pure a baseball stadium as it possibly could have been, and still is in most respects, but the signs sure don't improve her appearance. Regardless, it's still beautiful.

BEING CRITICAL OF THE HOME TEAM

We were, from time to time, critical of the Royals on the air, but we never really beat any guys up. For instance, in 1998 Royals shortstop Mendy Lopez didn't play for six games because he had a failed at-bat in a bunt situation. On the air I talked about how, if you're a middle infielder hitting .240, you need to be able to bunt.

There was a similar situation with Shane Halter. He didn't get a bunt down and, shortly thereafter, he was sent down to the minor leagues for a few days. Well, he wasn't sent down only because he missed the bunt, but also because he failed to come back the next day and say, "I've got to be able to do this...let's work on it." We talked about that on the air, and how it's disappointing to manager Tony Muser.

If a broadcaster keeps going back to the subject, and harping on it, then he is being too critical. But he can't come out and say, "Here we go again. Gee, this guy for the 18th time has failed to bunt." The word "again" can be a deadly word when referring to a player in a game. If we say he failed to get it down "again," that implies that it happens a lot, which may be unfair to the player. We pretty much have to take each little occasion by itself.

I don't like to hear guys just beat up on players on the air. I've got a theory, which I call the dirt theory. It says that the closer you are to the dirt, the harder this game is to play. For instance if you're standing on the dirt - the infield, home plate or the pitcher's mound - the game is very difficult. If you get in the dugout, it's not quite as tough. If you get about five rows up in the stands with a hot dog and a beer, it gets much easier. If you get all the way up in the broadcast booth where we sit, with an iced tea, it's easier still. I think you have to give the players credit for the fact that baseball is a very difficult game to play and they are trying to do it in a laboratory in front of 20,000 to 30,000 people. That's not easy. I always try to be very mindful of that.

Sometimes we point out that the manager and the coaches take these guys out everyday and work on different things. It's not as if the manager and the coaches sit back and don't do anything. They work very hard at getting these guys to do the right thing and make the right play, but sometimes the players simply don't execute. Some managers and coaches get fired over players not executing, and they often don't deserve it. When it's a lack of effort, then it's time to be critical of the players, and I'm not the least bit bashful about being that way.

One time a television guy sat down with us and said, "Why don't we approach it this way — let's not be critical, and let's not dwell on the negative." Our answer to him at that point was that we have to keep our credibility. If there is something there to be criticized, we're not going to ignore it.

Neither Royals management nor radio management ever came to us and asked us to be less harsh on a player. I never had anybody of importance in the organization come to me and ask me why I said something in particular on the air, not once in 25 years. I'm sure there have been times when someone probably wanted to, but then realized that, over 162 games, we were going to say a lot more positive things than negative things. And we could not do our job with people sitting on our shoulders saying, don't say this, do say that. I appreciate the fact that everyone let us do our job all those years.

WE'RE TALKING DENNY, FRED, SPLIT AND THE DUKE

During the 1996 season, Denny and I were joined in the booth by former Royals players John Wathan and Paul Splittorff. I enjoyed it immensely! This, again, goes back to how Denny and I grew up differently in this business. When Denny broke in with Buddy, it was pretty much you-do-your-innings-and-I-will-do-mine. I came up working with analysts in college basketball and football, and I have always been used to the interaction with the other guy in the booth. So when the Duke and Split joined us in the booth, Denny and I probably approached it differently.

Denny still does games the way he learned to do games - those are your innings and these are my innings. In fact, I've always enjoyed talking on the air to the guy sitting next to me. I've always believed the broadcast should be a conversation about the game, as it is going on.

So having said that, I really enjoyed having Paul and Duke in the booth to bounce things off of and to talk about things. Denny really enjoyed it, too. He worked with them very well; there was some terrific interaction there. I don't really know how it got started or why it lasted only for that one season, but it worked pretty well. The thing that helped was that we were working with two friends who were lifetime Royals, guys who knew the game and the organization. We could trust them and we could have fun with them. It was disappointing when it ended.

OTHER "DISAPPOINTMENTS," IF YOU WANT TO CALL THEM THAT

I am never really disappointed in how the team played. I feel badly for the people who invest their money and their time, in trying to develop players who, quite often, simply aren't going to improve very much, regardless of how much is invested in them. For example, I felt badly for Tony Muser and his coaches in 1998; they worked so hard. But they can't make a player better than he is capable of being. A player has just so much ability, and it's not his fault that he's not a great player, but it is his fault that he doesn't work to improve.

Some guys work exceptionally hard, and some guys don't. What really bothers me is guys who don't seem to understand what an opportunity they have, or guys who are just not willing to work hard. Remember, I grew up in baseball broadcasting watching the George Bretts, the Hal McRaes, the Frank Whites, the Darrell Porters, the Paul Splittorffs, the John Wathans and all those guys who worked to the max to get the best out of their ability. Those players worked very hard, played very hard, and got the most they could out of themselves. And therefore they got the most out of the game.

There are always going to be guys who retire, and when they look back at their careers think, "I should have worked a little like that...a little harder." I just hate to see guys reach the big leagues, become satisfied and think, "I made it," then let the opportunity slip through their hands.

It disappoints me every time I see a guy not run out a ground ball, or throw to the wrong base. I'm disappointed when I see a guy not get a bunt down, because, as a broadcaster I know whether that guy's head is in the game or if he is not giving his best effort.

Beyond those things, on a personal level, I was never disappointed while broadcasting games. Every night we still get to broadcast a Major League Baseball game, whether it's a bad game or a good game. We still get to do that, and it's a hell of lot better than a lot of things we might be doing. It's obviously more fun to follow the success of a winning team, when everyone is having a good time, and we can sit back and drink in the whole scene and think about how fun this is. But at it's very worst, even when the team is playing poorly, we are still doing a Major League Baseball game.

Watching a late season game in Baltimore, for example, is a great illustration. In August of 1998, the Royals were out of the pennant race, and the Orioles hadn't been playing well and were almost out of their race. Even so, there were 47,000 people watching that ballgame. On this particular Friday night the Royals won the ballgame, a one-run ballgame, and it was a lot of fun to watch. There is an awful lot of good in that, so instead of looking at the bad side of it, I've always chosen to view the glass as half-full. I would tend to always find something good in the ballpark. There is always something good at a baseball game, if you want to find it.

Maybe the Baltimore scene was helped by the fact that the Royals had won a few games. The club has not been a good club for a couple of years, so it is refreshing when the team does begin to play well, because you can sense a new vitality around the ballpark, and in the community; you can hear it on the talk shows, and you can see it in the newspapers. There's just no tonic like winning, even if it is for just a few games in the middle of a non-championship year.

THE ROYALS WILL SURVIVE

When I think about professional organizations that have gone through tough times and survived, the Cleveland Indians come to mind immediately. The Indians actually went through about a 50-year stretch of being bad, but they are a good team now. They did it right. They committed to the young players and they aimed their development at the year they went into their new ballpark.

The Oakland A's are another example. When they were in Kansas City, they were not a winning organization. Even through the early 1970s, the Royals chased them in the standings, and beat them. But then the A's came back and won the Western Division several times. The Minnesota Twins have gone from worst to first, and back again. The St. Louis Cardinals did the same thing. There was a World Series in the 1990s involving teams that went from first to worst and back to first again. It really does happen in baseball.

The Royals down cycle has probably lasted a lot longer than anybody thought it would. Hopefully, they will get back on top. They will, one of these days. The interesting thing in Kansas City is that the Royals and Chiefs have never really been good at the same time. When the Royals were really good, the Chiefs were down and not drawing well, and now it's the other way around again. As long as both teams aren't bad at the same time, we'll be okay.

Denny Matthews

It has been difficult watching the Royals go from being a newborn in 1969, to building a champion during the 1970s, to winning it all in 1985, and then falling back to where we are today. I have a buddy who says, "It is what it is." That is what it is and that is what you have to work with. At the same time, we understand the economics of the game and we know what is going on; so it is not a big shock when a small market team like the Royals can't compete with the Yankees and Red Sox.

From the outset of the 90s, it looked as through we might be headed for difficult times. In 1989, the Royals ended the season with 92 wins and a second place finish. The very next year, however, the team had a losing record (75-86), and finished sixth in the American League West. After two more toward-the-bottom-of-the-barrel finishes (another sixth place in 1991 and fifth place in 1992) it seemed that things might be coming back together some what in 1993.

That season the team had a good mix of players, with guys like Brian McRae, Greg Gagne, Gary Gaetti and Wally Joyner. George Brett was wrapping up his 20-year Hall of Fame career. Kevin Appier posted 18 wins, and Jeff Montgomery had a career-high 45 saves, tying him with Dan Quisenberry for the Royals single-season mark. Unfortunately, the best the team could muster was a record of 84-78, good for only a third place division finish.

Again, I understand what's going on with the team and with the economics of the game, so fretting about it or being frustrated about it serves no purpose. In fact, fretting and being frustrated would probably detract from what I'm trying to do. I try to remove myself from that. When you see and understand what's going on you can go about your business more routinely, and more consistently.

So, in essence, even though this has been a tough decade in terms of how the team has played, I try not to pay too much attention to the big picture — where we are in the standings, how many games we are behind, or how many teams are in front of us.

We see a lot of good ballgames and we enjoy those. The bad ones we hack our way through. And the merely average ballgames - we do the best we can with those.

THE DECLINE OF A CHAMPION

The Royals got caught up in a lot of factors, such as the minor league system drying up, free agency, the loss of Ewing Kauffman, and the strike in 1994, and, as a result, the team on the field declined as the organization has gone through the 1990s. Out of those key elements, the one I point to the most is the fact that the farm system had dried up a little bit, so to sign free agents, instead of giving up good prospects, the Royals have to give up a lot of draft choices. In essence when they did that, the team undermined its minor league system. That has had a lot to do with the team's performance.

The economics of building a minor league system like the Royals enjoyed in the 1970s and 80s, are there and are fine. The problem is keeping the players once they are developed. Bringing the players up, getting them through the system, into the organization and into the parent club is not that big of a deal. If the players develop to the point that they are really good, then there is a problem — just maintaining a contract with them. The question becomes can you afford to sign them when they become free agents? In this decade for the Royals, the answer is sadly, no.

The economics of the game finally began to take a toll in the early 1990s. It has not been until the last few years that what people had prophesized for free agency - the teams with the most money having the best players and, increasingly, the best teams - really came to fruition. That it did not happen right away surprised some people. In fact, it lulled some people into thinking that free agency really wasn't so bad. "Things are still pretty equal," they said. Indeed, in the early 1990s the gap was not overwhelming. The salary gap between the teams with the highest salary and the teams with the lowest salary may have been around $10 million. It is not out of the question today for the difference to be six or seven times that.

When the Royals were producing pennant-winning teams, Kansas City fans could relate to the players. Today no fans in any city can relate to any players because the guys move around so much. Free agency and the way players move around could be the subject of an entire book.

It is really difficult for a fan to make an emotional investment in a player when, in a year or two, the player is probably going to be with another team. It is almost as if the players of today, and not only the Royals, are no more than mercenaries. Players today generally go to the highest bidder and do their thing for two or three years, get a better offer, bigger bonus, better contract, more money, move on, and the cycle continues.

If teams don't have the money for good established players, they had better have a hell of a minor league system. Frankly, I'm really not sure what it's going to take to make the Royals a consistent winner again. I'm not trying to be flip about it, I just don't have the answer. No one has the answer.

So, free agency is another factor in the decline of the Royals.

The loss of Ewing Kauffman obviously is a big factor as well, because of his deep pockets and the way he would really prop the team up and acquire good players. Of course the strike in 1994 took away a lot of the enthusiasm from the fan base in Kansas City and the surrounding areas.

All of those things conspired against the team, and helped put us where we are today.

1994: HEY, THERE REALLY IS A SUMMER!

The 1994 season was a tough one on everyone involved in baseball, from the players, to front office people, to broadcasters, but especially to the fans. At the outset, it looked as though a strike might be avoided. Even when it became apparent that the strike was imminent, not many people dreamed that it would shut down the rest of the season. Major League Baseball was having a decent year; the first year with three divisions in each league. As it turned out, the Royals, in their new division (Central), finished the year in third place with a record of 64-51.

In Kansas City the strike really hurt, because the Royals took a double whammy, having no leadership in the form of a baseball commissioner, and none on the local level with Mr. Kauffman passing away the year before that.

The Royals are still feeling the blow of the strike and just haven't bounced back. Sure, they garnered a second place finish in the division in 1995, but they were behind the Cleveland Indians, certainly one of the best teams in the league. Oh, and that second place came on the basis of a smashing record of 70-74. Since then, they've been at the bottom of the Central Division.

When there is talk about a possible strike, as there was at the outset of the 1994 season, all a broadcaster can do is sit and wait. The way I approach a possible strike season is the way I approach any season. How else could I approach it? When there are games, I go out to the stadium and broadcast the games. If the work stoppage comes for the players, then it comes for the play-by-play guy. That's the way it was in 1994.

Once the strike hit, however, I was affected. Suddenly I discovered what summer is, and that people do things in the summer that I hadn't been able to do in 30 years. Our off-season is usually fall and winter, but all of a sudden it was summer, and it was a revelation. Hey, in the summer, it doesn't get dark until 8:00 or 8:30. Holy mackerel!

FROM ROYALS STADIUM TO KAUFFMAN STADIUM, TO A BALLPARK

Royals Stadium is a near-perfect baseball stadium. When it was built, prior to 1973, it was state-of-the-art, and a far cry from the old Municipal Stadium.

Noble Herzberg was the architect of Royals Stadium. Former Royals general manager Cedric Tallis was, conceptually, responsible for much of the design involved at both Anaheim and Kansas City. Here's how it worked: they (Herzberg and Tallis) took the best of Dodger Stadium and discarded what had proven to be ineffective, and they built Anaheim Stadium. Then they did the same thing with Anaheim, and the result is what we have today in Kansas City.

One thing not in Herzberg's original design was a construction strike. It caused a delay in the Royals occupying Kauffman Stadium in 1972, until 1973. In fact, I recall groundskeeper George Toma digging up home plate after the final home game in 1971 to move it over to the new stadium, to symbolize the move from the old to the new. A big deal was made about uprooting the plate after the final out of the '71 season to haul it over to the new yard. Instead, he was whacking it back in the ground at Municipal Stadium in early 1972, right where he dug it up. Sometimes the best laid plans get uprooted and then pounded back.

After the extra wait, everyone was pretty excited about Royals Stadium when it first opened in April, 1973. Everything about the stadium was so easy and convenient, especially compared with Municipal Stadium. Parking, for example, had been a problem in the old place. In the new complex there was ample parking, so people could breeze in and out, directly to the interstate. Now one can't help but wonder if people take it for granted. Even at some of the new ballparks today, parking and traffic are still a problem. Here in Kansas City, we have the best of it in that regard.

When it opened, it was really the start of something spectacular. But that was really just the start. For instance, there was nothing beyond the outfield fences; it was dirt, actually, because the stadium opened before they were able to get grass to grow out there. The trees behind the fences at the top of the hill weren't very big; they were hardly noticeable, they were so small. It was very stark. It took years for the trees to mature and for the grass to kick in. Then things began to fill in. The water spectacular was pretty neat, but it was pretty much all by itself out there. On that 39-degree opening night in 1973 the stadium was pretty cold in more ways than one.

In the original design of the stadium, there was one "mistake," one that was really out of Noble Herzberg's hands. Instead of real grass on the playing surface, the Royals went with artificial turf.

In fact, the first night at Royals Stadium, I made the statement that had there been grass on this field, then-Royals Stadium would be a perfect Major

League Baseball stadium. In 1995 they finally got rid of the turf and put in real grass. That same year, since the turf was gone, the fences were brought in and lowered.

At the time, it seemed like a good idea to bring in the fences in an attempt to produce more home runs and more excitement. The way baseball is now, though, makes that reasoning suspect. The fences probably didn't need to be brought in, or lowered. But, everybody else's fences had been brought in, so why not ours? Let's bring in the fences and change baseball to bash ball.

The other most significant change during this decade was renaming the stadium, from Royals Stadium to Kauffman Stadium, for former owner Ewing Kauffman. In recent years some stadiums have been renamed to appease corporate sponsors. The Kansas City stadium should always be named Kauffman Stadium. Keep the money out of the name.

When I first saw Royals Stadium I thought it was a palace. Personally, I think the stadium looks better today than it did when it opened (sans the extensive changes now underway for the 1999 season), with all of the trees around the outside, and with grass now on the playing field.

During the opening homestand in 1998, I said on the air, "When this place opened, it was a stadium. Now, with the changes they've made, it's a ballpark."

THEIR STADIUMS...THE NEW, SEMI-"OLD STYLE" STADIUMS

Throughout the 1990s we have seen ballclubs build new downtown stadiums in an old style, such as Oriole Park at Camden Yards in Baltimore, or Jacobs Field in Cleveland, and even the Ballpark at Arlington in Texas. Overall, I like these "new" stadiums. They've done a good job on most of the new ones.

One thing that some of these stadiums have in common is that they are in downtown areas. Some Kansas City fans have complained about our stadium being in, basically, the middle of nowhere. Again, the convenience of Kauffman Stadium is second to none. I don't live downtown, so a stadium there is not a big deal to me. On the other hand, downtown provides a nice environment for a stadium.

One thing about these new stadiums around the league that we miss, though, is the intimacy of our broadcast position. In the old parks we were right in the games as broadcasters. In every new ballpark, now, we are far back and far up. As good as the new ballparks are, we don't feel as much a part of the game as we used to. The most important thing for a baseball announcer over the course of a game is concentration. It's more difficult to maintain in some of these new settings.

That's really my only criticism with the new ballparks. As neat as they are, and as much fun as they are, damn, it's as if they said, "Oh, yeah, we do need to accommodate the sportswriters and announcers, so let's just stick them as far away as we can." That's tough. Distance from the field doesn't matter that much for a newspaper or magazine writer, or for a television announcer who has the aid of video monitors, but it does matter for a radio broadcaster. As a broadcaster I want to see every pitch to know what type of pitch was thrown as well as the location. I don't always know, but when I do, the listener is more in the game because of that.

The further away from the game the broadcaster is, and the more difficult it is to concentrate, the less the listener feels he is a part of the game. The farther away they put us, the better the chances that our attention, our concentration, will go by the board. We really have to fight it. My concentration is pretty good, but it has been trained to be. When we are in stadiums where we are way far away, and the game isn't any good, we drift. The concept is the same for fans who are in the nosebleed sections. Sure, they may be excited to be at the game and to be seeing it, but eventually their concentration isn't as sharp.

One thing that I've really prided myself on is being able to give an accurate description of the pitch. If my job were broadcasting on TV, the television could do the work. But in radio, if the announcer is going to do a good job, he needs to describe the pitch and tell where it is. Sure, I could say, "Here's the pitch...ball. Here's the next pitch...foul ball. Here's the pitch...strike." An important thing for the radio audience is knowing what the pitch is, and understanding how the pitcher is working the hitter. Some of the stadiums where we're at now, I have no clue. I still have great eyes; but in the new parks, we're way up, way back, looking through a screen. We could almost broadcast the game better in front of a TV in our house than we can at the ballpark. In the old ballparks the broadcaster was right on top of the action. It was great. He felt like he was in the game - he *was* in the game!

Detroit's Tiger Stadium is a prime example. We are so close to the action that we can almost literally carry on a conversation with the players. Everything that is hit in that stadium just reverberates. A hitter feels like he could go up there and hit a ball in the upper deck. Things are that close. There's a feeling of being closed in, but it's just so nice for a hitter. Psychologically, players walk into that ballpark and think, "Okay, 3-for-4, no sweat." It's just a nice feeling. Balls sound good when they're hit there. When a batter hits it solid...yeow!

Camden is about the best of the new-style stadiums for a broadcaster, but our position is still only decent there. We are back pretty far, but we aren't very high. There's an indentation where the press area is, apart from where the fans are. If they could have pushed us out as far as the very front of the upper deck we would have a wonderful vantage point, but they didn't, for whatever reason.

In Cleveland and Texas, the other two pretty new stadiums, we are higher than we are at Camden, and farther away. Texas may be the worst. It is brutal because we are way up high and extremely far away (as in upper deck, far away). We're about nine stories up and a mile-and-a-half back. The game is only a rumor.

Even some of the old stadiums aren't very good for a broadcaster. Oakland and Yankee Stadium, for instance, are the two I really dislike. Anaheim was totally changed before last season ('98), but not for the better, sorry to report. Before Anaheim was remodeled, the position wasn't bad. That stadium would have been in the middle of the pack, maybe even above the median, especially with its big, nice working area. Now we've got a little tiny board to put all our stuff on, real narrow, and it's a joke. In this age of high technology, where everything is supposed to be better...well, they ain't.

Oakland is one of those trips I'm not really fired up about, anyway, because there is absolutely nothing to do there. This year, for the first time, we stayed in San Francisco, and that really made the trip more palatable. There is really not a lot going on in Anaheim, either, unless you have a car, because things are spread out and we stay close to the park, in the Disney area.

Boston's Fenway Park used to be one I really liked until they changed the location of the press area. Fenway's pretty tired now, but 20 or 25 years ago it was super. It was right up there with Wrigley, but it's deteriorated, and when they moved the press area they put us a long way away from the game. Fenway has lost a lot of its charm. Don't get me wrong, though, Boston is still a fun city.

On the other end of the spectrum, Wrigley Field in Chicago and Busch Stadium in St. Louis are a couple of my favorite places. During interleague play, the Royals played the Cubs at Wrigley during the 1997 season - the first time I had been there professionally. I had made a couple audition tapes there when I was first starting out, but that was my first trip there as a "real" broadcaster.

Since we moved into Kauffman Stadium in 1973, our radio booth has been moved four times. We started out on the second level, press area, right behind home plate, which gave us a great angle to see pitches. Then we moved off-angle, still on the second level. That wasn't quite as good as the first spot. Then we moved downstairs, closer to the game with a much better view, but in a tiny booth. Then, in 1995, we moved again, a little to the right. Granted we have a bigger booth, which is a luxury in baseball broadcasting, but we are way off-line to see pitches and there's a screen in front of us. With the renovations being made to Kauffman Stadium, it will be interesting to see where the announcers will wind up.

AND THEN THERE WERE FOUR

For the 1996 season, former Royals John Wathan and Paul Splittorff were added to our radio broadcasts. That was fun. I've always said that everybody sees a baseball game differently. If we had five people in the booth, the listener would have five different perspectives.

The neat thing about having Duke and Split with us is their history in this franchise. Split played a season in the organization a year before we even had the major league club. Then Duke had the perspective of having been a Royals player, coach and manager.

While having each of them certainly gave us a different perspective, it also gave the audience a little different avenue to go down. Fred sees something one way, John would see something one way, Paul would see something a certain way, and I would see something another way. The listener may have a completely different opinion. Everybody had their own unique perspective on what happened or didn't happen. To me that makes a broadcast interesting. It was kind of nice having those guys with us.

THERE'S A NEW SHERIFF IN TOWN

During the 1998 season Bud Selig was voted in as baseball's new commissioner. He seems to want to get things back to the way they used to be, long before the strike of 1994, when stadiums were packed and fans of all ages enjoyed Major League Baseball. That's a noble venture, but there is a long way to go for something that may not be possible. Unless some things are changed, such as free agency, the rising salaries, and compensation for the small-market teams, the game is in big, big trouble. Something has to be done, and the sooner the better, quite honestly. If drastic changes aren't made in the very near future, then baseball as we know it on the big league level, on the professional level, is just going to go into the dumpster.

One needed change is consolidation of the umpiring staffs — the National League and American League — and the getting rid of umpires who are no longer interested, and who don't uphold the rule book. The majors need umpires who will call the game the way it should be called, move the game the way it should be moved, and run the game the way it should be run on the field. The way things are now, one umpiring crew calls a game one way, then in the next series, games are called in a different fashion by the next crew.

People thought the strikes were a mess; well, wait until all of this starts to crumble in their road. Then it'll really be tough to put the brakes on. The future of baseball is not very bright unless we get some bright people who can get the game to the point where it is competitive again and each team has an equal shot. Until then it's like jumping on the Titanic...you get that sinking feeling, and down you go.

3

Buddy and Denny: Early History of the Franchise

Denny Matthews

One of the responsibilities of a broadcaster during the course of a baseball game is the reading of live, on-air commercials for various sponsors. With the amount of time between pitches, and the (generally) limited amount of actual action on the field, Major League Baseball broadcasts are a natural for this form of advertising. During my second season with the Royals (my second season as a big league announcer) in 1970, Buddy Blattner and I were doing a game in Milwaukee. I was supposed to do an on-air spot for one of the Royals' big dollar sponsors, Guy's Foods, a food manufacturing company in Kansas City that makes various snacks, such as potato chips, pretzels and nuts.

We were doing the game on Friday night, July 2nd, which meant that Sunday would be the 4th. Guy's Foods has always been one of our sponsors on radio and we've always done commercial drop-ins during innings for them.

Our producer/engineer at the time, Ed Shepherd, handed me the card that simply had "Guy's Foods" written on it. That meant I was supposed to say a little one-liner which would be timely and appropriate. I was thinking that it was a holiday weekend, Sunday was going to be the 4th of July, there would be a lot of people outside picnicking, boating, camping, the outdoor scene. So I said, "For those of you planning a holiday picnic, we surely hope you take along plenty of those good Guy's potato chips."

Al Fitzmorris was pitching, and he was just really slow. Fitzy was fussing around on the mound and wasn't about to throw another pitch, and nothing was going on. I figured to myself, "Boy, that first promo came out really good, and since they are a good sponsor, I'll give them an additional plug."

The next line out of my mouth was, "And fans, while you're in the store, be sure to grab Guy's nuts."

The second that came out of my mouth, I knew it didn't air the way I wanted it to. Buddy, who always listened very closely to everything I said so we could talk about it later, was sitting to my right, and I was afraid to peek at him. So I just kind of glanced over my shoulder and saw this dumbfounded look on his face as if to say, "What in the hell was that? What did my young guy just say?!"

Shep was up behind us and he was laughing, so he was no help. There were two outs in the inning, and on the next pitch the hitter grounded out to end the inning. Thank God that was kind of a quick bailout! Obviously we laughed about that later.

When we got back to Kansas City I was convinced that my job was over. I saw my career flashing before my eyes. Guy Caldwell, who was an older gentleman, was the owner of Guy's Foods. He was out at the ballpark a couple of weeks later, so I told him the story (luckily he didn't hear it live). He thought it was the funniest thing he had ever heard. My job was safe for another day.

GROWING UP A STATE FARM INSURANCE COMPANY KID

For most boys (and possibly girls) growing up in the 1950s and 1960s throughout Illinois and Missouri, a summer day wouldn't be complete without hearing the likes of Jack Buck and Harry Caray call a St. Louis Cardinal baseball game on the radio; or without watching as Jack Brickhouse described the action of the Chicago Cubs on television. Many of us emulated these broadcasting legends, or pretended to be Stan Musial or Ernie Banks while playing in the yard.

In elementary school, when I listened to games, I would get on the floor with my baseball cards of the teams playing, with the lineups in order (the best I could). Whenever a guy came to the plate, I changed the cards around to put him on top. My favorite player was Don Blasingame, because he played second base and batted left-handed, just like I did. He is the only player I ever sent a letter to, requesting an autograph. He sent back a signed autograph postcard, and I still have it.

I was raised in that type of athletic environment where sportscasts were on the radio every summer afternoon; playing baseball, football, or basketball in the neighborhood was the thing to do; and going to Illinois State University football and basketball games with Dad was a regular occurrence.

I grew up in Illinois, in the twin cities of Normal and Bloomington, the oldest of four boys. My love of sports came largely from my dad, George Matthews. Dad had been an all-state high school basketball player in Danville, Illinois, as well as a baseball and basketball player at Illinois State. As a second baseman, he was the school's first All-American baseball player. He had a chance to sign with the Cincinnati Reds and with the Chicago White Sox; unfortunately, though, it was time for World War II and he was in the Navy.

When he returned from the war, with responsibility of supporting and caring for a growing family, baseball for dad was out of the question. He went to work in the personnel department for State Farm Insurance Company, headquartered in Bloomington.

Over the years, Dad passed his love of athletics down to his four boys, Steve, Doug, Mike and me. (Interestingly, today Mike is a radio analyst for Illinois State University basketball.) Home was very much a sports environment. My mother, Eileen, became quite proficient at warming up dinner after late practices. Usually once a summer, my dad would take us up to a game in

Chicago, usually to see the Cubs. Then, my grandmother, Gert Dohm, would take one or two of my brothers down to St. Louis on the train. We would spend the weekend in St. Louis and see Friday night, Saturday afternoon and Sunday games. That was a once a summer deal, so I probably saw four or five major league games a year while I was growing up.

For me, things just evolved from there, into becoming a decent athlete. After doing well in baseball at Trinity High School, I decided to go to college locally at Illinois Wesleyan. Originally, baseball was the main attraction of Wesleyan...originally.

The quarterback of the football team, Vic Armstrong, was one of my Sigma Chi fraternity brothers. One day while we were out throwing the football around, he asked me if I'd be interested in trying out for the football team. I had decent speed and pretty good hands. I didn't play football in high school, but it sounded like fun, so I did it.

To my surprise, I emerged from fall practice as Wesleyan's starting wide receiver. I will never forget my initial reception in a game. It was a break-in pattern that went for a 20-yard gain. Of course, I was concerned about being tackled for the first time, but I never even felt the hit. The thing I really will never forget is the roaring of the crowd when I made the catch. It seemed like a dream.

During the 1963 season, Armstrong finished 15th in the nation in passing in the National Association of Intercollegiate Athletics (NAIA), while I finished 8th in the nation in receiving. Considering the fact that I didn't play football in high school, my first year of collegiate football was quite an experience. One of the players who finished below me in receiving statistics was Otis Taylor of Prairie View, who went on to have a superb NFL career with the Kansas City Chiefs. (Taylor finished 12th in the nation in receiving in 1963.) We lost only three games in the three years that I played football at Wesleyan — undefeated in 1965, my senior year.

Ironically, while I was starting my Major League Baseball broadcasting career with the Kansas City Royals in 1969 in Municipal Stadium, Taylor was starring during the fall in Municipal Stadium with the Kansas City Chiefs, and would score a touchdown in the Chief's Super Bowl victory over the Minnesota Vikings less than a year later. The two of us have laughed about that 1963 season. He always jokingly reminds me that while I might have had the stats, he had the size, the speed, and the NFL career that I never had. There is no debate on that one.

MLB...the NFL...or Jack Buck?

Luckily, I had pretty good collegiate careers as a player in both baseball and football. Like Dad, in baseball I played second base. My middle infield partner was future major league shortstop Doug Rader, who signed with Houston after we finished our sophomore season. Opponents included future major leaguers Marty Pattin, Tom Murphy and Don Kessinger.

Pattin is one of my all-time favorite Royals, and he was a bulldog of a pitcher. When he was at Eastern Illinois and I was at Illinois Wesleyan, they came over to play us one blistering cold April day. I mean, snow flurries were flying around. Springtime in the midwest. Anyway, as the game got going, we had a runner at first, and the coaches wanted me to bunt him to second. A left-handed hitter, I laid a bunt down the first-base line, and as I was running to beat it out, Marty picked the ball up and fired it to first. Only it didn't make it to the man covering. It deflected off my batting helmet, and went into the right field corner. Our runner scored all the way from first base on the throwing error, and we beat him 1-0. I saved the newspaper clipping from that game, and I hauled it out and showed it to him a few years ago. He remembered the game.

He said, "Hell, I remember losing 1-0, are you kidding me? If I would have known it was you running, I would have thrown the ball harder, hit you in the head, and knocked you out."

To which I replied, "Well, you gave it your best shot and it ended up in the right field corner. No redos on that one...you don't get your mulligan."

After a solid season as a freshman at Wesleyan, the San Francisco Giants invited me to work out with their minor league team in Decatur, Illinois. They were very interested in signing me. Even though football was more my game at the time, I can't help but wonder what would have happened if I had signed with the Giants. Chances are I wouldn't have made the big leagues (the odds are about 25:1 that people who sign make it all the way). Who knows?

Not only did I have a chance to wonder about playing in the major leagues, I also had an opportunity to wonder about the National Football League. After my sophomore year of college, I had a workout with the Green Bay Packers. Keep in mind, this was in the mid-1960s, the hey-day of Vince Lombardi's Packers, when they were winning five NFL-NFC Championships between 1961 and 1970. This tremendous opportunity for me was set up by Wesleyan's dean of students, who was good friends with Norb Hecker, the defensive backfield coach for Green Bay.

I had a chance to go up to Wisconsin for three days and go through the paces with the team at Lambeau Field. A buddy of mine, Jim Bennett, went with me to take films and pictures. That was an unbelievable experience!

Alas, after trekking to the "frozen tundra" of Green Bay, and receiving letters from several NFL teams, I decided not to pursue a professional football career. In fact, even though football seemed to be more for me even when I worked out with the Giants farm club, my preference probably would have been Major League Baseball.

Instead, for a career path, I followed a trade I picked up during my sophomore season (that second year at Wesleyan was hectic!): radio. During that year, the local radio station in Bloomington, WJBC (a wonderful small town station), carried a lot of basketball games. In Bloomington/Normal there are two colleges, Illinois State and Illinois Wesleyan, plus four high schools. After my sophomore year of football, Don Newberg, the news director at the radio station, heard from Jack Horenberger, athletic director and baseball coach at Illinois Wesleyan, that I was interested in sports announcing. Lanny Larison from the station came out to the school and asked me if I'd like to help them with some college and high school basketball. And that's how all of this got started.

They offered me $5 a game. With all of the games that WJBC carried, they needed an extra guy to go with one of the regular sports announcers - to score games, get starting lineups, do the halftime show, and those types of things.

During my first year, I basically just tagged along, broadcast the starting lineups, occasionally a halftime interview with somebody and kept score for the guy doing the actual play-by-play.

In my second season, Newberg took me with him to do a Bloomington High School game. After the first quarter, Newberg stood up and said he had to go to the bathroom, and couldn't wait. He told me that if he wasn't back when the 60-second commercial break was finished, to fill in until he returned.

No big deal. Thirty seconds passed by. Then forty-five seconds are gone. The minute is up and Newberg is nowhere to be seen.

All of a sudden the second quarter is about to start and he's still not back! I just started doing the game. Newberg came wandering back at halftime.

"Boy it took you a long time to go to the john," I told him.

"No, I didn't have to go to the john," Newberg replied. "I just wanted you to do the quarter to see how you do. I figured if I told you about it, you'd get nervous, but if I just threw you in the water, we'd see if you could swim."

Evidently I made out like a fish. We split the second half of that game, and I continued to do more play-by-play throughout the season for WJBC.

During my last year, my senior year, I did a lot of the play-by-play, or I'd go out with Don Munson or Newberg, and we'd split up the duties. They also gave me a sports show (even during football season) for 10 minutes at 6:00 in the afternoon. Working at WJBC was neat. It was a gradual, weaning process.

By the time I graduated from Illinois Wesleyan in 1966 with a degree in Speech, the radio bug had taken a huge bite out of me, so I didn't know if I wanted to take a crack at professional football, baseball or broadcasting. In the meantime, I went to work with State Farm. Remember, I grew up in the community that the insurance giant has called home since its inception in 1922.

KANSAS CITY, KANSAS CITY HERE I COME

Heading into the 1969 season, it had been announced that the American and National Leagues would be adding two new teams, the Seattle Pilots (now the Milwaukee Brewers) and the Kansas City Royals in the American

League, and the Montreal Expos and San Diego Padres in the National League. Because of that announcement, there wasn't much question which route my life would take...broadcasting.

Seattle and San Diego were too far away from Illinois to suit me, and Montreal is in a different country, so I didn't have a ton of interest in those jobs. Kansas City is close to Bloomington (relatively speaking); yes, Kansas City would be the one to go after.

Even though the Royals were going to be new to Kansas City, professional baseball had a long history in the area, dating back to before the turn of the century. The earliest professional baseball team on record in Kansas City is the Antelopes in 1866. The Antelopes, an independent team, played before the National League was formed in 1876.

In the late 1800's, Kansas City was also home to the Kansas City Unions of the Union Association, a professional league which didn't last long. The team played at Athletic Park, now Southwest Boulevard and Summit Street. With the Unions able to draw Sunday crowds of as many as 5,000 fans, the National League in 1886 gave Kansas City the Cowboys. The League had been unable to find a home for an additional team, a team it needed to even out the league, so the Cowboys were placed in Kansas City on a conditional basis. Kansas City was the first, and to this day the only city which has been granted a Major League team on a conditional basis.

The Cowboys, who played their home games at League Park, a.k.a. "The Hole," were gone after that first year. Among less literal reasons, League Park earned its nickname by being 25 feet below street level. According to baseball historian Lloyd Johnson, in an article by Bill Richardson in the August 22, 1993 *Kansas City Star*, there was a sign in the outfield of "The Hole" which read, "Please don't shoot the umpire. He is doing the best he can."

Even though those Cowboys only lasted for the 1886 season, Kansas City quickly had another team called the Cowboys - an American Association team in 1888. Unfortunately, the National League had a hand in the demise of this version of the Cowboys, as well. The American Association was another major league, but it was hardly a match for the National League, and in turn, the Cowboys were forced out of business.

By 1915 baseball fans in Kansas City were treated to two teams: the minor league Blues and the Federal League's Packers. At the time, the Federal League was a third major league.

Keeping in tune with the tradition of Kansas City teams using recurrent names, a la the Cowboys, the 1969 version of the Royals was not the first team with that name in the city. According to former Royals assistant director of public relations, Phil Dixon, in his book, *The Ultimate Kansas City Baseball Trivia Quiz Book* (Bon A Tirer Publishing, 1992), in 1917 a man named Ben Powell organized a black team called the Kansas City Royals.

Actually, that Royals team was one of many African-American teams to call Kansas City home. In 1909, the Kansas City (Kansas) Giants amazed their fans with a 54 game winning streak. On the Missouri side, which is where almost all of the professional Kansas City teams have played, the Royals Giants and the Royal American Giants were predecessors to the 1917 Royals.

Due in large part to the strength of black baseball in the area, the actual Negro Leagues were founded in 1920 at a YMCA near the 18th and Vine district in Kansas City. In the 1920s that district was an area where players loved to hang out at night following a day game and listen to the sounds of legendary jazz performers such as Count Basie and Coleman Hawkins. Today that part of the city is home to the Negro Leagues Baseball Museum and the Kansas City Jazz Museum.

One of the most successful teams in the Negro Leagues was the Kansas City Monarchs. Through the years the team featured some of the best players in the history of baseball, such as Satchel Paige, John "Buck" O'Neil (who has worked with the Royals since 1988 as a special assignment scout) and Jackie Robinson.

For several years, the Monarchs weren't the only game in town; they "competed," albeit not on the same field, with the Blues. The Blues, an American Association minor league team which at one time was a farm club for the New York Yankees, won seven pennants while in Kansas City. (Early in his career, Mickey Mantle made a stop with the Blues.) The two teams, the Monarchs and the Blues, played in Municipal Stadium, originally called Muehlebach Field, which opened in 1923. Although not common at the time, it was possible to see blacks and whites sitting together at Muehlebach during a Monarchs game. However, when the Blues utilized the stadium, seating was a different story; there were separate sections for white fans and black fans.

THE KANSAS CITY ATHLETICS

The city received its first "modern-day" Major League Baseball team in 1955, when the Athletics defected from Philadelphia. Thirteen seasons later, in October of 1967, with no championship banners flying on the flag pole, team owner Charles O. Finley harassed the other baseball owners enough that he was allowed to bring in the moving trucks and once again move the Athletics. This time they headed west to Oakland.

To say the least, Finley was an interesting character. For some reason he was never really happy in Kansas City. Several times he threatened to move the team. When he wasn't allowed to move, he would just do something crazy and embarrassing. Why else would a city let out a synchronized cheer when it found out that he was moving to Oakland?

Finley always had something interesting up his sleeve. One of his more humiliating displays was the team's brown mule mascot, "Charlie O." He wanted to experiment with orange baseballs. While the Beatles were on their first United States tour, Finley allegedly paid the group more to appear in Kansas City than he paid that season's starting Athletics' lineup. The promotion didn't pay off for Finley or the Athletics.

Finley's move from Kansas City to Oakland left a sour taste in the mouths of Kansas City baseball fans, because Major League Baseball was gone. Many fans felt that it would be a long time before the city saw professional baseball again...if ever.

When Kansas City civic leaders caught wind of rumors that Finley was going to seek approval from Major League Baseball for the move to Oakland, they realized that they had to be prepared. How would it look, for their baseball team to move? So they got a delegation together and sent the group to that same owners' meeting. Once the approval was given Finley, the delegation immediately solicited the owners for a new franchise. They were guaranteed that the city would receive an expansion team before 1971.

Well, "1971" was not a good enough answer. United States Senator Stuart Symington (Missouri) urged and persuaded the owners to grant the city a team before then. The owners agreed to award Kansas City a new franchise in 1969, if they could get financial backing.

Long-time Kansas Citian and pharmaceutical millionaire Ewing Kauffman helped see to it that baseball would be back to the Midwestern city. Kauffman, after being nudged by some very intelligent, powerful, and high class people in the Kansas City community, such as Earl Smith and Ernest Mehl, financially backed the expansion franchise.

"THE" RESUME PACKAGE

Personally, I hadn't really followed the history of baseball in Kansas City and wasn't that concerned about the sport's status in the city until I learned expansion was on its way. (In fact, before I started with the team in 1969, I had been to Kansas City only twice. Both times were with the Illinois Wesleyan basketball team during the NAIA national tournament, to do some radio work with the team, during my sophomore and senior years.) Regardless of that, I decided to apply for the Royals job.

The St. Louis Cardinals made arrangements for me to use part of their press box during a series with the Chicago Cubs in order to make a demo tape of the game. The tape was good enough to send to a major league team. But was the tape enough by itself? Maybe not.

There was a guy by the name of Glenn McCullough who lived in Peoria, Illinois, and who was involved with the Central Illinois Collegiate League, in which I played during the summer. He told me to think of a way to make my tape stand out from the others. Schlitz Beer and their advertising agency, Majestic Advertising, were in charge of the Kansas City broadcasts at the time.

I went to a little restaurant in Bloomington and got one of those round, metal serving trays with the Schlitz logo in the center of it, attached a couple of pictures taken of me in St. Louis (one was with Chicago announcer Jack Brickhouse) along with my resume, and the tape. In the letter I wrote, "I hope you don't think I'm a Busch-leaguer for having done a Cardinal game, but this is my pitch for Schlitz and the Royals job."

When I told Glenn about it, he thought it was a good idea. He said, "It shows me a little creativity."

I didn't know if I'd ever get a job with an application like that.

With the Royals, the job that was open was for the number two man; the team had already hired veteran broadcasting legend Buddy Blattner as the main announcer. Blattner had most recently been with the California Angels.

When I applied for the Kansas City job in the fall of 1968, there were over 200 applicants vying for the same spot. Eventually those numbers began to be whittled down from 200...to 100...to 50...to 25. During this time, I kept receiving calls from the Majestic Advertising Agency - about once a month - saying that I made the cut. The calls kept coming, advising me that I was one of 25, then one of 10, then one of five. Finally, I was one of the three finalists.

The three who were left were asked to meet with Blattner for a personal interview. For me that meant a three hour drive from Bloomington to Buddy's home in St. Louis. I had been doing weekend sports for KMOX-TV in St. Louis, so the drive was no big deal. For the KMOX thing, I drove down to St. Louis on Friday, went to work Friday, Saturday, and Sunday, and then drove back to Bloomington on Sunday night. Even though the drive was not a problem, a meeting of such magnitude with someone like a Buddy Blattner might mean a lot of anxiety for some young announcers, but that was not necessarily the case for me.

I had met Bud about a year earlier in Anaheim. While I was visiting my uncle, we went to a game at Anaheim Stadium and met him. I don't know why I did it, but I did. I had done a few games with the Baltimore Colts football team during the 1968 season. Chuck Thompson did play-by-play for the Colts and for Orioles' baseball. Baltimore happened to be the team playing the Angels that night, so Chuck introduced me to Bud.

Doing some games for the Colts was a neat experience. I worked with John Sterling, who has been doing the New York Yankee games for the last seven or eight years. We split the games up to where on one game he would do the first half, and I would do the second; then the next game we reversed the order. Then we helped each other with the commentary when the other was doing play-by-play. It would have been fine to get into football broadcasting, but I really wanted to do baseball. Football, basketball, and hockey would have been secondary to baseball for me.

Before leaving Illinois for the interview with Buddy, I told my parents that I probably wouldn't be home until 10 or 11 that night. As it turned out, I stayed in St. Louis damned near all night. I got to Bud's house about 5:00 on a Friday afternoon. When we saw each other, he remembered our meeting in Anaheim. We went for pizza and beer, and had a great conversation.

I left his house about 3:00 on Saturday morning and got home around 7. My dad was outside mowing the grass. He asked me how the interview went.

"Well, I think pretty good...I stayed long enough," was my reply.

Two days later the Royals called and said we "Guess you realize you got the job." No, I didn't know, so I was glad they told me!

Later, Bud told me that there were three things that helped me stand out from the other applicants. The first thing was that I had done a major league game for the demo tape. Secondly, Blattner said he could tell that I had done my homework because I knew something about the players. The third thing noticed was that it was obvious I had played baseball because I had a good feel for the game.

I can't help but think about that resume package. Whether it was the tape, the fact that I had done a major league game, or the goofy serving tray, I don't know, but it worked.

THE YOUTH MOVEMENT...ON THE FIELD AND IN THE BOOTH

Since the Royals were an infant organization in 1969, it probably didn't hurt my chances that I was basically fresh out of college, and 26 years old. It enabled the franchise to have a young broadcaster with a young team.

It was fun watching the team take shape through expansion because the people on the player level were my age. That meant we were new together. The people who were older, who were in more authoritative positions, were so helpful to me and so nice. It was a wonderful environment.

My transition to the major leagues may have been helped by the fact that the Royals had a pretty good team even in their first season. It's easy to remember how many wins the team had in its inaugural season...69...69 wins in 1969. That record of 69-93 was pretty good for an expansion team. In fact, the Royals finished ahead of the other American League expansion team, Seattle, and they finished ahead of one of the other established teams in their American League West division.

Opening day, 1969, is one game I will always remember. The Royals, led by manager Joe Gordon, faced the Minnesota Twins, a team managed by a young and fiery Billy Martin, who was making his managerial debut. Gordon was a veteran baseball man who, strangely enough, had managed the Kansas City Athletics in 1960 for half of the season.

Gordon was excited about the opportunity to manage the first-year Royals. He had his first lineup almost complete after the final exhibition game against the St. Louis Cardinals. Ed Kirkpatrick and rookie Lou Piniella had been hitting the ball well, so they started in leftfield and centerfield, respectively, while Bob Oliver started in right. Around the infield were Chuck Harrison,

Jerry Adair, Jack Hernandez and Joe Foy. Ellie Rodriguez was behind the plate, with Wally Bunker as the starting pitcher. Not a bad opening day lineup for an expansion team.

The team was loaded with young, great talent, and a solid, if not strong, pitching staff. Hitting, however, was Gordon's main concern after the team struggled offensively during spring training. If hitting was Gordon's only worry, then he and his Royals should be in pretty good shape. Hitting usually comes along eventually, especially with a younger ballclub.

Kansas City's Municipal Stadium was possibly in the best shape of its storied life. It was converted to a big league stadium in 1955 when the Athletics moved from Philadelphia. Since it was 46 years old at the inception of the Royals, the facilities were spartan. The clubhouse wasn't state-of-the-art. We had a small pressbox in which to work, but it offered a wonderful view of the field. From our perspective it was a great place to work. Municipal was a typical, old baseball stadium.

But, on opening day, April 8, 1969, Municipal Stadium had been transformed into a gorgeous baseball cathedral for the festivities. A few of the things that stick out to me about Municipal Stadium, overall, are the smell of the old ballpark; the way the grass looked during both day and night games; the criss-cross pattern in which the grass was cut - it was the way a major league stadium should look, and smell, and feel. Three or four years ago, I drove past the area where Municipal used to be. Everything around the lot where the stadium used to be was still there; the houses beyond right field, the school behind the first base side, then another big building down the third base side. I could almost smell the ballpark again.

The playing field of Municipal Stadium had always been the nicest part of the complex. Opening day of 1969 was no exception, but the field was a little more crisp than normal. Groundskeeper George Toma, who has been with the club since that first year, turned the playing surface into something out of a baseball fairy tale.

George is an institution with professional sports in Kansas City, having worked for both the Chiefs and the Royals. He is totally married to his work. He loves it! He thrives on it. George loves playing in the dirt. From the time he was a little kid, he was playing in the dirt, and he's still playing in the dirt. He has a wonderful feel for his work; he's a perfectionist. George Toma did wonderful things with Municipal Stadium, and now he's perfected his trade at Kauffman Stadium and Arrowhead Stadium.

Some of the Royals have come in and said that the dirt is of such texture that they rarely get a bad hop. When I first started working with the team, I used to go out and take ground balls during batting practice at the old stadium, and it was true that you never got a bad hop. It was a wonderful playing surface. Today's surface is certainly no exception. George absolutely loves what he does, and it's obvious.

For the home opener in 1969, red, white and blue banners had been draped over the wall down the first and third base sides of the field. Flags representing each of the major league's teams hung from the roof. It appeared as though baseball belonged in Kansas City. And it belonged to the Royals.

As long-time *Kansas City Star* sports editor Joe McGuff wrote in his *Sporting Comment* column on April 9, the day after the opener, "A gusty wind blew out of the south, popping the pennants that ring the roof of the stadium. One of the pennants had been partly blown down and hung in a position approaching half mast. By the strangest sort of coincidence it was a green and gold pennant bearing the name 'Athletics.' "

The Royals, which were named in part after the American Royal, the annual horse and livestock convention held in Kansas City every year, took the field for the first time in their home white uniforms trimmed in royal blue with the team name scripted across the front of the button-up jersey. Their caps were the trademark royal blue with a simple KC in white. The uniforms were very similar to the ones the team still wears today.

Senator Symington, the person largely responsible for encouraging the owners to award Kansas City the franchise, threw out the ceremonial first pitch.

The Royals jumped out to a 1-0 lead in their half of the first inning, but the Twins answered with a run in the top of the second. The game remained tied until Minnesota got two runs in the top of the sixth. Rod Carew led off the inning with a single off Bunker. After Gordon brought in relief pitcher Tom Burgmeier, Tony Oliva singled, moving Carew to third. Harmon Killebrew lined to Foy whose only play was to first, but it scored Carew and put Oliva on second. Fortunately for the Royals, Oliva tried to steal third on Burgmeier. He really tried to steal on Burgmeier. He headed for third as soon as the Kansas City pitcher went in to his stretch. But Burgmeier alertly threw to Foy, who chased Oliva into a rundown. The Twins outfielder didn't make it.

That baserunning blunder was extremely beneficial for the Royals, because the next two Minnesota batters, Cesar Tovar and Rich Reese, each hit Burgmeier offerings hard. Reese doubled to score Tovar, but was thrown out at third for the final out of the inning, trying to stretch the double into a triple.

It seemed as though fate wanted everything to go in favor of the Royals in their career opener and to show Kansas City fans that this baseball team might be for real. Wouldn't you know it...the Royals battled back with two runs on a two-out rally in the bottom half of the inning. After Harrison and Oliver were retired, Rodriguez started off the rally with a double off the left-centerfield wall. Hernandez reached first on an error by Killebrew. The error also helped Rodriguez reach third. Pinch hitting for Burgmeier, Jimmy Campanis singled, which scored Rodriguez and moved Hernandez to third.

The hot-hitting Lou Piniella was the next batter. The rookie outfielder had already been instrumental in the game with hits in each of his first three at-bats. Even though Piniella had doubled and scored in the first to put the Royals on the board first, this at-bat in the sixth may have been the biggest of his young career. He came through against Minnesota relief pitcher Bob Miller with an RBI single to center. That's all the runs the Royals could muster in the sixth despite having the bases loaded for Kirkpatrick, but those runs were enough to tie the game at 3-3. (Kirkpatrick was retired by reliever Ron Perranoski.)

Neither team was able to score for several more innings. In fact as the game moved into extra frames, Perranoski and Royals relief pitcher Dave Wickersham each threw five innings. Each pitcher was on the mound through the 11th inning. Wickersham was pulled after the 11th, while Perranoski was lifted in the top of the 12th for a pinch-hitter.

After the Twins failed to get a base runner in the top of the 12th off the new Kansas City pitcher Moe Drabowsky, it was time for the young Royals to put some life into the remaining fans. After Foy reached base on an infield hit, and advanced to second on a wild pitch, Harrison was intentionally walked. The first pitch to the next KC batter, Oliver, was wild, moving the runners up 90 feet. Oliver was intentionally walked.

With the bags full, Joe Keough, who had come out of spring training as one of the team's top hitters, was sent to the plate in place of Rodriguez. Keough smashed the first offering from relief pitcher Rick Woodson over the head of Minnesota right fielder Tony Oliva for the 4-3 win. What a way to start out professional baseball's 100th year and the first year for the Royals!

I was on the air when Keough delivered.

People often ask me what my most outstanding memory is of the Royals, through the history of the franchise. My answer is the very first game. It was the club's first game, and it was my first game as a major league announcer. As it worked out, we won the game, and I was on the air when it happened. That means I was the first person to actually say, "the Royals win." That's kind of neat.

I mentioned Moe Drabowsky, who was the winning pitcher in that first game in Royals history. Moe was a nice, nice guy. He was one of the funniest and best practical jokers in the history of baseball. There are some great Moe stories out there. When he was with the Kansas City Athletics, he once put goldfish in the opposing team's clear, five-gallon water cooler in one of the bullpens.

Another time when he was with the Athletics, during a game against the Tigers in Kansas City, Moe got the number for the phone in Detroit's bullpen. The game was moving relatively slowly. So, in about the fifth inning, Drabowsky called the Tiger bullpen from the A's bullpen, and, imitating the Detroit manager he said, "Get Hiller up," and slammed the phone down. Nothing's going on, it's in the fifth inning of a 1-1 game, and

Hiller jumps up and starts throwing. You could imagine the reaction in the Detroit dugout, thinking, "What in the hell is Hiller doing up?!" So they called the bullpen and told Hiller to sit down. He sat down. An inning later, Moe did the same thing, and Hiller got up and started throwing again.

Drabowsky did all sorts of goofy things like that; harmless, but really pretty clever and funny. He did a zillion things that I have read about and have forgotten. But that was Moe Drabowsky.

With the win in the opener against the Twins, the Royals had an auspicious start to the history of the franchise, but it was difficult to tell by walking around the city. Maybe the attitude was because of the major league disappointment in 1967 with the departure of the Athletics, or maybe it was because of the cold and dreary April day; whatever the reason, only 17,688 fans saw the opening day victory at Municipal Stadium.

Kansas Citians were glad baseball was back, but it's not as though people were all abuzz about it. There was interest, and it was a festive day, but when the stadium is only a little over half-filled, we didn't have the feeling that everyone in town wanted to get in.

(On a side note, one of the umpires for that opening day game was a guy by the name of Don Denkinger. Don Denkinger...why does that name sound so familiar? A foreshadowing? Does the sixth game of the 1985 World Series and something about a possible blown call at first base jar any mental cobwebs? Prophetic beginnings for the franchise?)

The second game of the season had as much drama as the first, even though it wasn't opening day. After a 4-for-5 hitting exhibition on opening day, Piniella once again had a chance to make his mark. And did he ever!

The Royals struggled through much of the game with the Twins. Down 3-2 in the bottom of the eighth with two outs, and Pat Kelly at second base running for Jerry Adair, Foy ripped a ball into the leftfield corner. Kelly came around to score before Foy was thrown out trying to stretch the hit into a double. The important thing was that the game was tied, 3-3. With neither team scoring in the ninth, it went into extra-innings.

It went on in extra innings. And it went on in extra innings. Even though the game seemed like it might never end, we had only gone a little more than four hours by the time we reached the 17th inning.

Despite Piniella, who was a physical education major during the off-season, teaching the Twins and Royals about hitting in the opener, Minnesota pitchers returned the favor in the second game. During the marathon, Lou had gone hitless in six plate appearances heading into the 17th. With Jack Hernandez at second base for Kansas City in the bottom of the 17th, Piniella stroked a two-out single to left for the game-winning RBI. The Royals won 4-3 before leaving town for their first-ever regular season road trip.

From day one, or after those opening two games anyway, Lou Piniella was the team's first young star. He was definitely one of our best players, if not the best. He was a lot better defensively than anybody gave him credit for being. He had sure hands and deceptive speed; he caught a lot of balls nobody thought he could get to. He was just really a good hitter. A great competitor. Worked hard. And he had a good, outgoing, funny personality.

You could write a pretty thick book on the funny things that Lou Piniella has done. He did some unbelievable stuff. He was so obsessed with his hitting that he would sometimes take his offense to the outfield.

Just a quick story that comes to mind. We were playing a day game, and in the middle of this close game Lou grounded into a double play to end the inning. Okay, the inning's over and Freddie Patek brought Lou's glasses and glove to him, the glasses tucked inside, so he doesn't have to go all the way back to the dugout. Lou grabbed the glove and the glasses, and stalked out to left field still thinking about grounding into the double play. Whenever he became all worked up, when he made a big out, Lou would want to throw something, or tear something, or hit somebody - he just wanted to do something. So here were his glasses inside his glove.

Piniella took his sunglasses and fired them out into left field ahead of him, and kept walking out there. He picked them up, stuck them on, put his hat on, and got his glove, still thinking about grounding into the double play. What he hadn't realized was that when he threw his glasses on the ground, one of the lenses had popped out. As luck would have it, the second batter up in the inning hit a high fly ball toward Lou. He flipped down the sunglasses and started looking up in the burning sun with one lens out and one lens in. He started spinning around wildly in a circle trying to get an angle on the ball. He just kept spinning around like a top, out of control, and the ball fell to the ground.

There is just one hilarious story after another on Lou Piniella. That's just one of a zillion, each is funnier than the next. That's just kind of my favorite.

Despite a relatively successful inaugural season with a lot of good times, the trying year for the organization was the next year, 1970, when the team won only 65 games. (That was the lowest number of wins for a Royals team until the strike-shortened season of 1981, when they won 50.)

In 1971 the Royals really started to come along and make some noise in the American League. They finished the season 85-76 and came in second in the A.L. West. The vindictive Royals fan might point out that the team was able to put this winning record together in just its third year of existence; the Athletics were unable to put together a winning season during their entire 13 seasons in Kansas City. (Unfortunately those same fans may want to whisper...the Royals finished second in the A.L. West in 1971 to the Oakland A's.)

THE TALLIS TRADE MACHINE

The team's surge in 1971 was largely due to general manager Cedric Tallis, who had made some big trades in his first three years as G.M. All of his early trades were good ones. He was trading with the National League and at that point in time, it was clearly superior to the American League.

A couple of the more beneficial trades for Royals fans included players such as Lou Piniella, Amos Otis, Cookie Rojas and Fred Patek. Piniella became a Royal at the beginning of the 1969 season in a deal with the Seattle Pilots, the other A.L. expansion team. At the end of that first season Piniella was named the American League Rookie of the Year. Despite the deal to get Lou, most of the key deals the Royals made during the off-season were with teams in the senior circuit.

Within the span of one year, Cedric made three deals with National League teams that built the strength up the middle for Kansas City. On December 3rd of 1969 he traded Joe Foy to the Mets for Bob Johnson, a pitcher, and Otis, a centerfielder. Bob had a great year in 1970; and it was obvious after his first year with the Royals that Amos was going to be a star. Then in the middle of the 1970 season, Rojas came to the Royals from the Cardinals for an outfielder named Fred Rico (no, he never did anything in the big leagues.)

Almost a year to the day after the initial deal with the Mets, on December 2nd, 1970, Cedric took Johnson, who had had a good season, could throw hard, and was goofier than hell, and sent him to the Pirates for Jerry May, a catcher, Bruce Dal Canton, a pitcher, and Patek, a shortstop.

So in those three deals, Cedric got a catcher, a pitcher, a second baseman, a shortstop and a centerfielder. Boom, strength up the middle right away. Three deals with National League teams, the Pirates, Cardinals and Mets. That's pretty good. The Royals from that point on were pretty darn competitive. So those early trades were truly amazing.

It just seemed as though Tallis and the Royals scouting staff had an uncanny ability to identify young players who they thought would turn into terrific major leaguers, and did turn into terrific major leaguers. The Royals just stole good players from other organizations.

Tallis was doing a wonderful job. In my opinion, Cedric Tallis, in about a three or four year period, made some of the greatest trades in the history of baseball. Because of his spectacular deals, and the strong second place division finish by his young team, Tallis was named the 1971 Executive of the Year by *The Sporting News* magazine.

Once the Tallis trade machine had been set in motion, the Royals were able to start feeding players in from their minor league system. Some pretty good talent, including players like George Brett and Frank White, blossomed in the Kansas City farm system in the early 1970s.

I'd have to look at all the other trades, hundreds of trades that we've made over the years, to say if we've had more good or bad deals, but with the success of the organization, the Royals obviously have made a lot more good ones than bad ones. But those early deals always stand out in my mind because Cedric, very effectively, built strength up the middle.

The people who were doing all of this were great to work for and with. They had fun at what they did, but they worked hard. There was a great combination of those two ingredients in everyone, from the manager, to the coaches, to Buddy Blattner, to Cedric Tallis.

THE STUDENT-MENTOR RELATIONSHIP

During those first few seasons with the Royals, I learned the importance of having a great mentor in the booth and away from the stadium. Since the Royals job was my first full-time "professional" radio job, I soaked up all of the education I could from the seasoned Blattner.

Buddy Blattner was one of the true legends in this business, although he didn't need to be a character in the same sense as a Harry Caray. Buddy was very workman-like, very thorough, and had a great feel for the game as a former player. He had a great sense of the idea that we were producing a show from sign-on to sign-off. It was our show and our production. That's how he approached it.

Buddy was very good, with a great voice. He had a good sense of humor. To me, he was also a good teacher. He wasn't a goofy character at all, but he was very funny with some great stories. He was the whole package.

It was a great environment in our booth because of that mentor-student relationship. Bud was very good about taking me around with him and introducing me to everybody in the league, and making me feel a part of it. Bud and his wife, Babs, were just wonderful people. They had three daughters, and they treated me like a son.

Working with him was fun, revealing, interesting, pressure-free and comfortable. I couldn't have imagined a better working situation, starting out in broadcasting, than we had in our booth. All of the things that a young announcer could hope for in that regard fell into place.

My early memory of Blattner, however, is not baseball related. At one time Bud was also a top basketball play-by-play announcer with the St. Louis Hawks in the NBA. The Hawks enjoyed success in St. Louis from 1955-1968. In 1958, the team won the NBA championship.

Growing up in Bloomington we could pick up KMOX radio out of St. Louis. I would listen to Buddy do games for the Hawks. He was simply a terrific basketball announcer. People today talk about Chick Hearn with the Los Angeles Lakers, who is excellent, but Buddy may have been the best ever. He was superb.

Remember, that's coming from a grade school listener, but, he was outstanding. Even now, remembering him do basketball games, I remember enough to say how good he was.

Before heading into the radio booth, Bud had been a major league infielder for three teams from 1942-1949 (with a break from 1943-1945 during World War II), mostly with the New York Giants. In fact, Buddy was a true pioneer athlete-turned-broadcaster. Whereas it is fairly common nowadays to have former professional athletes in the booth, it wasn't that way 50 years ago. On a side note, while he was a teenager, Blattner was a world doubles table tennis champion.

Bud may be best known for his time with CBS radio and the Mutual Network with their *Game of the Day* in the 1950s. During most of those national broadcasts, he worked with former pitcher Dizzy Dean. Besides working with CBS and Mutual (and the St. Louis Hawks), Blattner worked exclusively for two other teams before joining the Royals, the St. Louis Cardinals and the California Angels.

Blattner is what some in the business consider to be a sportscaster's sportscaster. He was the type of broadcaster who liked to meet with his CBS or Mutual partners for breakfast on the day of a game to discuss the teams and the broadcast. While he was with the Royals, Bud liked to get together with me to discuss my progress.

One of the things he emphasized was to be myself, to do my own thing, and to not copy anyone else. I have always remembered that. He showed me quite a few things about the business. Once a week or so we would go out after a game and talk about how the game was handled, how I did, how I handled certain situations, how I could have done something differently, or how I wished I would have done something differently; basically a teacher/student discussion. That was great for me because he had a superb sense of how things should go. He used to say that we were producing a three-hour show every night.

Bud's last year with the Royals, and in broadcasting, was 1975. There have been a lot of rumors regarding his departure, whether it was on his own, or if he was fired. Bud's leaving Kansas City was probably a combination of a lot of things.

He was getting to a point where he was really tired of the traveling, and was thinking about at least shutting down part of his travel with the team. He and Cedric Tallis got along very well, but then Cedric left, so I don't know how well that set with Bud, or how upset he was about it. He was also very good friends with manager Bob Lemon, so when Lem left, Bud and new manager Jack McKeon didn't get along very well. (McKeon's last season was also Buddy's last season.)

Suddenly all of his friends, and all of the people he had come to Kansas City to work with, were all leaving. He wasn't real happy about that. That made the decision to leave a little easier for him. Without knowing all of the inner-politics of everything, those were the impressions that were the strongest to me about his leaving.

Bud never really missed broadcasting when he first left, because he had done it for so long and he really disliked the traveling. Most people in baseball, when they get out, say that traveling is the reason they got out, or, when they've been out awhile, they say they miss a lot of things but they don't miss the traveling. Bud packed a suitcase for a long time. He did an NBA schedule too, remember, which is far more frantic than doing a baseball schedule.

We still talk, on the average, three times a year. We just call each other to shoot the breeze, talk for 20-30 minutes. Knowing Bud, there are things about broadcasting that he missed but I'm sure there are a lot of things about it that he didn't miss.

TIME WITH OTHER LEGENDARY BROADCASTERS

In 1982 I had a chance to work the American League playoffs for CBS Radio with the legendary voice of the Detroit Tigers, Ernie Harwell. It was the Milwaukee Brewers against the California Angels. Like Buddy, Ernie is a very low key, old-time type broadcaster. He is a good man and a nice man. When we worked together, he didn't jump in on my innings at all. Once in a while he'd make a comment, but for the most part he just sat back and did his game his way, with me not making a lot of comments during his innings. That's the way he worked. That's the way he always worked.

His partners were Ray Lane for a while and then Paul Carey. That's the way all of them worked. Broadcasting alone was the style of baseball broadcasting when radio was in its infancy. That's the way the older announcers were brought up. That's the way they learned to do it. They did the game pretty much on their own; they didn't rely much on their partners, analysts, or color guys. They were "the guy," and they did the game their way.

Some guys bantered back and forth more than others. Vin Scully of the Los Angeles Dodgers doesn't have anybody breaking in on him, much. Harry Caray, when he was doing the Cardinal games with Jack Buck and the other people whom he worked with, was a one-man show; he did the game.

Ernie was that way. He was a little more amenable to a few little comments here and there. He didn't resent them, obviously. He was nice to work with, I didn't feel badly about making a comment if something needed to be brought up. He would say, "Anytime you want to say something, jump right in there." I knew how he did the game so I might make one comment for two half innings, if it was pertinent. It's the old thing with me, I always feel like if my partner has something to say, say it. If he doesn't, then shut up, because as soon as he tries to say something, it's going to sound like he is trying to say something and normally, it's not going to mean much because he is forcing it. If all of a sudden, something occurs and he sees something that needs to be commented on, then say it.

Ernie was enjoyable to work with and it was a fun experience. Ernie's southern drawl in Michigan may have sounded strange at first to some fans, but they loved it.

I have been lucky to be able to spend time with a lot of the great voices and characters in Major League Baseball. Bob Starr used to invite us to come out and play golf once in a while when we were in Anaheim. Merle Harmon had a nice house on the lake outside of Milwaukee, and he would have us out when he was doing the games for the Brewers in the 1970s. I remember going with Buddy out to Merle's on a couple of occasions.

There have been some huge names in this business, some true legends, and I've had a chance to spend time with quite a few of them. Since broadcasters have only a few people they work with on a regular basis, there is a great fraternity. It's gratifying to think that I've been a member of that fraternity.

ON THE BRINK OF SOMETHING HUGE

When Kansas City officials approached Major League Baseball about being awarded a team when the Athletics left, part of their argument was that a new stadium had already been approved. So from the outset we knew the team was not going to be in Municipal Stadium for too long.

After a second-place finish in 1971, with a record of 85-76, and a disappointing record of 76-78 to earn a fourth-place finish in the A.L. West in 1972, we could tell the organization was on the verge of seeing something really big happen. Mainly, we were ready to move into the new state-of-the-art Royals Stadium in the Truman Sports Complex, away from downtown Kansas City.

As the team played out its final season and approached the move, there didn't seem to be a lot of teary-eyed sentiment toward Municipal Stadium. In fact, the only thing I really remember about the final game at the old stadium is the digging up of home plate after the game to take over to the new stadium, but I don't recall a lot about the game itself.

In off-season moves going into 1973 to acquire more talent and fill in some holes, the Royals traded for such players as Gene Garber, Kurt Bevacqua and Hal McRae.

On the broadcasting side, since there was going to be additional excitement around the team because of the new stadium, there was some talk about some of the 1973 games being televised. We thought that would be exciting, but if that was going to be the case, Bud and I felt we could split the duties between radio and TV. We hadn't really thought about the prospect of another broadcaster joining us.

Yes, we were on the brink of something huge.

4 Hello, Everybody, This is Fred White

Fred White

The 1973 season marked an incredible time of change for the Kansas City Royals organization. The main change was the most obvious, as the team moved into its new home at the Truman Sports Complex, off Interstate 70.

Royals Stadium was a beautiful sight for a baseball fan's eyes. The stadium opened for business on a chilly April night with the Royals entertaining the Texas Rangers.

The 1973 season also marked new additions for Royals fans. Two young players, George Brett and Frank White, were brought up during the season from the team's farm system. One player was brought over to the American League from the Cincinnati Reds. I'm referring, of course, to Hal "Mac" McRae. These three players would later prove to be invaluable for the organization's success and they became the nucleus of the great teams. All three would later be added to the Royals Hall of Fame.

That was a momentous season in regard to the changes on the field. Obviously no one knew those three guys were going to turn out to be as good as they were. It took George a while to develop. Mac struggled offensively until the mid-point of the season. That's when he and George both got with Charlie Lau and went to work with him on their hitting. The fans didn't want Frank at second base, they wanted Cookie Rojas. Life as a Royal wasn't easy for Frank. Cookie was a fan favorite and even though White was a hometown guy, he was not readily accepted as our second baseman. A couple of years later, when Whitey Herzog was managing, and he chose to play Frank more than Cookie, the fans really gave Frank and Whitey a tough time. It was a very difficult thing.

In the mid-1970s Cookie made a great gesture toward Frank. In a ceremony at the stadium, he took his hat off and gave it to Frank; symbolic of saying, "This is your job now." Once Cookie did that in front of the fans here at home, life became a little bit easier for Frank.

But in 1973 veterans like Paul Splittorff, Steve Busby and Amos Otis were already with the club. The team was developing a winning habit, and the players knew it. They knew they were getting better every year. The atmosphere then was electric. They were a team destined for greatness and they knew it. The Royals were one big happy family. They would win. We would laugh. Then we would go on from there. Ewing Kauffman was the ideal owner, with

Joe Burke as the general manager and John Schuerholz running the farm system. It was just a wonderful time to be involved with this organization.

The 1973 season also marked my debut with the organization as a 37-year-old rookie major league radio announcer. With the new stadium and the excitement centering around the organization, the front office decided that several of the team's games that year would be televised locally in Kansas City. Buddy and Denny would split up the TV duties; I would fill-in and be the constant voice on the radio when games were being televised.

At the time I was hired to help with radio, I was the sports director and main sports anchor for WIBW-TV in Topeka, Kansas. In that capacity I occasionally went to Municipal Stadium to cover the Royals. It's safe to say that I was not a stranger to the Kansas City organization.

It's somewhat ironic that I ended up with the Royals four years into their existence, because I had applied for their radio job in 1968. But the Royals never contacted me again...until 1973. In the winter before that baseball season, officials with the Royals were in Topeka to meet with some station people at WIBW. I went to lunch with the group. The Royals people told me they were looking for a third announcer to use during television games and asked if I was interested. I mean HELLO. Are you kidding?

I immediately pinned the guy in the restaurant and wouldn't let him up until we had an agreement. We talked about it and essentially made a deal right there that they would add a third guy, me. It sort of surprised Buddy and Denny. The Royals hadn't even told them this was going to happen.

I remember going back from that lunch thinking, "You know, this is going to work; I'm really going to do Major League Baseball." I had always envisioned that when that day happened, it would require an application, an interview and a lot of those things. Instead, it just sort of dropped in my lap.

When Buddy and Denny arrived at spring training, there I was. We started with maybe some trepidation on Buddy's part. Denny never really felt like that. It worked out well and turned into a good relationship. We had a pretty good fit right from the beginning.

That first season I was the new guy and I was very aware of that fact. My goal was to not go into the new situation like an interloper, or like I wanted to take over. I really just wanted very much to be the third guy and test my wings.

As it turned out, I drove over to Kansas City from Topeka and went on the road trips with the team. (Again, the only time I worked with the Royals was when the games were being televised.) I was very comfortable with the situation, because it gave me a chance to become acclimated and to let my new partners decide if I was going to be able to help them.

Denny and Buddy didn't need help. They didn't need help in the sense of the broadcast style, but they had to decide whether or not they thought I could do the job well enough to continue the three-man rotation.

Interestingly enough, that first year I probably spent more time with Buddy than with Denny. Denny was a young, single guy and he was off on his own when the games were over, so I just sort of gravitated more toward Buddy, and he invited me to do things with him. Our producer/engineer Ed Shepherd, Buddy and I did some things socially together. I was divorced at the time, so I would occasionally go out with Buddy. In those days, Denny tended to hang out with the players more than he did with anyone else, because he was their age.

That's sort of how everything with the Royals happened — it just evolved. I came here in their mind as an experiment, but the position just sort of grew. There was never a great lightning strike, or a definitive moment when they said, "OK, we'll keep you." It was basically just twenty-five one-year handshakes.

If I had written a script and planned it, I could not have come to the Royals in a better year than 1973.

GROWING UP WITH THE CARDINALS

Broadcasting Major League Baseball on radio was quite a change from my childhood. I grew up in a small town of about 1,000 people in Homer, Illinois. My father, Eddie, slaughtered cattle in a packing plant while my mother, Mary, worked as a waitress in a restaurant (and owned the restaurant for a while). I had one brother, Jack, and a sister, Marilyn. My childhood was really a typical small-town childhood, which included playing every sport in school. In that type of setting, in a high school with only 89 students, a boy played every sport and was in the school plays.

For some people, including me, living in a small town is the greatest. Homer is a farm community near the University of Illinois, halfway between Chicago and St. Louis. In the summer, my buddies and I were constantly swimming or playing baseball.

While the baseball loyalties in our family were divided between the Chicago Cubs and the St. Louis Cardinals, I grew up a Cardinals fan listening to Harry Caray on the radio. It was an ideal childhood. My mom was a Cubs fan, my dad was a Cardinals fan, my brother was a Cubs fan, my sister couldn't care less, my uncles were divided right down the middle, and I was a Cardinals fan. In fact, the last thing my mother did publicly was go to the Cubs playoff game in 1984 (she was dying of cancer).

People in that part of the country used to say that they lived to see the Cubs in the playoffs. Mom literally did that. I got tickets and my brother took her to the game, brought her back home, and she really never ventured out again. That was the last thing she got to do. She had Cub earrings that she wore all the time. One of the debates we had when she died was whether to bury her in those earrings. We didn't; they're in our house.

I grew up in a family that loved sports and especially loved baseball. There were a lot of baseball discussions.

Deciding on which team to root for, especially in our household, was an important decision. In Homer, picking between the Cubs and the Cardinals was almost as important as choosing a political party. Maybe more important. My early allegiance to the Cardinals may have been aided by my first memory of listening to a baseball game on the radio. It was during the 1946 World Series between the Cardinals and the Boston Red Sox.

Our family and friends were all gathered at the house on Sunday afternoon, listening to the game. The most vivid play to me was a time when Enos Slaughter was on first base and Harry Walker was at the plate. Slaughter scored from first...on a SINGLE by Walker!

All the Cardinals fans in the family became excited. That is my first memory of really listening to a baseball game on the radio. That one World Series game in 1946 really turned me on to how good baseball could be and how good baseball was on the radio. Still, I never thought of being an announcer.

From that day on, whenever I went outside to play catch, or throw a tennis ball off the barn, I would announce the games, not to be an announcer, but rather announcing myself playing, making spectacular catches and doing other great things out there. I never thought in terms of wanting to grow up and be an announcer; I just needed an announcer to describe my fantastic feats out in the barn.

I also remember listening to the Army-Navy football game. That was one of those games we listened to every year. Dad was busy doing something else, but he wanted me to listen to the game and be able to provide scores when needed. Wow, that's a huge responsibility! It was my first time, so I wanted to do a great job. Every few minutes I would yell an update. My dad finally thought, "This can't be right." Oops! As it turned out, when I was giving him what I thought was the score, I was actually reporting first downs.

My friends and I listened to Bert Wilson describe the Cubs games in the afternoon and Harry Caray call the Cardinal games at night. As a Cardinals fan, I lived and died with Harry in the evenings.

We'd go play ball, then stop by Kenny's Drug Store (they closed at 9:00) to sit and listen to the game until it ended. Then when the game was over, we'd all kind of disperse and go home. It was great — there were the Cubs fans and the Cardinals fans, and we always had an argument going about baseball in those days.

When I was 12-years-old, my Uncle Bill took me to my first major league game to see the Dodgers and Cubs at Wrigley Field. It was magic! Just going to Chicago was a big deal. To go to Chicago and to see Wrigley Field and a major league game was really something special. Preacher Rowe pitched for the Dodgers. I don't remember who pitched for the Cubs, and I don't remember who won - I just remember we had great seats right behind first base. I can remember walking in there, looking at the field, and thinking, "Oh Wow!" For me, going to Wrigley felt something like going to Oz. We'd played in our yards or down at the grade school on the only diamond we had in town but I never dreamed that a baseball diamond could look like the one at Wrigley Field. There was just something special about it.

The second time I saw a major league game was at old Sportsman's Park in St. Louis. I'd heard Harry Caray describe it all those times on the radio, but when you're sitting there as a kid, after you've imagined this all of your life, and then all of a sudden there's Stan Musial, it's a little larger than life.

COACH WHITE?

I attended college at Eastern Illinois, and I began as a physical education major, with plans to be a coach. Coaching is what I really wanted to do but it didn't take me long to realize that I didn't want to teach. I didn't think I'd be a good teacher, so I switched to business. While I was in school I went to work for a terrific guy named Walt Warmouth. When they were in school, then-future Kansas City Royals Marty Pattin and Kevin Seitzer worked for him in the same restaurant where I worked. That was easily the best education I got in college.

Warmouth was a great sports fan and encouraged all his workers to be involved in sports. He sent me out one night to a Charleston High School football game, to spend pregame time with the coach, who threw up, looked at me and said, "I make $9,000 a year and I do this before every ballgame. Are you sure you want to coach?"

He was a good coach. After watching him throw up I thought, " Well, maybe coaching isn't for me." When I switched to a business major I thought I'd maybe still coach if it came up. In fact, I did coach the freshman football team one year at my old high school when I was in the area working. I really enjoyed it, and to this day I think I would have really loved it as my profession.

Life took me somewhere else and it obviously took me to the right place. It's interesting that my career allowed me to remain in sports.

After leaving Eastern Illinois, I still hadn't planned on going into broadcasting. Instead, I went into the insurance field with a friend of mine who had an established business. Another good friend, Dave Divan, was the sports director at radio station WITY in Danville, Illinois. After a long week at the office, I would go to ball games with him on Friday nights to unwind. It took a couple of years, but that friend talked me into working with him as his color commentator in football. Still, radio broadcasting as a full time "day job" didn't seem like a possibility, especially for someone from Homer, Illinois.

Being on the radio was a thing that guys from big towns did; small town guys didn't do that. Small town guys farmed and taught schools and did those types of things. I just didn't realize how much I fell in love with radio at the time. In my mind radio announcing was always going to be an avocation and a hobby for me. Up until the time I went into broadcasting full time, I kept going to games as a fan; in some ways I still do.

In the middle of that first season of helping out at WITY, Dave Divan quit and went to work with the Federal Bureau of Investigation as an agent. Station management offered me the job. I had had just enough of a taste of radio to love it, so I quit the insurance business and went into radio...full time.

I was only at WITY full-time for six months, as the all-night disc jockey on Saturday night, among other things. I was reading *Broadcasting* magazine in the spring of 1965 and saw an ad for a station in Hastings, Nebraska that needed a sports guy. The advertisement said they did 175 games a year, and I thought that job had my name on it. I looked at that as my college radio education and applied for the job in Hastings. That's kind of how it all happened to me. I started at KHAS radio in May of 1965.

FROM HOMER TO HASTINGS TO TOPEKA

In Hastings, Nebraska, at KHAS radio, as it is with people in most small stations, I basically did everything. I arrived daily by 5:30 a.m., and typed what was called a radiogram - a set of headlines on a sheet of paper. Then I mimeograph copies of what I had typed; then I'd jump in the KHAS station wagon with the lightning streak on the side of it to deliver the copies to all of the restaurants and coffee shops around town.

Sound like a full day? Well, as anyone at a small station would tell you, not quite. After the mimeograph copies were delivered, I'd go back to the station and do the morning sports report before putting on my disc jockey cap. Oh yeah, I also hosted two talk shows; one was called *The Trading Post Show*, and one was a "call me up and talk to me" kind of show about anything the listener wanted to talk about. At noon, I ran the board as the engineer for the noon news, and I did the sports for that segment.

Actually, that was just the morning schedule; there was always the afternoon. My main job during the afternoon was selling advertising; then I did the evening sportscast before doing play-by-play for American Legion baseball, or football and basketball, announcing for Hastings College and the local high school. Even if there was a game in Norfolk that night and I got home at 1:00 a.m., I was back at the station the next morning at 5:30. By any measure, a hectic schedule.

But working at KHAS was probably the best thing I ever did. Originally, I went there because they said they did 175 games a year. It turned out that they did do 175, and I did about all of them. I actually did three seasons there. It was great experience - a terrific education. I didn't make much money but I learned a lot about radio.

While I was in Hastings, we went out to do a late-season football game in a small Nebraska town. The field didn't have a press box, so people from the school brought a bulldozer over to the end zone and raised the blade up on it. My partner and I got in the blade and broadcast the game from there. At least we could see over the heads of the crowd.

The home team won the ballgame in the last second, and the bulldozer operator was so excited that he hit the wrong lever and dumped us out of the blade. That night it was so cold that when we hit the ground, my feet felt like shattered glass.

Working in Nebraska was an adventure. We did games from a library at one end of the field in a little town. The guy with me asked how we would know when the teams scored at the other end of the field. I told him the fans would honk their horns. And they did.

People in these small towns park their cars around the field and when a team scores, people honk their horns. At a baseball game, they honk their horns when somebody hits a home run.

We did a game in another small Nebraska town where there were no phone lines near the field, so we ran extension cords from a house into the back of a grain truck and taped the game from there. Another time when the gas station across the street gave up its phone line so we could broadcast the game live. But for a couple of hours the gas station couldn't answer the telephone.

I had a lot of wonderful adventures in Nebraska. I've always thought those experiences were a lot of fun and great add-on stories to everything else from my career.

As the months passed in Hastings, I looked into the possibility of going to other stations. The working hours seemed to be getting longer, and what happened to a couple days off during the week? As most people who have worked at small stations around the country can tell you, working long hours, seven days a week, doing everything from vacuuming the floor to hosting a drive-time talk show, is the norm.

The most promising opportunity at another station that I turned down came from Madison, Wisconsin. Something just told me to stay in Hastings and wait for a better offer. After two and a half years at KHAS radio, in October of 1967, that offer came from WIBW in Topeka, Kansas. WIBW is an outfit with both television and radio in the state's capital city. At the time, it was the dominant radio station in Kansas, with plenty of college and high school sports. So not only was it an opportunity to go to a bigger station, it was a chance to concentrate on sports.

When WIBW called, it was right and I was ready. I thought I had died and gone to heaven because sports was my main focus; I didn't have to do all the other stuff. It was a real luxury to be a sports guy and nothing else.

On the television side, I was the sports director, meaning I anchored the six and ten o'clock sports. On the radio side WIBW carried football and basketball games for Kansas and Kansas State. Gary Bender had gone from WIBW to KU as their announcer. Shortly after I arrived in Topeka, the station hired Max Falkenstien and divided the duties between us.

Falkenstien, who has been on the radio for the Jayhawks for more than 50 years, did the KU games, while I worked K-State. The radio station also did small-college games with Washburn, KCAC games, and other small colleges in Kansas. They also did a ton of high school sports, and coaches shows and various sports specials.

I worked about as much at WIBW as I had in Hastings, but now it was all sports. No more worrying about swap shows, general call-in shows, or working as a disc jockey. Now it never looked like work. Each new duty in Topeka was just the next fun thing to do. The hours and the number of days "worked" during the course of a week didn't bother me anymore. I loved this job!

Because I was a studio anchor, it gave me a chance to stay tuned to a lot of different sports, and a lot of different areas of sports. Television also gives broadcasters a chance to do more things. Announcers have a much broader knowledge of what's going on in the sports world when they do in-studio work, such as anchoring a talk show, because they have to stay conversant with so many things locally, regionally and nationally.

I could have been content at WIBW for the rest of my life, probably. However, I was always ambitious enough to want to try other things and, of course, Major League Baseball was always a goal. So when the baseball door opened, it was easy to walk right in.

MAGIC LAND

Sure, the Kansas City Royals had had their opening day in the inaugural season of 1969 at Municipal Stadium. Yes, going into the 1999 season they've had 30 home openers. But the home opener of 1973 was a little more special, a little more electric, because it marked the opening of Royals Stadium (renamed Kauffman Stadium on July 2, 1993). On a personal level, it also marked my beginning with the franchise.

The stadium was a marvelous new facility which not only got the team out of the decrepit Municipal Stadium, but it also hammered home the idea that the A's were officially out of Kansas City. The Royals were here to stay as Kansas City's team. The stadium, symbolically, said that Charlie Finley is not here anymore, Mr. Kauffman's here now.

There was no one thing that hit me when I first walked into the stadium. When someone walks in, they just drink in the whole scene, and think baseball. This stadium is only for baseball, and it is Kansas City's. This one belongs to our city and our area. No one can pick it up and move it somewhere else. This stadium is going to be here for a long time. To me it said that we were in the big leagues and it looks like we are here to stay. When we have a chance to travel and look at the other ballparks, it really confirms what we first thought, that Kauffman Stadium is incredible.

To me, it was, and still is, Magic Land. I don't know, but I guess it's like going on a blind date with Cindy Crawford. A person walks in the stadium for the first time, and thinks, "Oh my Lord! This is wonderful!" Even with all of the new ballparks in baseball today, Oriole Park at Camden Yards, Jacob's Field and the Ballpark at Arlington, I still believe this is the best baseball stadium out there.

After I found out that I was going to be one of the radio announcers, I made it a point to not come to Kansas City to look at the stadium before opening night. We did a story on it at WIBW, and I sent Ron Paradis to do the feature. I did not want to see the stadium until I walked in to do the game on opening night.

The stadium is a part of the Truman Sports Complex, which also features Arrowhead Stadium for the Kansas City Chiefs. On our side, Royals Stadium was the main jewel in Ewing Kauffman's crown. A gold crown is in fact visible to all as it tops off the 12-story tall scoreboard in centerfield. (According to the 1998 Kansas City Royals Media Guide, the mammoth scoreboard has 16,320 light bulbs, most of which are used on the 40 feet by 60 feet screen.)

By 1973 standards (and even by 1999 standards) Royals Stadium was a state-of-the-art facility, designed solely for baseball. And baseball fans knew it. The stadium offered every amenity imaginable to the 1973 fan.

In addition to the enormous scoreboard, fans were awed by the water fountains with colorful lights. They saw this from their seats, which are all angled toward the pitcher's mound. When they needed to stretch, fans could take a trip to the multitude of concession or souvenir stands. There was no problem finding a parking space in the massive parking lot, or leaving quickly after a game with easy access to the interstate. (Although many fans would stick around after a game to see a fountain spectacular with the colored lights.)

Fans weren't the only ones who enjoyed the amenities. The players, many of whom were young and had not been in the major leagues for long, savored their new surroundings. Players relaxed in plush clubhouses, or took some extra swings in the spacious batting cages under the stadium. When they were on the field, the Royals or their opponents reveled in the symmetrical field, while pitchers warmed up in the bullpen outside the fence in right or left field. For those chilly early or late-season games, there were also heaters in the dugouts.

Even the broadcasters were treated like royalty. Our broadcast position was relatively far from the playing field but it had a great vantage point. The radio team was on the upper deck of the press section but directly behind home plate.

IS THAT CARPET OR GRASS?!

Even though not many Royals fans or front office people brag about this now, Royals Stadium was the first stadium in the American League to have the fake grass.

Artificial turf (a.k.a. Astroturf) was introduced to the major leagues by the Houston Astros in the Astrodome in 1966. Ironically, when the Astrodome opened in 1965 (dome being the key word), it had real grass! They tried to do this with semi-transparent panels in the roof which, by the way, made them the first team to play in a domed stadium. Since fly balls were impossible to see with the panels as a background, the panels were painted, which blocked out the sun. No sun, no living grass. So, Astroturf was designed and was introduced to Astro fans on opening day in 1966.

Astroturf seemed like a great idea to Kansas City management; it seemed an obvious choice. Since the Royals were a team catering to fans throughout the Midwest from cities like Wichita, Kansas; Springfield, Missouri; Lincoln, Nebraska; and Des Moines, Iowa - cities 100 miles, 200 miles and more away from Kansas City - the thought was that fans should not have to worry about possible rainouts. It sounded like a great idea, but what may not have been taken into consideration was the fact that the start of the game may be delayed two or three hours while the field gets squeegeed after a rain.

The turf wasn't fun to look at for the spectators. The fake grass didn't give anyone chills the way real Bermuda grass does. For the players, the asphalt under the turf made the field extremely hot during the majority of the summer season. The surface was also tough on a player's legs and knees. Players who often had to make quick stops can still feel the effects.

Royals management, to its credit, did a great job of assembling a team crafted perfectly for the fast surface. The teams they put on the field were good artificial turf teams. With players like Amos Otis, Fred Patek and Willie Wilson, the Royals ran more than anyone else in the American League. It was good from that stand point, because we saw the Royals dominate teams and win at home.

Until my dying day, though, I am going to think that Kauffman Stadium is a better ballpark with real grass in it.

OPENING NIGHT, PART II

Obviously that home opener in 1973 against the Texas Rangers was a little more special than any other opening night, and really more important than any other game during that season.

People often ask me if I was nervous. You know, if I had "rookie" jitters. I was more excited, than I was nervous because I was part of what I thought was really going to be a good team; part of a new stadium opening; and a part of the Royals broadcast crew; and all of those things were happening at the same time. Each one of those things would have been very exciting by itself, but here they were all combined on the same night! I thought, "If I never do another one, I still did tonight, and I was asked to be here." That was all very exciting to me.

I'm just glad the Royals front office people decided to televise that first game in the new stadium, because otherwise I would not have done that game on radio. Probably because there were so many elements involved in it, we just didn't have time to get caught up with, "this is me and I've got to do this game" type of attitude.

The game started, we did the broadcast, and the game ended. Everything had gone so well that I stood around, smiled, and thought, "That was nice...I think I'd like to do that again." Stupidly, I didn't save a tape of that first game. Sometimes there were moments, such as George Brett's home run off "Goose" Gossage in the 1980 playoffs, when I thought I was really calm, cool, and collected, but I listen to it now and find that I was screaming! That's why I would like to hear a tape of that first game in the new stadium. But if I never hear it again, I know that it had those magical elements that I will never forget.

Whitey Herzog was managing the Rangers that season. Jack McKeon was the skipper for the Royals. An interesting note about McKeon: 1973 was his first season with the Royals. He came in under quite a bit of scrutiny after the firing of the popular Bob Lemon at the end of the 1972 season. I wasn't there yet when Lemon was fired, but from what I recall, from working in Topeka, there was a lot of flack surrounding the decision. Because of that, McKeon wasn't received as well as I'm sure he would have wanted to be. Lem was a guy who everybody loved and there was a lot of resentment when he was fired. My feeling was that when Jack McKeon got the job some players resented the fact that Lem wasn't there and McKeon was. That was probably fostered by people who weren't players who were around the players a lot. Jack was perceived by some as a lifetime minor league guy. It's funny because you can look at his credentials now and see that he has accomplished a lot in the major leagues.

Not a lot of people in the Royals organization ever gave Jack a fair chance, to be quite honest about it. He paid the price for Lem's popularity. Again, I wasn't on the scene when that change was made, but I was there for Jack's first full year and I do know what went on then.

McKeon's home debut with the Royals was against his future successor, Herzog. Paul Splittorff started for the Royals. It was a cold night, with the game-time temperature at 39 degrees. By the end of the game the temperature had fallen to 33 degrees. In fact, Kansas City had received a late snow a couple of days earlier, and it had to be cleaned out of the stadium. Up until the previous night there was some doubt about whether the game could even be played because of the snow and cold.

One of the things that sticks out in my recollection of the opening night ceremonies is that the dignitaries on the field were all wearing huge top coats. And what dignitaries there were. Then-Major League Baseball Commissioner Bowie Kuhn was there, as were Kansas Governor Robert Docking and Missouri Governor Kit Bond. It was a cold night but the Royals got us started well, and made the crowd of 39,464 forget about the weather.

The Royals jumped on the Rangers quickly. John Mayberry had a home run en route to Kansas City's win. Offensively, Mayberry was the star of the game with two hits, four runs batted in, and the two-run homer off Texas reliever Bill Gogolewski. Splittorff pitched very well, giving up five hits. An interesting side note with Split: he was the first pitcher to start a game in the Royals organization, when he did so with one of the farm teams in 1968. Then in 1973 he became the first pitcher in franchise history to win 20 games.

The Royals won that opening ballgame by a large margin, 12-1, in an ideal way to launch the stadium. With the blowout I thought, "Hey, what's wrong with this? This is the way it's supposed to be and this is the way it is."

BASEBALL'S REAL INTRODUCTION TO KANSAS CITY

The baseball world got it's introduction to the "new" brand of baseball in Kansas City on July 24, 1973, when Royals Stadium hosted the All-Star game. We didn't have to work but we were able to go watch the game. My tickets were down the left field line. When tickets went on sale, fans were lined up for what seemed like miles, and the final attendance was 40,849.

It was a night of celebration for the new stadium, and for having a major league team. The city had only had the team for four years when the All-Star game happened here, and the Royals had a player (Amos Otis) starting in the game, so that made it a pretty special night. The Royals were also represented on the American League team by John Mayberry and Cookie Rojas.

It was a lot of fun that night to mingle and see all the stars from both leagues. It was truly an "all star" game. Guys like Willie Mays, Hank Aaron, Thurman Munson, Brooks Robinson, and Ron Santo played in the game. Dave Concepcion and Carl Yastrzemski were voted to their All-Star teams, but were injured, so they were replaced in the game.

It turned out to be a fun game with some spectacular things, especially home runs. Two memorable home runs were off the bats of Johnny Bench and Bobby Bonds. Bench's home run carried all the way to the top of the general admission section in left-field. Bonds, who was the MVP of the game, hit one up on the grass between the water spectacular and the bullpen. Even though the American League got on the board first with one run in the second inning, the National League poured it on, and won 7-1.

FROM FAN TO EMPLOYEE

Even though I had lived within earshot of Kansas City for several years, and I had been in Hastings and Topeka when the Royals were created, it was not a difficult transition for me to go from being a fan to working for the team in 1973. For broadcasters who grew up as fans of their teams or schools it might be tough, but it was not for me. The transition was pretty natural.

By the time the Royals came along, I had been in this business for awhile and I looked at it more from a sports announcer's standpoint than I did from a fan's standpoint. Had I just begun broadcasting and started doing Cardinals games, I would have been more of a fan making that transition. Yet I was a Major League Baseball fan for sure, and in a sense, a Royals fan. I suppose there was some of me being a "fan," but if there was, it was subconsciously so, and it was not difficult to make the switch to worker.

It does not take long, when we see people (athletes) working, to get out of fan mode. We see them get out on the field and work everyday. We see them out there at 3 o'clock in the afternoon. We see the blue collar stuff they do and begin to appreciate them more as hard working people than as great athletes. We begin to appreciate them more as professionals than we do as gifted athletes. We see their work ethic.

If I did come in as a fan, I got out of that mode pretty quickly. It hit me that, "Hey, I have a job to do." The players are doing their jobs, so I have to do mine. Doing it that way helps to develop that good working relationship with them. An announcer has to show the players that they can trust him, and that he is not there to gossip. There is a code: what we see here, leave here; and what we hear here, leave here.

The broadcaster has to gain a player's trust as a person and as a professional. Once he has done that, he tends to look at the players more as teammates, or workmates, as opposed to the way a fan would look at them. The Royals organization was always very good about promoting that type of atmosphere, and player-broadcaster relationship.

BASEBRAWL

One time we probably wished the baseball world didn't know where we were came in the mid-1970s in Arlington, Texas. The Royals had a fight with the Texas Rangers and it was the biggest and worst baseball fight I've ever seen. It went on and on and on. The umpires and coaches couldn't get it shut down.

The brawl started when Royal catcher Darrell Porter and Ranger Bump Wills collided down the third base line. Then it just went all over the field. Everybody was in it and it seemed to go on for about 20 minutes. They had such a hard time getting the melee stopped that it reached a point where we were really beginning to be concerned for people's safety.

We had a fight in Oakland one time during the 1970s when Don Baylor charged Dennis Leonard. George Brett got between them, and it turned into a pretty good fight on the infield. Then when our guys got back to the bullpen, which is right next to the stands in Oakland, a fight broke out down there. The fans got after our guys down in the bullpen. That was incredible. Those were both very memorable brawls.

Broadcaster's hate to see brawls like these. In 1998 we had an embarrassing moment at Kauffman Stadium when then-Royal shortstop Felix Martinez sucker punched one of the Anaheim Angels during a scuffle behind home plate. Though most brawls aren't embarrassing moments in a broadcaster's career, when Martinez punched the Angel, even we broadcasters had to hang our heads.

My personal feeling that night was that the Royals should release him immediately and make a statement to baseball about not condoning this kind of action. They should have tried to get him some help too; but the organization definitely needed to make a statement to baseball on the order of: we've got a problem here and we are dealing with it. Instead, they sent him down to Omaha and got him off the big league team, which I guess in a sense is making a statement. Other than instances such as that one, fights are a part of baseball.

FINALLY GETTING OVER THE HUMP

The 1974 season was a long one for me because I wasn't doing the ballgames, even though I was in Kansas City a lot for WIBW. It was a disappointing season on the field for the Royals, with a fifth place divisional finish and a record of 77-85, which represented only eight more wins than the team had in its first season.

The next year, 1975, was really when I became full-time. It is also the year when things really started to click for the ballclub. The team finished in second place in the A.L. West behind the Oakland A's, with a record of 91-71. Another second place finish. Another finish behind those Oakland A's. If the Royals could just somehow get past that damn club that used to call Kansas City home they would be over that hump, a hump which had become a jinx. It was no wonder that the Royals (more so, really, the Kansas City fans) had two reasons to dislike Charlie O's team: the A's abandoned the K.C. fans, plus they stood in the way of Kansas City's new tenant reaching a divisional title.

At the end of that second-place season, McKeon was fired as the team's manager, and Buddy was let go as the main announcer. So in 1976, Denny and I started doing all the games together.

That was the year when the players really began to lock-in and get focused. That was when all those guys developed into a good team. They all seemed to hit their strides at about the same time. Brett became Brett. Frank White took over as the club's regular second baseman. McRae became a very good hitter. A significant move Whitey made that year was putting Al Cowens in the lineup full-time. That team really began to jell. That was when I was realized that this was really a good team.

McRae was a fun player to watch. Mac worked hard and was extremely aggressive. In fact, there's a rule named after him — the McRae Rule — referencing a play in which he hit New York Yankee Willie Randolph at second base in the playoffs; he knocked Randolph into left field. Even after the McRae Rule was adopted, Hal's behavior didn't change. He would do anything on the field to win a baseball game.

With all that was happening, it looked as though the Royals were going to finally catch the Oakland A's. Watching them battle the A's in previous years was exciting for us, but finally catching the Oakland team was something special. The Royals were rewarded for their persistent pursuit of the former Kansas City team with their first divisional crown, and the club's first trip to the playoffs.

A CARING OWNER

Since Ewing Kauffman always saw the players as his boys, he was extremely proud when they earned their first trip to the playoffs. Mr. Kauffman was a wonderful man and the perfect one to bring this franchise to Kansas City. He really cared.

Just the fact that he was around was a comfort.

He tried to take care of everyone involved in his organization, but he did it in an unassuming way. There were not many times that he even went down to the clubhouse, for instance. Usually when he did, it was just to see how the team was doing, or to offer support. For example, if the team was going through a losing streak, he was known for going down and handing all the guys a $100 bill and saying, "Take your wife to dinner tonight." He wanted to take care of as many people as he could.

THESE GUYS AREN'T THAT BAD...

For some reason, as the new guy, I thought baseball would be a difficult fraternity to break into, that I would have to work extra hard to earn people's respect (and maybe I did), but everyone was very helpful from the beginning.

From my point of view, even though I may have worked hard to earn that respect, I was really pleased to get cooperation from the players, the coaches and managers, and from the broadcast crew. It was apparent that I was going to be able to sit down and ask them questions; that I would be invited out for a beer with them after a game to talk baseball. People in the organization were very impressive; professional in every sense of the word. I really appreciated that.

I often took a deep breath and thought, "This is going to be good; they're going to help me and it's all going to work okay." I hope I showed them a little bit of something — that I cared about them, that I wanted to do well and that maybe I had some ability. It was a lot easier and a lot more fun for me than I thought it would be. Let's face it, I was still a neophyte as far as Major

League Baseball was concerned. I still looked at things with the eyes of a fan and I wondered what it was going to be like. Well, it was every bit as good as I thought it was going to be.

STICKING WITH THE WILDCATS IN TOPEKA

I was not with the team on a full-time basis at first. In fact, even though I started doing Royals games full-time in 1975, I stayed at WIBW until December of 1979, all the while, for a total of 13 seasons, doing Kansas State basketball on WIBW. It was a full schedule, but I wouldn't have it any other way.

Basically, I did only selected Royals games during 1973, then I didn't do anything with the team in 1974, and then I came back in 1975 and worked every game. In 1974, I just wanted more money than I was getting and they wouldn't agree to it. Apparently they felt that I would just come back and do it anyway. Then spring training rolled around and they still thought they could get just anybody to come in and work for whatever they were going to pay.

I thought about it and decided that I had proven I could do it, plus I was still the sports director at WIBW. I worked almost every day that year, and didn't get the winter off. When I wasn't doing a Royals game, I was back at Topeka working and I never got any time off. If I had gone to spring training in 1974 without a decision from the Royals, I probably would have talked to another club somewhere. But I finally determined that if I was going to broadcast Major League Baseball games I wanted to do it in Kansas City. But I really thought they would come around. They didn't.

So I stuck it out in Topeka for a few years. In 1979, a new all-sports cable network came on the air...ESPN. I did a ton of stuff for them. What with ESPN and the Royals, I was on the road a lot, which meant WIBW quite often took a backseat.

I really felt pulled in all directions. Then, during this same period in 1979, the Pirates offered me a job. I didn't want to move to Pittsburgh, but for the record, WIBW told me they couldn't equal the financial package I was offered by the Pirates.

My thought was to tell the station to just give me the winter off, and I'll worry about making up the financial loss later with ESPN.

Having to work in Kansas City this summer and Topeka in the winter, living two different places was just wearing me out with ESPN.

So, in the middle of the 1979-80 K-State basketball season, I closed my final basketball broadcast for WIBW.

Mr. K...Building a Champion

Denny Matthews

The Royals organization decided to change the name of Royals Stadium to Kauffman Stadium in 1993. It was extremely appropriate that they used Ewing Kauffman's name, considering he was the person who brought baseball back to Kansas City when the A's left, and built a winning organization so quickly.

FROM NON-BASEBALL FAN TO MLB'S IDEAL OWNER

Ewing Kauffman may have been one of the least obvious of people to bring baseball back to Kansas City after the A's bolted for Oakland. He had developed a name for himself in pharmaceuticals, and had become a billionaire through hard work. He was not a baseball fan at all, and actually did not know much about the game, but he had the wherewithal to buy the team. Maybe it's safer to say that once he was pushed a little bit, he realized that he should buy the team for the city.

There were a lot a businessmen, most of them friends of his in Kansas City, many of whom were very involved in the A's, who really prodded Ewing to buy the team. Guys like Earl Smith and Les Milgram really got the thing rolling and then Ewing's wife Muriel put him over the edge. Muriel was the last one to kick him in the seat of the pants and say, let's do it. Major League Baseball awarded them, and the city, the team.

I do not know how many individuals actually sought to buy the franchise, but the people who wanted Ewing to become involved, people like Smith, Ernie Mehl and Senator Stuart Symington, sensed that he would be the best one. The others, for whatever reason, didn't work out.

To their credit, the people who pushed Mr. K to be involved somehow sensed that he was the right man for what they needed. They knew baseball, but they needed money and needed someone willing to back the team to show Major League Baseball that a professional team could work in Kansas City. Ewing had never been involved in sports very much. He played golf and gin rummy with his buddies at the club, and other things like that, but that was about it. The main thing about Ewing Kauffman was that he was very competitive. So, he liked that part of baseball. He wanted to be better than a George Steinbrenner. He wanted his team to be better than the Orioles and everybody else, and, most especially better than the Oakland A's.

He and Charles Finley got into it every once in awhile. In 1969 Ewing offered to buy Reggie Jackson for $1 million. Finley toyed with the idea, but turned it down. Could you imagine Reggie as a Royal?

I used to see the two owners at the old ballpark, when Ewing invited Finley up to his box at the press level. They would sit there through the baseball game and play gin rummy. They would be betting with $500 bills and trying to outdo each other in rummy while their teams were trying to outdo each other on the field. It was pretty humorous. But that's the way Mr. Kauffman was.

BEHIND EVERY GREAT MAN...

Ewing's wife Muriel was extremely important in the building process of the Royals. She pushed him along. He was very conservative with everything including his money, and with his thought process, in a sense. She was the one who made him spend more than he probably would have otherwise, given his background and given his conservative nature. But he put the brakes on her, too.

He wasn't afraid to say, "No, we're not going to do that." But, she'd still push Mr. K, which was good for him. If both of them were at first base, she would try to steal a base before he would. She was more of a driver and a gambler.

Muriel was a very bright person, and independent, with her own money. She had a law degree before women did things like that.

Even though I wasn't very comfortable with Mr. Kauffman early in my career, Muriel and I always got along wonderfully well. I talked to her a lot. For some reason some people - especially women - were not at ease around her. But I could say things to her and people would ask me, "How do you say that to her?" People misjudged her. She was a very outgoing, gregarious, fun-loving person. He was early to bed, early to rise, and she was late to bed, a party-goer. He would hang with her about twenty minutes and then she would grab 17 other people and they'd stay out until two in the morning, just having a good time. "The old guy is going to bed," she would say, "so I'm going to go out to party." And she would. She was a person I felt comfortable with from the beginning.

Ewing and Muriel were a terrific pair.

THE KAUFFMAN STEAL

One of the people Mr. K hired early on to really get things going for the franchise was Cedric Tallis, who had been with the California Angels. Cedric, as Royals general manager, is the one who made those great trades I alluded to earlier, which made the Royals a pretty good team pretty darn early. It was difficult to be an expansion team at that time, because baseball's economics were different than they are today, and free agency was not around yet.

Despite that, Mr. K quickly built a winner in Kansas City. It is not difficult today to be an expansion team because if an owner has money he can buy almost any player; but given the structure of baseball at that time, it was. The Royals did remarkably well because of Ewing's attitude toward getting the good people.

Ewing first met Cedric on a trip to Anaheim. Before Mr. K agreed to put the money up for the Royals franchise he, as was his nature, wanted to study other teams and learn more from other owners about running an organization. The first owner he met with was the late Gene Autry, who owned the California Angels. When Ewing and Muriel went out to Anaheim, their "tour guide" around the stadium was Tallis, the Angels vice-president in charge of operations, and the business manager. It was immediately apparent to Mr. K that Cedric knew baseball, and that he knew stadiums (Cedric was instrumental in designing Anaheim's stadium). So that seed was planted in Ewing's mind dating to the early days of his interest in ownership.

When Kauffman decided to buy the franchise, which some say he did on the flight back to Kansas City from that trip to Anaheim, one of the first people he hired was Cedric. Besides serving as general manager, one of Cedric's duties was also going to be helping with the design and construction of a new stadium. Cedric assumed the position of executive vice-president of the Royals on January 16, 1968. At that point, Tallis and Mr. K assembled a staff that knew baseball and would be perfect for the expansion Royals. One of the first people Cedric hired was Lou Gorman, as the director of player development. They put together a front office staff that may have been one of the best in baseball.

THE RIGHT MAN AT THE RIGHT TIME

Ewing Kauffman may have been one of the best owners in the history of baseball. He put his money into it and let his people make the decisions, and pretty much let these people do what they thought they needed to do to win. As Ewing progressed in his ownership tenure there were times when he needed to be more involved, so he was. Otherwise, we didn't see him very often.

Owning the club was good for Ewing and he was smart enough to realize that he was getting into a business that he did not really know anything about. That's the reason he hired Tallis and Gorman, who, in turn, hired Joe Burke, John Schuerholz and Herk Robinson. He put those people in place and simply let them run the business. He had final approval over everything, obviously, but he let the baseball people do their thing. It was largely due to that willingness to get baseball people that the team prospered so quickly.

Mr. K was very loyal, and he expected loyalty in return. That was high on his priority list. He gave and wanted back. That's one of the few things he wanted from the people around him; loyalty and dedication to what they were doing. If he knew he had that and knew they were productive, he would leave them alone; then in return he would take care of those people in a lot of ways. So it was a pretty good reciprocal deal.

In 1997 there was a lot of talk about the Royals moving to the National League. Major League Baseball owners left it up to the Royals board to decide if they wanted to move. The board decided to stay, and the Milwaukee Brewers went to the N.L. Had Ewing Kauffman been alive, he would have had enough trust in his baseball people to have left it up to them, but I think he would have wanted to say no to the switch.

The general managers, Tallis, Burke, Schuerholz and Robinson, in their turn, all dealt with him. If one of them was going to make a trade, he would set it up and then call Ewing to get final approval. Probably 99 times out of 100 Ewing would say, "If you think that's the right way to go, then let's do it." All of them, as a courtesy, would call him and inform him about what they were thinking about doing, or tell him that they had a certain trade in place and wanted his feelings on it.

One time when he was not hands-off was during the expansion draft and he was asked to be involved. The Royals were on their 25th pick (they had 30 picks overall) and couldn't decide whom they wanted. I could imagine the conversation among Cedric Tallis and the other people involved in the draft going something like this: "Maybe we ought to let him pick one, what do you think?"

They did, and as it turned out he picked the oldest guy - Hoyt Wilhelm. He was the only player I had heard of, and it was probably the only one Kauffman had heard of also. By the way, the Royals turned around two months later and used Wilhelm in their first-ever trade, when he was sent to the Angels for Ed Kirkpatrick. Kirkpatrick went on to have a solid five-year career in Kansas City.

Ewing pretty much stayed out of the way during the entire time he owned the team, but as years went by he enjoyed ownership more and more, and he learned more and more about baseball. He was not one to get into anything without first learning about it. He asked a lot of questions. He just became interested. Plus Muriel liked it. She liked the action and they both had a great time with it. I think owning the club was great for both of them.

Even though he wasn't a baseball fan when he bought the Royals, over the course of time, he became a fan of both the sport and his team. And because of the great baseball people he had around him, he was very knowledgeable.

THE ROYALS AS A MEASURING STICK

Ewing Kauffman and the Royals were very good for future expansion clubs such as the Toronto Blue Jays and the Montreal Expos. Toronto said, "Yeah, we're going to do it exactly like the Royals." Yes, and a tough act to follow, at that.

The Royals created their farm system in 1968, and that meant they had minor league players in place a year before the big-league team played its first game. They signed a ton of guys, players such as Paul Splittorff, and they sprinkled them throughout the minor league system. Splittorff, incidentally, pitched the first game ever for a Royals team at any level. He did so at Class-A in Corning, New York, in the New York-Penn League.

Then in October of 1968 they picked their 30 players through the expansion draft, as all new teams do. Most of those players were put on the field that first season, and they took it from there.

Insiders say that often the other owners would call Mr. K if they wanted to really get something rolling. He was a mover and a shaker in baseball. He was, quietly, very effective in that role, and he accomplished a good deal on a league level and on a Major League Baseball level.

THE ROYALS BASEBALL ACADEMY

One of the unique plans that Ewing devised to develop the franchise (not copies, incidentally, by other franchises) was the Royals Baseball Academy. Basically, his thought was to take players who had not been drafted - and who were good athletes - train them through intense work, and make them baseball players.

He felt that the organization could take great athletes and turn them into great baseball players. So in August of 1970 he started the Royals Baseball Academy in Sarasota, Florida, with long-time baseball man Syd Thrift as the Academy Director.

Forming the Academy was an example of the way Mr. K's mind worked. He was very competitive, always looking for something different, looking for an edge. Some of the other baseball minds in the organization thought that the Baseball Academy had some merit and decided to give it a shot, and even if they didn't like it, it was something that Mr. K wanted to try.

Before the Royals Baseball Academy's first year the team traveled around the country holding tryouts. More than 7,500 high school athletes turned out.

The Academy was designed as a two-year program (including college), so a high school diploma was a must for a hopeful. During the morning, at Ewing's insistence, each player was expected to attend school at Manatee Junior College in Florida. He insisted that they take some speaking courses and some personal finance courses. He wanted them to be able to mingle in society, to talk to the press and to be able to handle their money. So the players went to college in the mornings, and studied baseball for the remainder of the day.

It was interesting, because in a much smaller sense Finley was doing the same thing with the A's by taking track athletes and using them only as pinch runners. In fact, most of those guys didn't even have gloves. A lot of people have copied that in the Dominican and other Latin American countries and now have camps and academies down there. When Mr. K opened the Royals Academy the other teams were kind of laughing about it. Baseball, in general, is extremely slow to accept new ideas. It's almost as if they're saying, "This is the way we've done things for the past 117 years so why should we change? Baseball is perfect the way it is."

I can only imagine the conversation when all of that took seed. I'm sure Ewing went to Cedric, or someone like that, and said, "Why couldn't we do this?" Or, "What if we did this?" Cedric probably said, "Well, maybe we can." To which Ewing would reply, "Well, let's try it." I'm sure that was the conversation, or something close to it.

After a few years the Academy wasn't panning out financially. Less than four years after it opened, in April 1974, the Royals Baseball Academy closed. But, as it turned out, it was too bad that the experiment ended. The Royals got their middle infield of the late 1970s and into the 80s out of the Academy; Frank White (Academy's first "graduate") and U.L. Washington.

Some of the older baseball heads around the Royals were never totally in love with the Academy. The organization was somewhat divided over it. A lot of people with the Royals felt they were spending too much money, in terms of what they were getting in return. They felt that if they took that money and spent it in more orthodox avenues, such as the minor leagues, signing players, scouting, as it had always been done, the team would have been better off.

GUARDING HIS INVESTMENT

One amazing thing is that through all of those years, even though people in the organization might not see him, we were aware of Ewing Kauffman's presence all the time. It almost felt like a Godly presence; where we may never see him, but we know there is one. It was eerie how we always felt his presence at the ballpark even though we rarely saw him.

Our broadcast booth was on the way to his suite, and about once a year he would poke his head in and ask how we were doing. Then he would go on to his suite.

Personally I did not feel too comfortable around him early in my career, but as I got to know him, that changed. As a broadcaster it just was not my place to try and buddy up to him; he was a lot older, and I was just starting with the organization. It took about two years, but after that time, I felt comfortable with Mr. Kauffman. We talked quite a bit during the last 10 years he was around.

I would just go down to his suite and talk to him, sit for 10 minutes, and shoot the breeze. A lot of times there were people there, and if that was the case, I would not go in. But sometimes in his box there would just be him and Muriel, or sometimes just Ewing.

The last time I saw him was shortly before he died; about three weeks before, and he was in his suite all by himself. I went in and sat with him for about 15 or 20 minutes, and chatted. We didn't really talk about anything specific; it was just a situation, like the others as we got to know each other, in which we talked about different things such as the club, baseball and investing.

Ewing was very good about getting all his Royals ("associates," as he liked to call them) and everyone who worked for him, and saying, "We've got a lot of investment people now, and we want you to save your money and make good decisions with your money." He encouraged all of us to tap his investment people. It was one of those things he wanted us to do. He'd say, "You go in there and see them." He was just like a father. It was obvious how much he really cared.

He wanted to make sure that he could make as many people as possible happy and comfortable, but he would not give anyone anything. That is best summed up in a story he used to tell when he would say, "When I see a guy, a beggar, along the street and the guy asks me for food, I won't give him fish. I'll give him a fishing pole."

SAY IT AIN'T SO, MR. K!

During the baseball strike in 1981, Ewing underwent surgery for removal of a benign tumor from his chest. Around that same time word began to surface that he was possibly interested in selling part of his interest in the Royals. Obviously people were concerned. But, looking at it from Mr. K's side, the Royals were not a high-yield investment; they were, in a sense, his donation to Kansas City. In fact, former *Kansas City Star* Vice-President and Sports Editor Joe McGuff, who (at this writing) is a member of the Royals Board of Directors, has estimated that Mr. Kauffman spent around $250 million on the Royals in order that the club could remain competitive, and stay in Kansas City.

Kauffman loved the Royals and Kansas City too much to let something bad happen to the franchise. He wanted them to remain in Kansas City long after he had passed away. I think that is obvious from his elaborate plan to find a new owner.

When he first started thinking about finding another investor, he hoped he could find someone in Kansas City who would step up to the plate; someone who might be able to take over as much as 49 percent, initially, and who could also absorb the possible financial blow. It was not a get-rich-quick scheme.

Although Kauffman could find no local investors, it appeared he had one with local ties: Michael Shapiro of Los Angeles. Shapiro had grown up in Kansas City, until high school, when his parents moved to California. Still, it appeared he was the one to buy this minority interest in the Royals. The two parties were so close to a deal in early 1983 that it was reported in the paper as being a "done deal." Evidently, though, Shapiro did not meet all of Mr. K's conditions and the deal fell through.

Soon thereafter - actually, three months later - Ewing announced that he was selling 49 percent of the club to Avron Fogelman of Memphis. Fogelman was involved in commercial real estate and apartment developments, but he wanted to become involved in Major League Baseball.

Fogelman is responsible for introducing the concept of the "lifetime" contract to the Royals, and maybe to all of professional sports. Three players were signed to "lifetime" contracts. They were George Brett, Dan Quisenberry and Willie Wilson. Frank White was offered a similar deal but he turned it down. The concept may have been intriguing at first, but I don't know how successful it was.

In 1990, after Fogelman had some bad luck on his business side of things, Mr. K bought back Fogelman's portion (which had since become 50 percent) of the Royals. I didn't get a chance to know Avron very well while he was in Kansas City, but I do know that he was very enthusiastic and very interested in baseball. Later in 1990 Ewing announced the succession plan of the Royals, which we are nearing the end of now.

THE ROYALS FATHER FIGURE RAISES A WINNER AND LOYALTY

Ewing Kauffman realized that playing in the World Series was the culmination of what the team had been trying to do, so, like a father figure in his quiet way, he was proud when the Royals went in 1980, and he was especially proud when they went again in 1985. He never did get close to the players, he was seldom in the clubhouse, and he didn't socialize with them, but he was "a proud father." It was almost as if he was saying, "Here's my boy finally becoming a man, and establishing himself as a champion."

I don't recall even seeing Ewing much in 1985, the year the Royals won the World Series. He didn't come to the clubhouse much after the games or go to the parade after the team won the Series. He didn't do any of that. He was pleased for all the people who had been working toward that end, and he was happy for the fans who came to the ballpark and supported the team. He was very happy to see them rewarded for supporting the team. That was his mindset all the time. He could see that they were being rewarded, so he was being rewarded.

Ewing wasn't big on all the side shows and all the extracurricular activity they do now at ballparks. He just wanted to put a good solid product on the field. The Royals had two people in marketing back then. I think the main guy who was in marketing at that time also took care of booth sales. The marketing plan, such as it was, was to put a good team on the field, give the fans a nice clean ballpark, and a nice environment to watch a game. It was no more complicated than that, and neither was Ewing.

Herk Robinson has told me that Mr. Kauffman refused to spend money on advertising - in the paper, or anywhere else. He didn't believe in it. He felt that if the team was good enough radio and TV would talk about it and the newspaper would write about it; so the "marketing" emphasis should be on winning.

He also put a lid on season tickets at 15,000, so that fans could walk up and buy a ticket if they suddenly decided they wanted to come and see a game. He said, "We won't sell more than this because I want people to be able to drive out here, buy a ticket and see a baseball game." He fought to keep prices down. In fact, he lost money so that ticket prices could be kept low.

You can look back on what he has done for this community and see that his depth of caring about other human beings was truly profound. For a man in his position, it would have been easier for him to take his money and do whatever he wanted to do. In fact, he did.

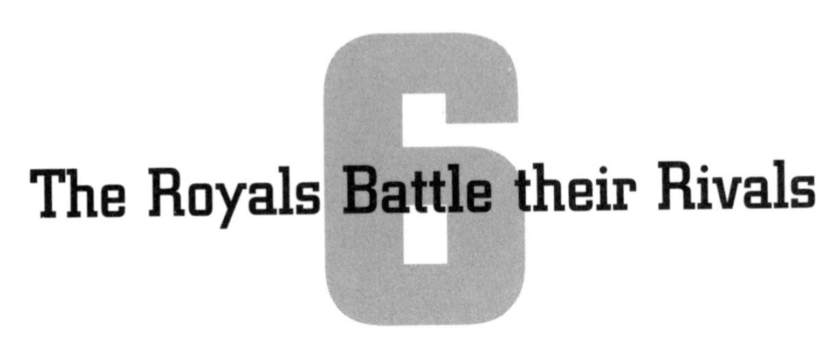

6 The Royals Battle their Rivals

Denny Matthews

The first really exciting night the Royals ever had in Municipal Stadium was on a weekend night when Vida Blue, early in his career, came to town with the Oakland A's. There were so many fans who came to that game that the Royals were totally unprepared, ticket-wise. There were lines of people stacked up outside the ballpark. It turned out to be one of the best games ever.

During the course of the game the Royals turned over six double plays, but the A's came back late in the game to win, as they usually did in those days. That was the first time, though, that we really had the feeling that the Royals were beginning to click with the city. There was the obvious connection, and the obvious reason to dislike the A's, since they had been in Kansas City and deserted. They had been gone for one year when the Royals came into existence in 1969.

That game was not until 1971. But it was a big, big night. It was the A's. Vida Blue was the draw. There was still that connection with some A's fans in Kansas City.

WHERE DID THESE A'S COME FROM?

It's odd to realize that while the A's were in Kansas City for 13 seasons, they never had a winning record. Then, as soon as they moved to Oakland, they turned around with guys like Reggie Jackson, Sal Bando and Jim "Catfish" Hunter, and became near-instant champions. They had all those young players when they were in Kansas City, but those players just hadn't learned how to win yet.

The latter-day Kansas City Athletics were good big league players, but they weren't big league winners; they hadn't come together as a team. But everything was in place when they left Kansas City. Believe it or not, that was a real good team that left Kansas City but nobody knew it because they had never had a good record.

WHY WE LIKE TO DISLIKE THE A'S

For the most part, rivalries in baseball simply don't exist anymore. Yes, the Red Sox and Yankees still dislike each other and probably will until the "Curse of the Bambino" – the sale of Babe Ruth from the Red Sox to the

Yankees – is lifted off of Boston. (Which, in theory, would only happen if Boston wins a World Series.) Long-standing feuds such as the Dodgers and Giants, or the Cubs and Cardinals (with the exception of the 1998 home run duel between Sammy Sosa and Mark McGwire) have toned down almost to the point where they are just some other regular season series. With the current economics and structure of baseball, generation-long rivalries may just be a memory. For obvious reasons, the Oakland A's and the Kansas City Royals had a pretty strong rivalry going during most of the 1970s.

During the rivalry there was a sense of revenge for people in Kansas City. The Royals were trying to establish their own identity, front office people and players, so I don't think they felt a need for revenge against the A's as much as the fans did. After all, Charles O. Finley was not a pleasant household name. To add insult to injury, the first loss in the club's history, in 1969, came at the hands of the Oakland A's, 5-0. Try this on for size, though. The first home run in Royals history was by Mike Fiore - against the Oakland A's.

With the city's reaction, maybe the organization could feel the undercurrent in the mood of the fans. As far as the players were concerned, the A's were the best team in baseball, and had been for some time. They were the team to beat. The players knew that if they wanted to be the best they had to somehow get past Oakland. The A's were in our division, so they were a pretty good barometer for how good the Royals were becoming. If the Royals could beat that team, they knew they were pretty good themselves. And they did beat them. But those Oakland teams had an attitude. They strutted, and they would fight anybody. As the rivalry developed, there was genuine bad blood between the two teams.

One game that sticks out was one in which a fight broke out between Don Baylor and Dennis Leonard. Actually it wasn't really a fight between those two, because Baylor charged the mound and Leonard ran away. But, Brett tackled Baylor. We had a melee. A brawl. Everyone got involved.

1976: A.O., A.O., A.O.

I still have vivid memories of when the Royals clinched a tie for the division title against the A's in 1976. It was truly a defining moment for the Royals; it proved to Kansas City that the Royals had finally caught the A's. (We clinched outright a few days later at home.) The two stars of the game, one likely and one unlikely, were Amos Otis and Larry Gura.

Manager Whitey Herzog made a shocking move by starting pitcher Larry Gura and catcher John Wathan in that game. Everybody thought Whitey was out of his mind. Didn't he realize this was a game to clinch the pennant...the Royals first pennant? Didn't he realize that Dennis Leonard and Buck Martinez should make up the battery in this important game? Evidently not, as Whitey demonstrated the kind of manager he really was by making that move. He felt that the A's lineup would have more trouble against Gura, a left-hander obtained from the Yankees in exchange for Fran Healy in May of that season, than they would against any other pitcher in the Royals' rotation. He was right. Gura and Wathan did a number on the A's with a 4-0 shutout. That game established Larry Gura's ability as a legitimate starting pitcher for the Royals for years to come, and it showcased John Wathan's ability as a catcher.

There was a question mark surrounding the status of the other star of the game, Otis. It wasn't a matter of whether he would play or not, but rather of how he would respond facing Oakland pitcher Stan Bahnsen. You see, Otis had been hit in the head with a pitch by Bahnsen two weeks earlier in Kansas City. But in this clinching game, he responded remarkably well. After Cookie Rojas laid down a bunt for a single, Otis came to the plate and homered off of Bahnsen, to help give the Royals the win.

Amos was a funny guy, and one of the key leaders for many years. He was one of the key guys who was always willing to help younger players. He wasn't a take charge, yell (rah-rah) type of guy. He was very quiet and did things very much in his own way, at his own pace.

Amos had several clutch home runs during his 14-year career with the Royals. In fact, even 16 years after he retired, Otis still is in the top four in every career offensive category for the Royals except batting average (although that was a respectable .280). He ended his career with 193 home runs, 992 runs batted in, 340 stolen bases and 1,977 career hits. On top of that he collected three Gold Glove awards and five All-Star game invitations. He was the first Royal to actually play in an All-Star game, in 1970, and the first Royal to start in an All-Star game, in 1973 in Kansas City.

One of his most impressive home runs, one that most Otis fans remember, was in 1976 at Royals Stadium when he hit a ball halfway up the flag pole. Had it not actually hit the pole it probably would have gone out of the stadium.

THE PROMISE

Cookie Rojas was so excited and in so much awe of the new stadium when it opened in 1973 that he said when the Royals clinched their first pennant, he would jump in the water fountains in left field. A few hours after the Royals finished their game with the Twins in Kansas City, the A's lost to the Angels on the West Coast, clinching the title for the Royals. Because their game was in Oakland, we didn't find out we had clinched until about 2 o'clock in the morning.

The next day, after the regular season finale, Rojas and Freddie Patek went out to the fountains in left field for a swim; they jumped in the pond. The maintenance people had to turn off the electricity so the two players wouldn't be lit up like the Kansas City Plaza lights during the holidays. That may be one of the funniest things that has happened in the stadium, at definitely one of the most joyous times.

IGNITION SWITCH ON

The Royals barely had enough time to breathe between passing the A's and developing a new team to battle, a new team to dislike, a new team to draw fans into the stadium: the New York Yankees. In fact, the Royals had no breathing room when they faced the Yankees in the 1976 playoffs after capturing their first A.L. West title.

The rivalry really ignited in 1976, but there were some good games in previous years because the Yankees were becoming a good team again. The Yankees were trying to establish themselves as a power in the East, while the Royals were trying to do the same thing in the West. We found out that those great regular season games were just preludes to the playoffs. The playoffs brought things to a fever pitch.

WELCOME TO THE PLAYOFFS

After getting off to a slow start in the 1976 League Championship Series, losing the first game at home 4-1, the Royals bounced back behind the strong pitching of Paul Splittorff to take the second game, 7-3. The Royals seemed fairly poised after that opening game. Part of the reason for that was because they knew deep down that they were a better ballclub than the Yankees.

Later, with the best-of-five series tied at two games apiece, the Royals jumped out to a quick 2-0 lead in the top of the first inning in the Bronx. Unfortunately, the Yankees didn't really intend on losing the series finale at home, and they tied the game in the bottom of the inning. The game rolled along until the ninth. Kansas City pitcher Mark Littell, the fifth Royal pitcher used by manager Whitey Herzog that night, faced Chris Chambliss to open the bottom of the ninth with the score tied at six. Yankee fans, as they have been known to do at times, had thrown a bunch of trash on the field, and forced a 10-minute delay before the game resumed. Not to over-dramatize it, but on paper this was a classic match-up. Littell had not given up a home run at all during the 1976 season. Chambliss had teed off for a homer in the third game of the series to help give the Yankees the win in that contest. After the delay, Littell threw a pitch and boom...it's gone (barely)...and it's over. Game. Set. Match. It was a shocking end, it really was.

The thing about that situation that a lot of people may not remember is that Otis had broken his ankle in the first game of the series, so obviously he didn't play in that final game against the Yankees. Instead of having Al Cowens in right and Otis in center, Whitey had to put Cowens in center and Hal McRae in right. There is a gate where Chambliss hit the ball out, and I can still see McRae, who isn't very tall and can't jump exceptionally well, going up at the gate, and the ball just getting past his outstretched glove. Cowens, who was taller than McRae and could jump better, might have caught it. But who knows?

It would probably be more accurate to say that the home run was more shocking than it was disappointing. If the Royals had been expected to win that series, then losing would have been disappointing. But the Royals and Yankees were very evenly matched that season, so the Series could have gone either way. In fact, the two teams were so close that it came down to the last pitch of the series.

The teams were dead even in 1976, the Royals were superior in 1977 and the Yankees were better in 1978. Whitey has said, and there really isn't much doubt about this, that the 1977 team was the best-ever Royals team, so losing to the Yankees that year was disappointing. Those two teams played evenly all through the years, even though you had the feeling that, in any one year, one team might be a little better than the other.

THE ROYALS AND THE DODGERS?

Every game during the regular season in the late 1970's between the Yankees and Royals was as hotly contested as the playoffs were. There was a real rivalry, a real electricity in the ballpark, every time they played, whether in New York or in Kansas City. The games were well-played; fundamentals were good, there weren't a lot of goofy mistakes, sloppy games, bad pitching or bad defense. It was good, quality pitching. Most of the games between the two teams, for about four or five years, were pretty close; nearly every single pitch counted for something in the outcome. Fans never left the stadium feeling they had wasted their time or money.

In April of 1977 the Yankees opened the season in Kansas City on a beautiful, unseasonably warm night. There was the crowd and the electricity in the stadium a couple of hours before the game; the atmosphere was that of a postseason game. If you ever wonder whether a game is important, walk into the ballpark two hours early; you can feel the electricity, you can hear a buzz. That feeling can't be explained, it can't be manufactured, and it can't be invented; it's just there. It's a special feeling everywhere in the stadium, from the stands, to the pressbox, to the clubhouse, to pregame batting practice.

It's fun watching players before big games like those, because they are often down on the field before the game giving each other a hard time - good-naturedly, for the most part. Funny stuff with a little knife to it, but just typical ball player banter. It's a mind game. They like to play mind games with each other, and try to find that little edge. The Royals and Yankees of that era realized that the teams were so well-balanced and so close in ability that any little edge was important.

Positional match-ups give an idea of how closely matched the Royals and Yankees really were. Darrell Porter and Thurman Munson behind the plate. Frank White and Willie Randolph at second base. George Brett and Graig Nettles at third base. The only place where we didn't match up was in was in the bullpen. The Yankees had Sparky Lyle and then Goose Gossage.

Whitey didn't really have a sure-fire closer - someone like a Dan Quisenberry or a Jeff Montgomery, someone who was almost guaranteed to come in and shut the Yankees down. Sporadically during the rivalry we had decent closers in Steve Mingori, Doug Bird and Al Hrabosky, but not a dominating closer like Quiz, who didn't come on the scene as a force until 1980. We were so thin in that department that in 1977, with the ALCS tied at two games apiece, and the Royals leading 3-2 in the ninth inning of the finale, Whitey felt he needed to bring in usual starter Dennis Leonard, But it didn't help; the Yankees scored three runs in the final inning to win the game 5-3 and take the series. I truly feel that if the Royals had had a dominating closer, the Yankees would not have won all three Series from 1976 to 1978. It's interesting to think back on those three Series. We remember so much from the World Series and the two battles between the Yankees and the Los Angeles Dodgers. Do people realize how close it came to being the Royals and the Dodgers in one or more of those Series?

BRETT CATCHES A FISH, YANKS GO TO THE SERIES...AGAIN

The 1977 regular season was incredibly impressive for the Royals, winning a franchise best 102 games. It was a team that seemed destined for the World Series. But once the team gets into postseason, it's a whole new ballgame. And once they hit postseason play that year they met up with the Yankees again.

Behind home runs by McRae, Cowens and Mayberry, and a strong pitching performance by Paul Splittorff, the Royals coasted to an opening game victory, 7-2, in front of a typically hostile New York crowd. It was the best-of-five, with the first two games at one site, and the final three, if needed, at the other site. In 1977 we opened play in New York, with games three, four and five in Kansas City. The shared thought around the Kansas City clubhouse after the first game was that even if we didn't win the next night, we could take at least two of three from the Yankees at home; especially after that fantastic regular season. The Yankees won the next night. That sent the series, tied at one game, to Kansas City.

Dennis Leonard, a 20-game winner in 1977, tossed a masterful four-hit complete game on Friday night, as the Royals won 6-2. Okay, two down, and two more chances to win one. Well, it didn't happen. New York was able to stretch the series out to the fifth game, and scored three runs in the top of the ninth inning to win the game. Sparky Lyle came on to pitch in the eighth inning, shut the Royals down, and ended up with the win for the Yankees. Even today some of the Royals from that 1977 team say they felt they had a good shot at going to the World Series. It came down to a closer; they had one, we didn't. They go on to the World Series...we go home to play golf.

The Royals went more quietly in the 1978 playoffs, winning only one game. That was the second game, in Kansas City. When the Yankees went home and won the next night, we knew it would be tough to win the next two. Roy White of the Yankees hit a cheap home run in the fourth and final game in New York, down the right field line, barely reaching the seats. That was one of those years when I had the feeling all along that it just wasn't going to happen for Kansas City.

The highlight of that series was George Brett's three home runs off Jim "Catfish" Hunter in Game 3. That was pretty exciting. What people don't remember, though, is that he almost hit a fourth. On his fourth at-bat in that game, George hit one to the wall in right center at the 385-foot sign which was caught, and pretty much pinned the outfielder to the wall.

That was typical of the Catfish style of pitching. If there was no one on base, or there was no chance of an opponent's home run bringing his team back, Hunter would challenge hitters. There was nobody on base each time George came to the plate. It was a personal challenge he issued to all the batters he faced. The fun thing about his offering that challenge to George is that Brett wasn't backing down, either. George had four great at-bats in that game.

.400, BY GEORGE

In 1980 the Royals couldn't do anything wrong. They blew everyone away early. During the first few months of the season the Texas Rangers were the closest team to the Royals in the A.L. West in the standings, and in talent; and there was still a huge difference between them. The Royals went down to Arlington in late May, Memorial Day weekend, and won. There was basically no race for the last 100 games - the final four months - of the season.

That was also one of the hottest summers in Kansas City history; it was hotter than hell. The Royals played a game every night and said they couldn't wait until October when it would be nice and cool, and they could do some postseason work. It really wasn't an exciting season, except in the sense of individual guys putting up numbers; but as far as the race goes, there wasn't one. In fact their lead was so big that for the last two months of the season they played only about .500 ball, but it didn't matter.

For us, for much of the season, the main focus was George chasing the batting average of .400. Since there was no pennant race to be concerned with, George became our focal point. The team had it on cruise control, while George was smoking everything thrown to the plate.

In the middle of August the Royals hosted the Toronto Blue Jays. On his way to a 30-game hitting streak, on August 17 (day 29 of the streak), Brett lined a two-out, three-RBI double down the left field line to go over the .400 plateau for the first time. In a picture that will live in the minds of Royals fans forever, Brett stood at second base, raising his arms, tipping his helmet to the Kansas City crowd as his batting average climbed to .401.

Other players, like Willie Wilson, were having good years, but this was a year for George. For the last part of the season, it was like, "Well, let's see how

George does today." It was very similar (although their teams didn't have big division leads) to everyone in 1998 watching Mark McGwire and Sammy Sosa chase Roger Maris' home run record. In 1980 in Kansas City, George was all there was to really talk about, despite the team's juggernaut toward the pennant.

NOW CAN WE BEAT THE YANKEES?

When I say 1980 was George Brett's year, I mean 1980 was George Brett's year. For some reason, when the Royals met the Yankees in the playoffs in 1980, even though some doubt had been planted in three previous postseason series, there was a feeling that maybe, just maybe, this could be Kansas City's year.

As it turned out, somewhat surprisingly, the Royals took care of the Yankees in much the same fashion as they had demolished their opponents in the regular season. Kansas City hosted the first two games of the playoffs.

Behind strong pitching performances by Larry Gura and Dennis Leonard the Royals won the two games in K.C., 7-2 and 3-2. During the regular season, Gura had a career-best 18 wins (he had 18 also in 1982), while Leonard won 20 games for the third time in his career. Who am I leaving out? Oh yeah, the sure-fire closer the Royals so desperately needed in the previous three playoffs. They had him in 1980, in the form of submarine-style pitcher Dan Quisenberry. Quiz recorded the save in the second game. Earlier that season he set what was then an all-time single season record for the Royals with 33 saves.

With the Royals leading the series two games to none we headed to New York. Despite the team's luck in previous years, the guys felt pretty optimistic going to the Bronx, needing to win just one of the next three games.

That win came on Friday night, October 10. The Royals got on the board first in the fifth inning, via a solo home run by Frank White. But the Yankees came back in the bottom of the sixth and scored two to take the lead. Things were beginning to look doubtful for the Royals. With two outs in the top of the seventh inning and Willie Wilson on base, U.L. Washington beat out an infield single to set up a meeting between George Brett and "Goose" Gossage. On the first pitch, a fastball (imagine that), George launched it into the right field upper deck to put the Royals up 4-2. He knew it was going to be a fastball, and he started swinging about the time Gossage started winding up. Imagine the force of a 98-mile-per-hour fastball making contact with a bat as quick as George's, and it's easy to see why it turned out as it did. Everything was just going his way, and we could feel it coming. And it did. And it went.

Ironically, the two pitchers of record for the final game were not the starters. They were Dan Quisenberry and "Goose" Gossage, as the Royals swept the Yankees to earn a trip to their first-ever World Series, to meet the Philadelphia Phillies.

CLOSING A RIVALRY

The Royals and Yankees have not met in the playoffs since 1980. Sure, both teams have been to the playoffs more than once since then, but not against each other. Maybe it's fitting then that the rivalry basically ended the way it did. The thing that will always stick out to me about that rivalry is the excellence of play from good players, good managers and good coaches. Just baseball excellence. The excitement. The drama. The determination. The fact that many guys were capable of rising up to make the big play, and they did.

THE "OTHER" WORLD SERIES

I don't remember a lot about the 1980 World Series with the Phillies because we didn't broadcast the games. We could tell the Royals might have a tough time. The worst thing we did was stay an extra three days in New York before going to Philadelphia, instead of going home first.

Once we got to Philadelphia, since we weren't doing the broadcasts, we just sat around. I thought that was really brutal. I couldn't wait to get home.

In the first game, the Royals jumped out to a 4-0 lead behind home runs by Amos Otis and Willie Aikens, but the Phillies came back with five runs in the bottom of the third. It was pretty much over from that point on.

The Royals figure that their World Series was the Yankees. They put so much effort, physically and mentally, into beating the Yankees that when the World Series came around, it was anti-climatic. At least it was for us. There was a period of time when the local announcers couldn't do the World Series, but Fred and I still went to Philadelphia with the team.

For the first two games of the Series we sat in the stands and watched. We came back to Kansas City for three games. I went to the first game in Kansas City as a spectator, gave away my tickets for the last two games, and then I didn't go back to Philadelphia for game six. Philadelphia won the series four games to two. The Royals may have been a better team than the Phillies that year, but Philadelphia's ace was Steve Carlton, a pitcher we weren't going to beat, so we were down two games before play even began.

BECOMING A CHAMPION

The Royals went on a couple of wild rides in the 1970s with both the A's and the Yankees. They went through the complete process of becoming a champion. In the beginning the A's were so good that we knew in our hearts it was going to be another year or two before the Royals could really challenge them, but we could see that steps were being made in the right direction.

I could tell that while these players had a lot of potential they were going to have to improve, they were going to have to gain the experience and learn how to win. That's the whole key. A team comes together, guys get to the big leagues and they have to establish themselves as major league players. That takes a year or two. Okay, now I am a major league player. The next step is to learn how to win. So, for the first two or three years, they are trying to figure out how to be a big league player; the next two or three years, they are trying to figure out how to win at the major league level. That's six years right there, give or take a year, so that's why winning a title doesn't happen overnight.

Right up until 1975 or 1976 they were still in the process of learning how to win. Most of the key players had proven to themselves and everybody else that they were viable big league players. 1976 was their break-out year. That was the year that they learned how to win.

7

No. 5, George Brett

Fred White

If beating the Yankees in the 1980 playoffs is as good as it gets for some Royals fans, then George Brett is probably as good as it gets in terms of players for Kansas City fans.

Brett's heroics in the 1980 playoffs against the New York Yankees helped propel the Royals into the World Series to face the Phillies. One dramatic game by Brett against the Toronto Blue Jays in the 1985 playoffs helped push the Royals into the World Series that year and, eventually, to a World Championship.

Some of his statistics with the Royals are staggering, including: leading the team in every career offensive stat except strikeouts and stolen bases, 3,154 career hits (215 in 1976), a .305 career batting average (.390 in 1980), 1,595 runs batted in (118 in 1980); five five-hit games, 16 two-home run games, and three three-home run games. Oh yeah, there are also his three American League batting titles, a 1985 Gold Glove Award, and the 1980 American League MVP award. Simply stated, a Hall of Fame career.

Surprisingly, Brett is very similar to another legendary icon...Elvis Presley. Brett was drafted out of high school; Elvis cut his first record out of high school. Brett had batting titles in each of three decades (the only player ever to do this); Elvis had gold records in each of three decades. Brett flirted with a .400 average in 1980; Elvis was spotted at a gas station off Georgia highway 400 in 1980.

Elvis is best known for his music and his movie roles (OK, to the general public maybe just his music.) Behind the scenes however, he was an extremely generous person. This side was usually seen by only his beneficiaries and his close friends, who, for the most part, were not famous people. His friends were his friends because they were his friends. (Say that five times real fast.)

George is best known for his defensive play at first (OK, again, maybe his hitting and his play at third.) Away from the field, Brett was, and still is, an extremely generous person. Like Elvis, this side of George is usually seen only by his beneficiaries and his close friends, who, for the most part, are not famous people. A lot of them are people he grew up with in California. Some, like former Royal player and current bench coach Jamie Quirk, advanced through the Kansas City organization with him.

George never measures his friends by anything other than how good a friend they are to him — he doesn't care what walk of life they come from. His is the most eclectic group I've ever known. He never sought people who had star power. He gives loyalty and expects it in return. George lives life - he's just a fun guy to be around.

He is the best tipper, taking care of the clubhouse guys, the waiters or waitresses, and hotel maids. One of his best friends ever worked in the clubhouse - Al Zych, the equipment manager. He sat next to Al in the dugout during games; they loved each other. George will be embarrassed for me telling this, but when Al retired, he and his wife Jackie were going to the lake and George wanted him to have something special so he bought Al a houseboat. George simply thought it was the right thing to do. He did a lot of things like that. God knows how much George has done that no one knows about but him. He is just like that.

A lot of George's generosities have been through charity work for ALS (aka Lou Gehrig's Disease). Working through the Keith Worthington ALS Chapter, he has served as Honorary Fund Raising Chairman, and has hosted such events as the George Brett Golf Tournament, the ALS Auction and Lou Gehrig Night at Kauffman Stadium. Worthington was a friend who died of ALS.

When George started his golf tournament, the slogan was, "I made a promise to a friend and I'm going to keep it." That's really a telling slogan about George Brett. If he says he'll do something, he'll do it.

One of the greatest displays I ever saw of George's kindness was in Detroit at the Hyatt. This one particular year at the hotel there was a little people's convention; midgets and dwarfs. As I walked into the bar I saw George sitting on a tall bar stool. Suddenly, someone grabbed my hand. I looked down and saw a very diminutive person, who asked, "Do you know George?" When I told him I did he asked if I would take him over to George to have his picture taken.

I took the guy over, and here's the scene: a dwarf standing next to George, and a dwarf with a camera. George picked the guy up, had his picture taken, put him down, looked over and there's another one; he gets his picture taken, then George looked down the bar at a whole line of midgets, so now George is getting into it; this is fun.

That was George, though. I've never seen anyone be more inundated by people than George was, and still is. I've been to dinner with him when people wouldn't leave him alone, but he was very gracious. People just keep coming up to the table and say, "I don't want to bother you while you're eating, but..." George, very graciously, wipes his hands, then signs the autograph or has his picture taken. I think George's thing with autographs is, "Don't lay a trap for me, hide out and ambush me. If you bump into me by chance and you genuinely want an autograph or picture, I'll do it."

GOOD GRIEF, CHARLEY LAU

George Brett was drafted by the Royals in 1971 fresh out of high school, but he wasn't really tabbed as the next superstar. When he first came up to the major leagues in 1973 he was just another young player. No one not connected with the Psychic Friends Network (sorry, that wasn't around in 1973) thought Brett would be the Royals superstar in two to three years; nothing he did in the minor leagues indicated that he was anything special. Nothing he did early in his spring training camps with the Royals indicated it either.

George was a kid who had promise; but then we saw him out there in 100-degree weather shagging fly balls for other guys, taking extra batting practice. That was the key.

He became great because he worked hard and willed himself to be great. Shake his hand during the season and you could feel the calluses he got from his overtime work at the plate, perfecting his swing. It could make anyone become a fan of his, as a human, and not just as an athlete.

Originally George was just a young player trying to get to the big leagues. Once he made it, he was a young player just trying to stay there. Once he stayed there, he was trying to be a big league player who could do things and could hit well. Then something strange happened: a need for a transformation. Royals coach Charley Lau got ahold of him. At the time, George was struggling at the plate, batting under .200.

Denny tells a story of when we were on a road trip in Baltimore, and he was in a cab with Brett and Lau. Charley asked George, "Are you tired of hitting .138?"

"Yeah."

Charley replied, "Well, I'll see you at the ballpark [in Kansas City] tomorrow at 2 o'clock."

Lau took Hal McRae under his tutelage at the same time. Mac came over to the Royals from the other league and he was struggling, too. Charley had Mac and George out there working hard. That's how the project really started. It was Lau who really made McRae and Brett excellent big league hitters.

Charley's whole take with the players was that when they finally buckled and finally became so frustrated that they finally realized it wasn't working their way, and they were ready to work with Lau, at that point he would take them on. He never went to players and said, "Come over here...I can help you." He waited until they were ready to come to him. What George Brett and Hal McRae did, in all honesty, was outwork everybody else.

Everyone talks about what a great natural hitter George was, but it was going out to the ballpark at 2 o'clock in the afternoon when it was about 134 degrees on the artificial turf that helped make him a great hitter. People don't understand that Brett and McRae hit until their hands bled; they were out there working, working, working.

It was not automatic; it was not as though the light came on and they were both suddenly terrific hitters. They began; Charley's system started working and they believed more. It worked a little better and they believed more, to the point where they became supremely confident and great hitters, both of them.

Hitting excellence for Brett and McRae was a step-by-step process. Some of the nuances of Charley's instructional method are interesting. For instance, he noticed body types. He said, "To get started you need to rock back in your hitting motion." Then he would concentrate on the head. He wanted them to bow their heads to the ball, because the ball was going to be coming into the hitting zone. Then make an aggressive move toward the pitcher. The goal with Lau was to hit the ball up the middle.

Charley could get players to believe in him. He was almost a hitting guru. People forget that when George won his batting championship in 1976 Charley Lau called nearly every pitch for him that year. George would look in the dugout and Charley would give him a sign of what the pitcher was probably going to throw him. Charley was seldom wrong. I think George would verify that. He began to develop confidence. Once he had that confidence, he never looked in the dugout to Charley again.

But he had that much of a belief in the "system." Charley could get him out of a slump pretty quickly. I remember when George or Mac would be in a slump, Charley would say to me, "I think he's going to get it going tonight," or "I think he's going to have a couple of hits tonight." That would go on for a few days and then he would say, "I think he's about ready to hit it out of the park. I think he might hit one out of the park tonight." And it would happen! It was uncanny how Charley could read those guys and know what was going to happen. Charley had a mystical element to him.

Charley Lau had a great teaching tool: his voice. He was so soft-spoken that when he was talking, you'd get closer and closer, and you stuck to every word because you had to if you wanted to hear it. He also understated everything. If George or Mac got five hits in the ballgame, we'd look at Charley and he might say "heavens" in almost a whisper. That's as loud as he ever got. Sometimes he wouldn't say anything. Sometimes he would just shrug his shoulders.

Another thing about Charley, though, was his work ethic. We talk about George and Mac working, but Charley did too. Lau had a bad back most of the time. When he was meeting with George and Mac at 2:00 in the afternoon, he may have worn things out the night before, and might be a little hung over. When it was time to go hit, he'd get his cup of coffee, they'd get the bag of balls and he'd walk down the tunnel all crooked because of his back, then go out in 100 degrees and throw to his pupils for an hour. He worked at it as hard as they did. The three of them formed a bond that was just incredible.

MR. ROYAL, MR. CLUTCH

George Brett may have been one of the best clutch players ever. He liked it. He liked that challenge of the clutch situation, and he responded to it. He never sought the spotlight, even though he was comfortable there. A Reggie Jackson, for example, wanted the undivided attention and all the glamour that went with it. George never showed anybody up, and never made a hot-dog move anywhere. When the game was over, with him it was, "Well okay, that's what I was supposed to do. I did it, so let's move on."

The only time I ever saw him be demonstrative was in the third game of the ALCs with Toronto in 1985, on his second home run, when he jumped in the air and pumped his fist. That's the only time. And that, even, was the right gesture at the moment, as if to tell the city and the team, "We are alive and we are in this thing."

He never hit a ball and stood at home plate like a Reggie would, to bring attention to himself. When he hit the one off Gossage in 1980, there was no doubt it was gone, but when we looked at him, he was just out there running the bases doing what he was required to do. The rules required him to go and touch 'em all, so he did it. That's how he was.

Maybe he could deliver what the team needed, when they needed it, better than anyone else. It was amazing how he could come up with exactly what the Royals had to have, whether it be a single, double, triple, or home run. He did it many times.

There were knocks on him as a defensive player, such as the way he threw when he came up from Omaha. But he worked hard at his defensive play, just as he did with his hitting. I remember thinking a year or two before he won a gold glove that he had made himself into a gold glove third baseman. That he deserved to win that award. A couple of years later, in 1985, he did. Even though, on the defensive side, he was known more for being a third baseman, he had solid skills at other positions. During his career he played some short-stop, some second base, some in the outfield and some at first.

The thing about George is that he just loved playing baseball. He was put in left field one night because people were hurt and the team was short of players. He was out there like a little kid just having a great time playing left field, celebrating. He played very well that night.

George was the cornerstone for the Royals, even though there were so many other important players. Guys like McRae, Frank White, Darrell Porter, Al Cowens, Amos Otis, Paul Splittorff and Dan Quisenberry were all a part of the success. They wouldn't have been as successful without him but they may not have been as successful without Cowens, Splittorff, or those other people. Who knows? They were a terrific team. But if the team had to take one guy away, George would have been the last one to go.

I remember Splittorff kidding Brett when George hit the home run off Gossage in 1980, laughing at him, saying "It's about time you got us in the World Series; you kept getting us close." Split recognized George by saying that, and by adding, "You're the guy who got us here and you're the guy who got us over the hump."

CHASING .400

The 1980 season was a magical one for the Royals as a franchise, but it was really special for George. Long before he hit the home run off Gossage to help the team win the American League pennant, George tried to reach the unthinkable, a .400 batting average. To get there, though, some extraordinary things would have to happen.

One that helped was his 30-game hitting streak. The streak lasted from July 18 until August 18. As the streak matured he'd go through a stretch of games in which he'd get a hit his first time up and take the pressure off for the rest of the game, but then there were a few times he had to sustain it on the last at-bat. He hit so many balls so well that year. It's a wonder he didn't have a 50-game hitting streak, as well as he was playing.

On August 19, as the Royals were playing the Rangers in Texas, Brett was facing Jon Matlack. Hitless, George came up late in the game and lined a pitch down the right field line that everybody thought was fair, but it was called foul. That would have put the streak at 31 games! He didn't get a hit that night. But what a streak it was!

For much of the season he flirted with .400, a feat last accomplished by Ted Williams in 1941. The Royals had such a huge lead late in the season, that the main excitement was watching to see if Brett could reach .400.

The most unforgettable day in the chase came fairly late in the season, on August 17 in Kansas City against the Toronto Blue Jays, when Brett scorched a double late in the game to push his average to .401 - over .400 for the first time. One of the most memorable images in the history of the Royals is George standing at second base waving his helmet to the crowd, receiving a standing ovation.

He missed a lot of games in 1980 because of injury, but he always came back. And when George came back, he always came back hot. One such occasion was August 26 in Milwaukee. Cecil Cooper, the Brewers' first baseman, was also challenging the .400 mark. On this particular day, Cooper's average was right around .385. George went in there and went 5-for-5. After his fifth hit he was standing at first base next to Cooper and the Milwaukee fans gave him a standing ovation.

George helped cap off an incredible run in 1980 during game three of the American League playoffs with the New York Yankees. With the Royals leading the series 2-0, but down in the game, 2-1, George faced his nemesis again, "Goose" Gossage. With Willie Wilson and U.L. Washington on base, Brett smacked Gossage's first pitch into the rightfield upper deck. New York tried to put together a rally in the eighth, but a great defensive play by Washington helped prevent it, and the Royals won the game, 4-2.

If we had thought to ourselves about the perfect baseball moment before the 1980 season began, we would have thought that it would happen at

Yankee Stadium with George against Goose, and that it would mean it all. Then to have it actually happen, and to have him do what he did, was just an incredible moment in Royals history.

WHITEY AND GEORGE AND DICK

Through the years it has been interesting to watch how managers act, react and interact with their superstars. With the appreciative approach George Brett took to the game and to the Royals, he and his managers were able to adapt to each other, usually fairly quickly. It was not like watching a Reggie Jackson and a Billy Martin, for instance, who seemed to always butt heads. Two of the higher profile field leaders who managed George were Whitey Herzog and Dick Howser.

George and Whitey are very good friends to this day with a great deal of respect for each other. There was a time when Whitey was managing and George was in a slump, and he hadn't had a day off in a long time. We were in Boston; Brett made an out, kicked at his batting helmet, and missed it. Whitey said, "Well hell, when he kicked at his batting helmet and missed it, I knew it was time to give him the day off."

George and Dick had a different type of relationship. It was O.K., although George did not really know it when he was playing for Dick. The day Dick went into the hospital to have surgery for his brain tumor he called me to see if I would call George and have him come to the hospital.

Other than a picture of his family, Dick had one other picture up in his room and it was a picture of George and him together. I had seen Dick quite a bit leading up to that time and had been there a few minutes when George came to the room. I said to George, "I'm going to let you talk to him." Later we rode together out to the stadium. On the way he said, "All this time I had never known that he felt that way about me."

Dick really loved George, respected him and admired him. Dick was not the kind of guy who would show his feelings right off the bat. I remember George being very surprised that Dick wanted to see him and when he saw that picture in the room, it just buckled him — it really got him.

When the team won its first playoff game in 1985 over Toronto George ran the game ball over to Dick and buried it in his chest. Dick remembered that and told me that was the first time he knew that George really cared that much about him.

The Royals had planned on having a night at the stadium to honor Howser. The last time we had a chance to talk to him was right before another road trip. Dick wanted George to come by the house, so again we went over there together. As we were talking, Dick said "They want me to ride this exercise bike and I don't like to do that." George said, "Well look, we're going on a road trip and when we come back we're going to do this special night and either somebody's going to push you out there in a wheel chair, or you're going to walk. I want you to walk like a man, damn it! So get on that bike and ride."

Dick just broke down; it really got him. He went into a coma shortly thereafter and that's the last time we talked to him. There were those two personal moments between George and Dick, which were pretty telling about how they felt about each other, and I just happened to be there for both of them. They were close at the end, very close.

They came to that relationship late. George and Whitey were buddies almost from the beginning. The Royals and those two grew up together. When Dick got there, George was the guy, established, and had beaten Dick in 1980 when Howser was managing the Yankees. Their relationship was more of an arms length affair until after Dick was no longer managing, and when George began to realize how much Dick thought of him.

JULY 24, 1983...A.K.A. "THE PINE TAR GAME"

New York's Yankee Stadium seemed to be Brett's ball yard. He did more dramatic things there than anywhere else, including Kauffman Stadium. Yankee Stadium was his stage - a great ball park for a great left-handed hitter.

One game that helped mold the legend of George Brett at Yankee Stadium came on July 24, 1983. The game that came to be known as the "Pine Tar Game" was a pretty typical Yankees/Royals game in the Bronx. The score see-sawed back and forth. With two outs in the top of the ninth inning, and the Yankees leading 4-3, U.L. Washington beat out an infield single to help bring up Brett to face his nemesis, Rich "Goose" Gossage. If "Goose" could get George to chase a couple of high fastballs, he could record another save. Well, Gossage did try to get the fastball past Brett, but George ripped the offering into the right field seats. Even though it wasn't really an important game, it was a fairly dramatic moment. The Royals went up 5-4.

Yankee manager Billy Martin had been thinking about the pine tar on George's bat throughout the series. He intended to protest at the particular point in time when it would be most meaningful.

Martin had a knack for doing things like that and I think we were pretty attuned to what he was doing almost immediately, but it was a classic case of over-reaction by everybody involved. Billy Martin, George, the umpires; everyone over-reacted and didn't get the thing right. Pine tar on the bat does not affect the flight of the ball. In fact, if anything, the sticky substance would restrict the ball's flight.

Protesting was actually Graig Nettles' idea. He was the guy who put the idea in Billy's mind. I remember Denny was on TV and I was on radio alone at the time, and I said, "They are talking about pine tar." But we found out there was really not a penalty for that because a bat had been taken out of a game earlier in the season in Anaheim. All they did was say clean it up, which Al Zych or trainer Mickey Cobb did, and then the bat was put back in play.

Tim McClelland was the plate umpire in the "Pine Tar Game," Joe

Brinkman was the crew chief. They kept talking it over. They were rolling the bat around, measuring it with home plate, and goofing around. What they did, eventually, was combine three different rules to come up with their decision. I remember saying at the end of the whole thing, "Rarely do you ever see a protest upheld in baseball, but here's one that I bet will be." And it was.

When I guessed they were talking about the pine tar on the bat, I figured there was nowhere the umpires could go with the call; so, when they called Brett out it was startling, and that's when all hell broke loose. I have never seen George that mad. He was livid. Needless to say, he was ejected. The Royals protested the game.

We were at the airport after the game, getting ready to leave, and umpire McClelland was there. George was on the phone and Tim walked by and said something to George. George ignored him. It really pissed him off. McClelland tried to make a joke out of it, but it was not funny.

Three days later, American League President Lee MacPhail overturned the call. It was the first time he had ever overruled the decision of umpires. When we went back to New York to finish the game on August 18, it was almost a big joke, even though it was really interesting. For one thing, there was a different umpiring crew. MacPhail and the umpires had brainstormed about all the things that might happen when the game resumed. Remember, the Yankees weren't real pleased with MacPhail's decision, and Billy Martin, the team's manager, could always have a couple of tricks up his sleeve.

So the game resumed, and the Yankees threw to first base to protest, saying that George had missed first. Dave Phillips, one of the new umpires, pulls an affidavit out of his pocket that the umpiring crew that was there that day saw him touch first base. So the Yankees threw to second base. Here comes the affidavit from the previous crew saying that he touched second. That was when the Yankees really got frustrated. It was like, hell with it, go ahead and beat us and get on out of here.

Both teams had convoluted lineups out there. Ron Guidry, who was usually a tough left-handed pitcher, played second base for New York. The Royals had McRae at second as well. The two teams finished and we went on down to Baltimore, or wherever we were going. What did George do during all of this? Well, he and a friend of his, Larry Ameche, were over in New Jersey having lunch, watching the game on TV, and waiting for us to get back to the airport. Oh, the Royals lead held and won the game, 5-4.

THREE BATTING TITLES IN THREE DECADES

One feat that George accomplished that we may never see again in baseball is getting three batting crowns in three different decades. He led the league in hitting in 1976 with a .333 average; in 1980 with his .390 mark; and in 1990 by batting .329.

The first batting title for George came down to the final day of the 1976 season. The Royals were hosting the Minnesota Twins. As we came down to that last day of the regular season in 1976, George Brett, Hal McRae, and the Twins' Rod Carew all had a chance to win the batting title.

Going into the game McRae led Brett and Carew by less than a percentage point. In the ninth inning George hit a routine flyball to left field. The Twins' left fielder, Steve Brye, either didn't see it or he let it drop on purpose, resulting in an inside-the-park home run for Brett. (Sun did not seem to be a factor.) I think he took a step in and all of a sudden, for some reason, he turned and started back, then realized he was wrong, and he couldn't get back in to catch it.

McRae was the next batter, and he grounded out to the shortstop. Hal was upset because he thought Minnesota manager Gene Mauch wanted Brett to win the championship. McRae said later that there were racial undertones. The Twins were chapped about it because they felt the same thing in regards to Carew. A lot of people blamed Gene Mauch for that, and whether that was fair no one knows. There was a lot of controversy around that title, the one that left a bad taste in a lot of people's mouths because of the circumstances around it.

George and Mac continued to be good friends. Whitey gave the team a couple days off before the playoffs and Mac went home to Florida. At the workout afterwards, Mac walked into the dugout and greeted George by saying, "How are you doing?" They were friends and they didn't allow this to be a problem.

There is an interesting anecdotal post-script to this episode. On the Wednesday afternoon before the playoffs Whitey held an intra-squad game. He didn't have enough position players, so he asked Denny to play left field. The weather that day was basically the same as it had been on the final day of the season. Ironically, Brett himself hit a fly ball toward Denny in left. It was very similar to the one George hit in the ninth inning on the previous Sunday but this time Denny caught the ball without any problem. Denny said that all sorts of thoughts went through his mind about it, but of course no one made a big deal about it, because it was in an intra-squad game.

Mauch was with the Royals for a year and he will tell you to this day that he has no idea what happened when that ball was hit. I don't think he ever asked Brye about it. He just didn't want to talk about it, or even know about it.

Here's another interesting batting title story. George's last batting championship, in 1990, came down to Rickey Henderson and him on the last day of the season. George needed one hit to lock the crown. We were playing in Cleveland, and writer and Brett friend Steve Cameron actually came up with the strategy to keep George out of the game until there was a sacrifice fly situation; so if he makes an out, he's got another chance.

Sure enough, the Royals had a runner at third base, and manager John

Wathan pinch hit George, who hit a sacrifice fly. The next time up he hit a ball so hard to right field that when it cleared the second baseman, it just went "whippppp." He hit it so hard, with so much top spin, that he just killed the ball. He did the same thing twice in that game and in the process, clinched his third batting title.

NUMBER 3000

The 1992 season was an incredible one for George and anyone who followed his exploits that year. As the season went along (a season in which George had not missed any games due to injury) he inched closer and closer to the 3,000th hit of his career. At the end of September the team went on a road trip which included Minnesota and Anaheim.

In the series finale with the Twins Brett strained his left shoulder. The injury forced him out of Monday's and Tuesday's games in California. He was heading to the west coast with 2,996 hits. People kept telling him to skip Wednesday's game and wait until the team got back to Kansas City - to get 3,000 there. He said, "There's no guarantee I'm going to get four hits. I've been in slumps." I remember going down to the tunnel next to the Royals dugout and finding George swinging the bat. That was 30 minutes before the game and there was still a question about whether he would play. He was down there with trainer Nick Swartz swinging the bat, and he nodded his head yes. He's in the lineup.

What was that about George being a clutch player? Even though he really did not think he would do it that night, George got four hits; four hard hits, September 30, 1992, to become the 18th player in history to reach the plateau of 3,000 hits. In fact, each ball he hit, he hit harder than the one before.

It was funny how it worked out for Denny and me, because we alternated calling the hits. Brett's first hit came in the first inning, a fly ball to left that had a chance to be caught but wasn't. It ended up as a double. The second hit was a line drive to center in the third inning. Denny called hit number 2,999, as Brett dropped the bat head and hit the ball to center field, in the fifth. The fourth hit, the magic one, was scorched over the head of the second baseman, Ken Oberkfell. It was nearly right at him and I remember thinking, "Hold just a second, make sure they call it a hit. You know you want to say this is it." Then we heard the call from the scorer...it's a hit! There wasn't any doubt in my mind that it was, but the human thing came in — the official scorer is involved. One of the hardest things to do in broadcasting is to hold back on a call, especially a call like this one.

Going into the game everybody thought that it would be nice if George could get a couple of hits and go back to Kansas City for the record. But, boy, when he got one, then when he got two, it became a matter of self-fulfilling destiny. On the third one Denny was on the air and said, "He's at 2,999 and charging." Tim Fortugno threw him a first-pitch fast ball on number 3,000, and George just absolutely smoked it.

The funniest thing was that after he got 3,000 he was picked off first. Now-former Royal Gary Gaetti was playing first base for the Angels. George was wandering around first base when Fortugno threw over there. Gaetti caught it and tagged Brett out. George looked at Gaetti like, "What are you doing?!" It was hilarious! It was like George was saying, "Wait a minute, we're having a good time."

Even though George didn't get number 3,000 in Kansas City, he got it in the second-best place - Anaheim. It's the stadium where he played his last high school game, thirty miles from where he grew up. Some fans may have wished he would be taken out of the lineup after his first two or three hits, but there is no way George would have gone for that. He was like racehorse Secretariat, with the bit in his mouth, ears back, hell-bent for the finish line.

There was not any doubt. I think everybody there wanted it. And when he got to the finish line, number 3,000, it was first-pitch fast ball...boom...and it was over. See you later. That was how George did everything in his career.

THAT THING YOU DO

George did some amazing things in his 20 years with the Royals, but it all goes back to his approach to the game. To him, baseball is a game, a kid's game. It was a perfect fit, because George was, and still is, just a big kid. He loves to have fun and surprise people. He did things during his career that caused me to step back and think, "My goodness, he did that?!"

One amazing thing he did that didn't really set any records, but was incredible to see, was hit a home run out of Tiger Stadium in Detroit. George hit the 22nd home run to actually go out of Tiger Stadium. He did it on a Sunday afternoon in April, 1988, when he crushed a Jeff Robinson fastball for a homer that hit the roof in right field and then left the stadium. It was estimated at 450 feet. Our broadcast location in Detroit is extremely close to home plate. The thing that I remember most about that shot is that it was high and it made a hell of a noise. It was so obvious that it was out that George (uncharacteristically) watched it for a few seconds before he ran the bases. When George hit that ball it made a loud "whap" sound. Any big hit can make that kind of noise there, but evidently when it goes out of the park it is even louder.

One "George" game that always sticks out in my mind is one in which the Royals were playing the Yankees at home on a hot Sunday in the 1970s. The Royals were trailing something like 11-2 in the 9th inning. George hit a ball into the right field corner and ran so hard to get a triple that his spike got caught and he fell and busted his chin, but he got up and made it to third. I looked at that and thought, "Good Lord, they are 9 runs down. It's hotter than hell, it's the ninth inning. They've got no chance of winning, but George knew one thing to do, and that was to bust his butt on every play."

He ran out every ball he ever hit. If a fight broke out he was the first guy in. If the Royals needed a big hit, no matter what kind of a hit they needed, he was the guy who could do it. He's the best player I've ever seen. I do know that. George Brett could have played with anybody, anytime, anywhere. On top of it all, a good friend, and loyal to his team.

Charley Lau had a friend in Baltimore named Bobby Watson. We had a weekday day game in Baltimore, and Bobby invited us out to his house for a feast in the backyard. The party was rolling along pretty well, and we're drinking beer and having a great time. Bobby's son played lacrosse and he had a bunch of equipment in the backyard. George picked up this lacrosse stuff and started fooling around with it. Next thing we knew, George was a goalie, using a chair to defend himself, while we took shots.

Whitey walked out and asked us what we were doing. "Oh, we're playing lacrosse."

"Get him the hell out of there with that stuff! He'll get hurt!" George was down there with a chair having the best time. He just wanted to play goalie and have us fire at him.

This story is told in more detail elsewhere in the book, but there was a time several years ago when George wanted to go out and play hockey with Denny and his friends. He had never played the sport, but he wanted to learn how to play hockey.

That's how George lived. That's the quintessential George Brett. He wants to do everything!

FORE!

There is another story that has been circulating for years about a time when George was playing golf and was about to be hit by an golf ball flying toward him: he pulled out a club and hit the ball in midair. It's a true story.

George loves to play golf. In 1980 he injured his foot. The team had just finished playing the Baltimore Orioles and for some reason Oriole pitcher Scott MacGregor stayed in Kansas City. George and Scott were high school teammates and long-time friends. There was also a writer from Boston, George Kimball, who wanted to do a story on George. Brett said, "Let's go out to Lake Quivira and play golf. We'll play with Scotty and Kimball so we can talk while we play." - Brett and MacGregor were in one cart together, and I was in the other with George Kimball.

One particular hole, Brett and MacGregor had already hit first, and were up by the green. Kimball decided to hit a nine-iron. When he hit it, he pulled it. Brett, sitting in the cart with one golf shoe on his good foot, got out and hopped over on one foot with a club in his hand and took a swing, and smacked Kimball's ball. We were standing there and he hit it right back to us!

I looked at George Kimball and said, "Now do you think he can hit?" (Keep in mind, that was the year he ended the season with a .390 batting average. His eyesight and hand-eye coordination were just incredible!)

As if to prove that his feat that day was no fluke, he did virtually the same thing on another occasion, on the same course. He had just smoked a ball that hit a tree and came right back at him. George, calm and collected, hit it again out of the air!

FOREVER A ROYAL, AMEN

If someone were to ask George what he's most proud of about his career, he might say that it was hitting the home run off of Gossage in 1980; or helping lead the Royals to the 1985 World Championship; or becoming the 18th player in Major League Baseball history with 3,000 hits; or collecting three batting titles; or being the only player in major league history with at least 3,000 hits, 600 doubles, 100 triples, and 200 stolen bases; or, maybe even how he went about playing the game. But, don't be surprised if he were to say that he is most proud of having played his entire career for one team.

It is amazing to think that a player of George Brett's caliber played for just one team during his entire Hall of Fame career: 20 years. At the press conference announcing his retirement in 1993, he said, "The one thing that I'm proud of most, and I say this sincerely, is spending my whole career with one team." Over and above everything he did, he feels that that made him unique, especially in this day and age of players hopping from team to team and league to league. He takes as much pride in that as he does in all the numbers he accumulated.

George always said that he wanted his last at-bat to be a ground ball to second, so he could bust his butt to first and make the fielder throw. That's really how he played. He would never dog a ground ball. I don't know that anyone ever respected the game the way he did.

It showed during that retirement press conference when he said, "The game became a job. It wasn't a game anymore. And baseball shouldn't be treated that way."

One can't help but wonder how a teammate of George's could sit in the dugout, watch him play, or run out a ground ball, and not want to play just like that. How could someone sit there and not learn something watching him play?

People will probably never understand how much he hurt, or how many times he was hurt and came back. There were times toward the end of his career when he would play when he didn't need to because he was tough, and he wanted to keep driving himself. You have to be mentally tough to play when you're physically hurt. George proved he was tough both mentally and physically. Even as he got older, and he didn't have the skills he had when he was 25, he could still find a way to produce and win by sheer force of his will.

There will probably never be another player like him for the Royals, at least not in our lifetime. You don't get two of those very often. The Cardinals are still waiting for another Stan Musial. The Cubs are still looking for another Ernie Banks. The Pirates are still waiting for another Roberto Clemente. George would be the first to hope there would be another like him, but I don't think there will be.

REALLY, FOREVER A ROYAL?

During the winter a few years ago a story broke about George and his brothers wanting to buy the Royals. They approached Royals Chairman of the Board David Glass, and expressed an interest in purchasing the team. David told them that the club was not for sale...not yet. When the "official" process began last year, George and his brothers, who are involved with other professional sports teams, once again put the Brett name in the hat. The only problem this time was that, even though they had Kansas City's best interests at heart, they were going up against a couple of bigger cash cows.

George would have liked to own the club, but I don't know how really important it was for him. It is important, however, that he still be associated with the franchise. I don't even know if he would stay in Kansas City were he not involved with the club in some manner.

Hopefully, whoever ends up with the club will see how important it is to include George with the Royals. The main question is, if he doesn't own the club, what position could he hold in the franchise? What many people don't know about George Brett is how bright he is. But he doesn't want to be a figurehead. He doesn't want to be the general manager, and I don't blame him. I don't think we will ever see George in uniform again, so coaching or managing is out. There just has to be something there for him.

Theoretically he could, and would, be what Stan Musial has been to the Cardinals, or Joe DiMaggio has been to the Yankees. *Just* being an icon. Is that enough for him? I don't know. But I do know that they can't cut the ties on George. He has to be always and forever a Kansas City Royal. (Not to mention the fact that Kansas City fans would go nuts if he were not involved.) Cutting the strings with George would be the worst public relations move the new owner(s) could make. On the other hand, making him a vital part of the organization would be one of the best things the new owner(s) could do.

He is smart enough, and knows so much about the game, that he would be very valuable to the Royals in a consultant capacity. There has to be a place for George Brett in the Royals organization.

THE END OF THE ROAD

On October 3, 1993, after 2,707 games spanning 20 years in the big leagues, George Brett hung up his spikes for the final time. He ended his career with a .305 lifetime batting average, 3,154 hits, and 13 trips to the All-Star game.

Brett's final game at Kauffman Stadium, September 29, was in front of a crowd of 36,999. The Royals played the Cleveland Indians. After going hitless in his first three at-bats, George came up in the eighth inning with Kevin Koslofski on second base and the Royals down 2-1. In typical George Brett fashion, he delivered a single up the middle against Cleveland's Jeremy Hernandez to score Koslofski and tie the game. The Royals scored a run in the bottom of the ninth to beat the Indians, 3-2.

After the game George was escorted around the field on a golf cart. When he got off the golf cart, he got down on his hands and knees and kissed home plate.

Maybe the most telling thing of all, though, was his final game, October 3, in Texas. It was in the same city, Arlington, and against the same team, the Rangers, that George had hit his first major league home run in May of 1974. To say that this October day was a special one would be a severe understatement. It was a game that not only marked the end of George's career, but also that of another future Hall-of-Famer, Nolan Ryan. Originally Ryan was supposed to pitch in the game, but he was hurt. Wouldn't that have been something to see George and Nolan face each other under those circumstances? Even though Ryan didn't pitch, he and Brett took the lineup cards to the plate; they received a standing ovation for that.

On his last at-bat all of the Royals and all of the Rangers were out of the dugouts standing on the field as Denny told the listeners to "take a good look," and I said, "savor it in your hearts and savor it in your minds." That moment may have said as much about him as anything ever could. Guys who played with and against him were standing and applauding. I thought if there's ever been a tribute to a guy, what he is and what he stands for, that's it. To the Royals, he represented the consummate teammate. For the Rangers, those guys had played against him, and they knew he had earned their respect and admiration.

By the way, in that last at-bat, his final career appearance at the plate, if you can believe this, George singled up the middle, then came home on first-year Royal Gary Gaetti's home run in a 4-1 Kansas City win. (Ironic...remember Gaetti was the California first baseman when George was picked off base after his 3,000th hit.) That was George.

I feel very lucky to have been able to follow the career of George Brett. The first year I was with the Royals was also George's first year. There were great moments for him, which turned out to be great moments for us. It was incredible and I was lucky enough to be a part of the ride.

8 The White Rat and other Field Leaders

Denny Matthews

One night in the late 1970s, the Royals were hosting the Oakland A's. This was after the Royals had become a better team than their old rivals. By this time Whitey Herzog, also known as "The White Rat," was managing the Royals. There was a big crowd on this particular night with an electric atmosphere all over the ballpark; as with most games in Kauffman Stadium in the 1970s, it was a near-capacity crowd. In the top of the first inning Oakland's Joe Rudi drilled a double into the corner. Then somebody else came up and smoked one. The next hitter, Sal Bando, hit a rocket into the alley. Wow! Three batters, three bullets! For some reason, the A's were just all over the Royals pitcher.

Almost immediately, Whitey hopped out of the dugout and went up to the home plate umpire and started talking to him. No one in the stadium could figure out what was going on. Then Whitey walked down the third base line and said something to Steve Boros, the A's third base coach. Then he called the third base umpire over. I thought, "maybe, he thinks that the bullpen is stealing signs." I didn't know what else he could be talking about.

So, I said on the air, "Maybe Whitey thinks they're stealing signs. You can do that from the bullpen if somebody had binoculars. That person could look into the Royals catcher to see the signal, then take a towel, and if a fastball's coming, put the towel on his left hand. If the curveball's coming, he could put it on his right hand. Very subtle."

I was just throwing it out as a possibility when suddenly everyone began walking toward the left field bullpen. Sure enough, Whitey, the umpires and the third base coach all went out to the bullpen, opened the big fence door, and walked in. The Oakland players were seated near the fence. As the men walked down the line of chairs, hmmm, there was a towel. Somebody picked it up, and there were the binoculars. The umpire held up the binoculars.

Whitey and I may have been the only two people in the stadium who had any idea what kind of shenanigans the A's were trying to pull. I was guessing — Whitey apparently was dead sure.

THE WHITE RAT

Whitey Herzog had managed in the league before he joined the Royals, so I knew him before he started in Kansas City in 1975. He knew a lot of the players and he actually lived in Kansas City at that time. That made it easier for him. And it helped me form a quicker relationship with him.

Whitey had a real good sense of what to tell the players to motivate them and to help make each of them feel equally important. The players loved to play for him.

He was very smart, and was never out-managed. He had a great sense of timing on offense, and on pitching changes. He was an excellent tactician; opponents had to work exceptionally hard to beat him. Whitey loved team speed; so evident with teams he managed in both Kansas City and St. Louis.

He was the guy who took the Royals organization to the next level. While he was here his teams won three straight A.L. West titles, and a couple of those teams were an inning or two away from going to the World Series. He won more games (410) and had a higher winning percentage (.574) than any of his Kansas City managing counterparts.

As Royals manager, Whitey had a successful run for a little more than four seasons. But he got into trouble with the front office and there was a conflict there, and of course that's not good. The trouble with the front office mainly stemmed from two instances. The first came after the 1977 season when Whitey and first baseman John Mayberry had a falling out, and the popular "Big John" was shipped to the Toronto Blue Jays. The second came a year later when Whitey fired hitting coach Charley Lau. Charley had been with the organization since the early 1970s, and had helped develop the hitting of players like George Brett and Hal McRae.

Despite all of that, his firing came as something of a surprise, after the team's second-place division finish in 1979. I don't think Whitey was completely surprised when the team got rid of him, but it wasn't a situation in which there had been a lot of rumors flying around all season about him being on the proverbial "hot seat." With some managers, and even ones in Kansas City, there are times when it becomes a concern, or a major story, for the media. When those rumors do start to fly, as announcers, we deal with what we have to deal with. We put those things aside and deal with the task at hand...doing our interview and letting the guy go win some ballgames.

PUT ME IN COACH...I'M READY TO PLAY

Having Whitey here was a lot of fun because he gave me the opportunity to play with the team a few times during in-season exhibition games. That all started when I used to go out during spring training and take ground balls to stay in shape. Whitey's thought was that we have these in-season exhibition games with Omaha (Kansas City's Triple-A affiliate), the Naval Academy, and a couple major league teams (Pittsburgh and Atlanta), so the regulars would play the first three innings, then I'd come in and play — usually in the outfield or third base.

On a 25-man roster there aren't enough position players to fill a team when the starters all leave the game. As Whitey used to tell me, "With you playing, I know one of my regular players won't get hurt." That was his theory. It didn't matter if I got hurt. I could just go up to the booth and talk.

Playing in these games was a blast, but it also helped give me credibility with the players. They knew I had some credibility in describing a difficult play, or saying a ball took a crappy hop, or saying that a player should have had a ground ball. It was a no-lose situation for me because, in the players' eyes, why wouldn't I screw up? On the other hand, if I did anything positive, that's a plus, because I'm not really supposed to be able to do anything well on the field. It was a lot of fun for me being able to play in a big league uniform, and it was fun for the players to get on me in a good-natured way because of my deficiencies as a player.

THE WIT AND WISDOM OF THE WHITE RAT

Whitey Herzog loved Casey Stengel; he idolized Casey Stengel. Whitey can do a great imitation of Casey; I mean a great imitation. Casey was infamous for having that double-talk and being able to say things without saying things. The longer Whitey was with the Royals as manager, unwittingly the more he began to sound like Casey during our interview. In fact, Whitey's wife, Mary Lou, asked me one night, "Don't you think Whitey is beginning to sound more and more like Casey?"

Whitey had some great comments on his pregame show; that would really startle me. Sometimes they aired, sometimes they didn't.

One night when the team hadn't been playing real well, in his best Casey Stengel truism (he didn't do it on purpose) he said, "Yeah, we haven't been playing very well, but you're only as good as you are, and you can't do what you can't do." I thought about that one, and thought about it. We should have put that before the Harvard Debate Club. See if they can refute that one.

Whitey had a couple of other theorems I loved. One was, "It's hard to be lucky when you're horseshit." That pretty much applies to everything, doesn't it? The other one that I always liked, and always favored as a broadcaster, was when he once said, "If you're going to play horseshit, play fast." I really liked that one.

The wit and wisdom of "The White Rat."

THE ORIGINAL MANAGER

Joe Gordon was the Royals first manager and really a great pick because he had a bunch of guys who came in without knowing anybody. But Joe was a player's manager, which helped the transition for the new club. He was with the Royals only during that 1969 season, but that was the agreement he had with the organization.

Cedric Tallis asked Joe in 1968 if he wanted to manage again. (Gordon had been a major league manager, and actually had done a stint with the

Athletics, briefly, when they were in Kansas City.) Joe said he didn't know, but Cedric asked Gordon if, as a favor, he would manage the team for one year. So he came back to Kansas City, at Cedric's request and managed that one year.

Joe was a great player himself, they say. He was a second baseman with the Yankees, terrific defensively, and very good offensively. Apparently he was one of the better second basemen in the history of baseball.

As a manager he was really loose, which was very important that first year. He just let everybody go out and play. He was a nice, friendly guy. He loved Chinese food. If we played a Saturday day game on the road, it was not uncommon, after the game, for him to get a bunch of people together and say, "Let's go have some Chinese food and a couple of beers and sit around and talk." Even though I wasn't the main play-by-play guy at the time, I was still able to spend quite a bit of time with Joe, and I had a great time with him.

THE METRO STOPS HERE

Manager Charlie Metro was just the opposite. He was more of a stickler for detail; very regimented. Whereas Joe was free and easy, Charlie was a stern disciplinarian. That rubbed some veteran players the wrong way, and Charlie had problems in the sense that the players were jerked from one extreme to the other. They went from Joe's method, to Charlie's method and it was such a shock to them that it didn't work out well for Charlie. So, early in the 1970 season, 52 games into his managing tenure with the Royals, he was fired. He may have been the right guy, but he was definitely there at the wrong time.

I still see Charlie here and there, and it's always fun to talk to him. He was really solid with regard to his background in baseball. He was a good evaluator. Bob Lemon came on board after Charlie.

THE PLAYER'S MANAGER

Bob Lemon was more like Joe Gordon, a player's manager. He was very loose. Like Gordon, Lemon was a great player in his playing days, which means he let the guys do their thing. He gave the young guys confidence — they didn't feel a lot of pressure because Lem was a very low pressure manager.

Gordon and Lem played together in Cleveland, and their personalities were really a lot alike, so it was kind of an interesting contrast. The Royals went from Gordon to Metro to Lem; so they went from one extreme to another extreme and back to the other extreme.

Bob Lemon was pretty successful and pretty popular as the team's manager. By that time, Cedric Tallis had acquired some good players, and the Royals were just starting to develop into a good team. Lem had the beginnings of the real good teams, real good players. After almost three full seasons, and as the only manager so far with a winning record, Lem was fired. His best season was in 1971 when the team went 85-76.

To a lot of people, it was a shock when he was fired. I don't know why he was. I didn't spend much time in that inner circle and I didn't spend a lot of time with the manager or the coaches then, because they were all a lot older than I was. I was more involved socially with the players than I was with the manager, coaches, writers, etc. They were all of a different era. My contemporaries were the players. Jack McKeon was brought in to replace the ever-popular but now departed Lemon.

TRADER JACK

A lot of guys swore by Jack McKeon, and a lot of guys swore at him. He was more of a disciplinarian than they were used to. Personally, I always liked Jack. He had problems with certain players, and I think the longer he was in Kansas City the less the players listened to him.

Two of the Royals' worst-ever trades came while McKeon was managing. Two players he didn't necessarily see eye to eye with were Lou Piniella and Gene Garber. After becoming the team's first star, Lou was sent to the Yankees after the 1973 season for Lindy McDaniel. That was one of those trades that left Kansas City people completely baffled. Needless to say, it wasn't a very popular trade, and may have been the worst trade ever.

The other clincher under McKeon was when the Royals traded Jim Rooker to the Pirates in exchange for Garber immediately after the 1972 season. Gene, during that stint, was in Kansas City for only two seasons, 1973 and 1974. The Royals used him both as a starter and a reliever. But McKeon didn't like him, and, following the 1974 season, he just sort of gave Garber away. After Gene left the Royals he had 10 or 11 really productive years as a relief pitcher. Ironically, as he was approaching the end of his career, the Royals obtained him again, late in the 1987 season from the Atlanta Braves for Terry Bell.

Gene Garber was one of my all-time favorite Royals. I loved to just sit and chew the fat with him. He always had interesting things to say. I don't think a lot of people took time to know him, and I don't know why I did, but I did. We got along very well.

Things finally reached a point under Jack where hardly any of the players were listening to him. The Royals' front office figured something had to be done. That's when they got Whitey Herzog.

JUMPING THE HUMP

Jim Frey was brought in after Whitey, before the 1980 season. When Frey came to Kansas City, he didn't have any managerial experience, but he had been a long-time coach with the Baltimore Orioles. The thinking by the Royals was that Baltimore was such a successful organization; it's like the old idea that when you have a real successful head coach, his assistants are usually the first ones considered for jobs. That idea holds true in baseball. The Orioles were so successful for so long under Earl Weaver, and had such a very solid system, that other teams looked at his assistants as potential managers. That was the biggest reasoning behind getting Jim Frey as Royals manager in 1980.

And evidently it was the right move because in his first season as the Royals' skipper Frey led the team to its first-ever World Series. That was the year they swept the Yankees in the playoffs, then lost to the Philadelphia Phillies in the Series. There are a couple of arguments in regard to Frey's brief stay in Kansas City. One is that he is responsible for getting the organization over the hump by taking the ballclub to that World Series. Others argue that he did it with Whitey's players, who were already in place. I say, yes it's true, the great team was already in place, but Jim took that great team and managed it very well.

FROM CELEBRATION TO SADNESS

In the first half of 1981 the Royals got off to a slow start. Then the strike hit. When the strike ended, Jim Frey was fired, and former New York Yankee manager Dick Howser was named the new Royals leader. I wasn't privy to all of the inside information, but it may have been a situation where they simply didn't want to let Howser get away. Dick wasn't managing at the time, and Frey was expendable.

Our front office had a sense that Dick would really be a good manager somewhere, and it might as well be in Kansas City. When he managed the Yankees in 1980 the team won 103 games, but lost to the Royals in the playoffs. Owner George Steinbrenner fired him. I guess winning 103 games was not enough for that owner.

I liked Howser. He was more distant from the players than other managers had been. He was rather a stickler for detail. He was fairly reserved and quiet. I didn't have the feeling that he was really close to many of the players; he didn't want to get close to them. He was sort of aloof — he might have been more aloof than any of the other managers, but that was just his personality. I played golf with him occasionally; he and Fred were very close.

THE DUKE

After Dick passed away from a brain tumor during the 1987 season, former Royals' player John Wathan was named the full-time manager. (Actually, Billy Gardner led the team through the first 126 games in 1987 before Wathan took over.) Working with Wathan was very easy, but I knew it would be. I had known him so well and liked him so much as a player, that I knew things would be easy, and they were. I thought, and still do think, that John could have been a real good manager.

But he had a lot of things going against him. The Royals had been grooming him to become a big league manager, but because of Dick's illness he had to become one before he was really ready. He hadn't really managed enough in the minor leagues to become a big league manager. Then he came to the big league level trying to fill the shoes of Howser, managing guys whom he played with, and boy, that is a killer — that is deadly. He was friends with them and then he suddenly became their manager; that's real, real tough.

For the most part, he did a great job. From late 1987 until early 1991 Wathan posted an overall record of 287-270. In 1989 his team posted 92 wins, which is tied for third on the all-time single season list for the Royals. Unfortunately, those 92 wins were only good for a second-place finish in the division. In 1991 he was replaced by interim manager Bob Schaeffer for one game before another former player took over.

FROM ONE FORMER PLAYER TO ANOTHER

Hal McRae was in a situation similar to Wathan's, although to a lesser extent. Hal had never managed; had never thought about managing. He was a great hitting instructor and he learned, from the ground up, to manage on the major league level, which is the toughest way to do it. He had no minor league experience, but Hal McRae is so bright that he was learning very quickly.

The reason he took the job fairly prematurely was because it was an opportunity he couldn't really afford to turn down. General Manager Herk Robinson was pretty persuasive. Herk told Hal that he really wanted him to consider it. They negotiated and Mac finally acquiesced and said, sure.

He really didn't like it at first, but the more he managed, the better he liked it. By the time the strike came along in 1994, despite the team having won 14 or 15 games in a row prior to the stoppage, Mac was fired and replaced by Bob Boone in 1995. But, Mac was doing a hell of a job and really enjoying it. He had a good feel for the job.

Hal McRae is really a fun and funny guy. He has a great sense of humor, is really smart, and really knows hitting. I would rather talk hitting with Hal McRae and Charley Lau than anybody I've ever talked to in baseball. They both had such an interesting insight and perspective on it. McRae really has an interesting way of explaining things; straight and direct and to the point. He has a great way with words; so great that he can create incredible pictures with words. He is one of the smartest people I've ever met.

Mac once gave me one of the best compliments I have ever received. One day after I had played in a couple of those exhibition games, he said, "Denny, you've played the game."

CHOOSING THE ALL-STAR MANAGERS

If I had to pick the top managers from the history of the Kansas City organization from an impact standpoint, I would say, in order, Whitey

Herzog, Dick Howser and Joe Gordon; Gordon, for setting the tone for an expansion team with his personality. I don't know that there have been any more than that who have made a huge impact on this franchise. Others really weren't around long enough to have an impact. I think Tony Muser, if he stays long enough, could fall into that category. Tony is one of the nicest people in baseball, and a great baseball person.

THE INSIDE SCOOP

I've done the manager's show every day since 1976, and Royals managers have told me a zillion things. We tape the five minute pregame interview, then we just sit and talk without recording anything. So they say things to me; they are frustrated sometimes, and they've got to get things off their chest. Okay, here's Denny, let's lay it on him. Things like that. Obviously many of the comments could not be repeated. It went without saying. It seemed the longer we did the show, and the better I got to know the manager, the more they would talk, the more comfortable they were with me, and the more they would tell me things off the air.

Having a good relationship with these managers makes my job a lot easier. Absolutely. It helps not only with the pregame interview, but also in terms of knowing their thinking, what they are trying to do with the team, the insights, some of which we can use or say on the air, some of which we can't. It all kind of melds together to paint the whole picture, it gives us a lot better view — I don't feel like I am looking through smoke trying to figure out what's going on. I have a pretty clear, concise image of what they are trying to accomplish.

For instance, I know tendencies. I know whom Tony trusts for the hit and run and whom he trusts for the bunt in certain situations, and certain types of bunts. Sometimes it helps to know they are going to run. With the inning factor, the score factor, the pitcher factor, the pitcher's control factor and the hitter, it's possible to make a pretty reasonable guess as to what the managers are going to do.

COMMUNICATION IS THE KEY

In my opinion, the first part of the formula for a good manager is the ability to communicate. I would say that, on the big league level, the most important thing is to make all the players feel they are a part of the team, from the best player to the number 25 guy. The number 25 guy has to feel just as important as the top dog, and everybody in between. A good manager has a way of doing that.

Making the lesser players, or bench players, know that they are an important part of the overall picture is really the first step. Communication, obviously, is a big part of that. The ability to teach, to get points across, to make the players be less concerned with their own individual stats and more concerned with helping the team win the game; that's what it takes.

The ability to evaluate talent, obviously, is important. Strategy is not a big deal because major league managers know all the things to do — they play the percentages, so nobody really out-manages anybody. So, just tending to their own business in that regard and solving the problems that come up every day and night, because managing is an everyday thing. The ability to solve people problems goes a long way in determining how effective a manager is, too.

FROM PLAYER DEVELOPMENT TO PLAYER SWAPPING

Another key for a manager to be successful, and one that he really can't control, is the team's general manager. The Royals have been lucky to have had four very good general managers in Cedric Tallis, Joe Burke, John Schuerholz and Herk Robinson. That doesn't mean they have always seen eye-to-eye with the field managers, but they have usually worked well enough together that things have gone pretty smoothly.

As I mentioned earlier, Cedric Tallis was a great general manager and pulled off some of the greatest trades in franchise, if not baseball, history. He turned out to be the perfect first general manager for this organization. It was a position he held until 1974.

In the meantime, the Royals hired Joe Burke in 1973. When Joe Burke joined the club, his background was more in business than it was in baseball. He had no experience in scouting, player development or player evaluation. He was purely on the business side. All of a sudden, in 1974, he was thrust into the baseball side as the general manager, but he maintained his hand on the business side, too. But Joe made some excellent trades, and he was really a stabilizing force in the organization. Some of the key players he traded for include Larry Gura, Darrell Porter and Willie Aikens. Joe was a very nice man, a very honest man. Everybody liked Joe Burke. He did a terrific job.

It's worth mentioning a side note. Whitey had been with the Texas Rangers, and when he started there, he was hired by Joe Burke. Then, when Whitey came to Kansas City, he was hired by...Joe Burke.

John Schuerholz and Herk Robinson originally worked together under Lou Gorman in the minor league department. They both eventually worked their way up the Royals' organizational ladder. Herk really had more experience scouting than John did when he started to work for the Royals. He had scouted on the grass roots level and he had scouted both on the amateur and the pro levels. As a matter of fact, he had spent a year scouting in the Baltimore organization before joining the Royals just after the 1969 season.

After the 1981 season Joe Burke was promoted to team president, so he and Mr. K had to find a replacement; but which one? Herk made the decision easy, because his daughters were young and he wanted to be able to spend more time with his family; so he said he didn't want the position. He didn't want to travel. He got into the business end. He became the director of stadium operations for years and years.

John chose to stay in the baseball side, so he became the general manager. When John left to go to the Atlanta Braves, Herk was Mr. Kauffman's choice to take over as general manager. So John and Herk both had really excellent backgrounds in player development at the times when they were named general manager. That's one of the things that people didn't realize. They thought when Herk came out of the business end of it — stadium operations — that he had no experience on the baseball side of the business. Actually Herk had more experience early in his career in scouting than John did. That was not a common perception.

They were both eminently qualified to do the job. It just so happened that John became the general manager first because Herk elected to be more of a home body and stay in the business side in stadium operations. He was as qualified as John when Mr. K asked him to take over as GM.

Schuerholz and Robinson each had to work with an entirely different set of circumstances. Obviously John had the best of it with regard to the good players and the team nucleus when he took over. When Herk eventually took over in October of 1990, the minor league system had pretty well dried up and he had to start all over again in the scouting and minor league development. That's why I say, given what they were given to work with, all four general managers did, and have done, a wonderful job.

THE DUST KICKING SAILORS

Two of the most infamous managers in the 1970s and 80s were Billy Martin and Earl Weaver. Both left their mark, good or bad, on the game's history. Billy was with several teams including Minnesota, Oakland, and New York, while Weaver stuck with the Baltimore Orioles.

Billy Martin was a very good manager for a short period of time. He had a way of finding a quick fix. He'd go in — clean up a team in a hurry — they'd win, then they'd get tired of him and that line of talk he had. Whether the players or the front office got tired of him first was kind of a toss up. Sometimes it was one way, sometimes the other; but for short periods of time, Billy was a pretty darn good manager.

I didn't really know Earl that well, although I did some interviews with him early. He was kind of a showman. Earl had great teams in Baltimore and he was good with those great teams. Just because a manager has great players doesn't mean he is going to win; Earl had to make those guys into a great team. He platooned a lot, and his teams didn't run much. A three-run home run was a big deal for Weaver, but the Orioles always had great defensive teams and great pitching, which can make any manager pretty smart. He managed those very good teams really well. He was a personality, a character.

THE ULTIMATE CONVERSATION

Hall-of-Famer Ted Williams managed the Washington Senators for a couple of years and it was fun listening to him talk about hitting. It is not uncommon for a former great player to go into coaching and have a difficult time figuring out why his players aren't as good as he was, or don't work as hard as he did when he was playing. Ted Williams was one of those managers. He couldn't, or didn't, understand why his players were a lesser talent than he was. And, of course, who could be as good a hitter as Ted Williams? Anyone who played for him was under the gun in that regard.

From my side, though, it was outstanding to sit around and talk to him about hitting. One of the greatest conversations I've ever heard (I would love to have a tape of this) was in spring training the Royals first year, 1969, when Joe Gordon and Ted Williams were behind the batting cage talking hitting. They had opposing views, and the conversation was fascinating.

Joe Gordon's theory was to hit down on the ball, while Ted Williams' theory was a sweeping upward type of stroke. Hearing them argue back and forth, the pros and cons, was absolutely scintillating. Their debate went on for about twenty minutes. It was unbelievable. Can you imagine being 26 years old, your first year in this business, listening to a conversation like that?! The exact views and ideas they shared are somewhat fuzzy, but that is a conversation I will never forget.

9

1985: It Was Worth the Wait

Denny Matthews

During the interleague portion of the 1998 season (I'll say it that way since those games only happen certain times in the season), one of our series was in St. Louis. That was the first time since 1985 that we had been in Busch Stadium to broadcast a game, but, I didn't look at it that way. For me, having grown up a Cardinal fan (as I did) and having seen so many games in St. Louis, it wasn't "Well here we are back for the first time since 1985." That really wasn't a part of it in my mind.

It was just going to St. Louis for baseball, which, from the time I was 5, 6 or 7 years old, was always fun. This interleague trip was just as enjoyable. It was a regular season series in St. Louis and it's always fun to go there, especially a trip like this (interleague) which is good for the obvious fan-interest reasons. So, like a lot of fans, I didn't really reminisce about the 1985 season while we were there. Considering how a couple of those early years during the 1980s went for the Royals, it's maybe more impressive that 1985 turned out the way it did.

THE A'S AGAIN? DO WE HAVE TO DO THIS?

When the strike hit in 1981, the Royals had not been playing well, especially considering that they were coming off of their first-ever trip to the World Series. Actually, after the first 70 games, the team was 30-40. After the strike, manager Jim Frey was fired, and Dick Howser was brought in. We're always a little surprised when a manager is fired, in some ways; and in some ways we're not, because there is almost always rumbling somewhere from someone. In part, since the Royals had not been playing very well, Frey's firing may not have been a complete shock.

Howser came in and did a respectable job in the second half, finishing the season with a 20-13 mark, but things were in such chaos at that point, with the split season, that to me, it was a lost year. The 1981 season wasn't that interesting, or exciting. Even the playoffs were a mess. The way the post-season worked, the best team from the pre-strike season in each division played the team with the best record from the post-strike season in a mini-playoff series. For instance, the Royals and A's, both A.L. West teams, played each other.

By the time the post-season rolled around, not many people cared what happened. It wasn't that much fun. Anytime there is a strike like that, as we saw in 1994, fans lose all interest in the season, and really, in baseball. The Cincinnati Reds, who had the best record overall, were not in the playoffs because they lost in the mini-playoffs. Some people thought that canceling the strike-shortened season of 1994 was such a travesty; well, for all intents and purposes, the 1981 season was canceled too.

A LOT OF OTHER TEAMS HAVE HAD SCANDALS... NOW IS OUR TIME

Things didn't get much better for the Royals over the next couple years after the 1981 strike. Sure, the team won 90 games in 1982, the first full year under Howser, but they finished second in the West. During the 1983 season, a season in which the team finished under .500 for just the first time in a non-strike season since 1974, with a record of 79-83, four Royals were involved in a drug scandal. Willie Wilson, Willie Aikens, Vida Blue and Jerry Martin all pleaded guilty to drug possession charges, and all served some short jail time.

The scandal didn't affect the people who were playing on the team at the time, but I think it did affect the people who were running the team. It caused them a lot of headache and a lot of embarrassment. It wasn't the first time some people in sports had gotten off the track, but it was the first time it had happened in Kansas City. The convictions certainly impacted and soured a few fans. It didn't do as much damage with the fans as the strike did, but there was some disappointment, and a feeling that these guys had let us down.

Since the players served time during the off-season, it didn't really affect the team and the way they played, but obviously it had an impact on the individual players involved, as to how they either came through or didn't come through in particular situations. Since most of the players indicted were not vital to the Royals success, it didn't have much effect on the team. Blue was on the downhill side of his career; Aikens was a one-dimensional player; Martin probably was not headed toward stardom; Wilson, on the other hand, still had a couple good years left in him.

Mr. Kauffman was probably more disappointed than anybody, just for obvious reasons, and he was probably hurt by it more than anybody. He felt the vibrations not only because it was the first incident like this for the Royals, but because these were his players.

As announcers, with things like team drug problems, there really isn't much we can, or need to, say. Our job is to do the game, it really isn't to get involved in those personal types of things. Not that we avoid them, but what can we say over and above what has already been written and said? That's what we run into. People say, "Well, you didn't talk about that enough." Well, what's enough? What else needs to be said, or can be said? What else is there to say?

Okay, Willie Aikens was taking drugs and got caught. What can I add to that? I wasn't at his house, so I can't give an insight on how he got them in there or what the guy looked like who delivered them. Offering our opinion, or doing a 20/20-type investigation, is not really our job.

Some people would prefer us to say, in the eighth inning of a close game, "Willie Aikens grounds into a double play. You know, if he hadn't been taking drugs he probably would have gotten a hit." I think some people would want us to actually say something like that.

We get on our soap boxes on certain subjects. We bang on the umpires here and there for some calls; and when our guys make a bad play or a series of bad plays, we'll say something about it. The game itself, how it could be improved, our ideas on realignment, things like that may get our attention. Fred and I sometimes agree on certain subjects and sometimes we differ on things. Either way, that's good. Opinions are food for thought for the listener, and they make for interesting listening. If we had agreed on everything, the broadcast would have been a little duller.

There are a lot of things that we know that the general public doesn't need to know and won't ever know. That's the way it should be. There are certain things in most every company that their employees know but will never talk about, so why should broadcasters be expected to reveal everything?

REBOUNDING FROM THE SCANDAL

I didn't see any evidence of the drug setback affecting the team in 1984. In fact, it came out strong and ended up winning the division with an 84-78 mark. Dan Quisenberry was still the closer. The team also added the young arms of Mark Gubicza and Bret Saberhagen. The Royals that year were a very good, very solid team.

Unfortunately, the Royals faced the Detroit Tigers in the League Championship Series. The Tigers were magical that year, coming out of the gate at 35-5. It was apparently their year. That was going to be their year just like it was going to be the Royals' turn in 1985. There are times when certain teams are destined to win, and things are going to happen so that they will. Everything went right for Detroit in 1984.

The Royals had a good year and that was the year that the pitching rotation was established. The team was still good, still young and still productive.

It was not necessarily disappointing when the Tigers swept the Royals in the playoffs, because it was what we almost expected. Career years abounded among Detroit players. Winning was in the cards...it was their turn. Even Johnny Grubb, who was not normally known for his offensive output, had a good year with a batting average at about .325. Destiny happens a lot in sports. Teams win games late on goofy things, and sometimes they just win on their own ability. But everything falls in place for champions; it has to, that's part of it.

NOW IT'S THE ROYALS' TURN

The attitude heading into spring training ahead of the 1985 season was pretty much just like any other year. We knew we had a good team and if they'd play well over the majority of the 162-game schedule, then they'd have a chance, depending on what the other teams did. So going into the 1985 season, as with any other, we wondered whether the Royals were going to over-achieve, under-achieve or simply achieve. Then we wondered about the other teams in the division. This may sound bizarre, but some years teams over-achieve and everybody else under-achieves and the over-achievers win going away. Sometimes every team achieves and it's a close match down to the end.

Everybody knew the Royals would be a solid big league team in 1985. There were some other teams in the West that were going to be pretty good, too. But the breaks were really going the Royals' way, especially late in the year.

Normally, if you lose three in a row in Seattle, and three in a row in Minnesota at that juncture in the season, you're out of it if another team is good enough. Well, as luck would have it, the Royals did lose six straight games on the road, at the end of September, but they weren't out. Their main competition in the West was the California Angels, who weren't good enough to take advantage of the Royals slide. In fact, as the Royals came back home for an important series with the Angels on October 2, after losing the six straight, California was only up in the standings by one game. All the cards were aligned for Kansas City.

The ballclub came home, caught a second wind, took care of the Angels, then turned around and beat the Oakland A's. The Royals won the A.L. West crown with a 91-71 record. And, for the second time in as many years, they were headed for the playoffs. And, for the second time in as many years, they wouldn't be facing the New York Yankees for a trip to the World Series; instead, they met the Toronto Blue Jays.

The first two games of the A.L.C.S. were in Toronto, the first time the city had hosted the playoffs. Toronto forced Charlie Leibrandt out of the game by the third inning, and went on to win the opener 6-1.

The second game looked a little more promising throughout, as the Royals led pretty much the entire game. They were still ahead 5-4 heading into the bottom of the ninth, with Dan Quisenberry on the hill. Wouldn't you know it...the Jays scored the two runs they needed, and took a two games to none lead to the United States.

The mindset in the series for the Royals, once they were down 2 games to 0, was interesting. They said there's "No pressure on us. Now we are not supposed to win," so they figured they could play loose and breathe easy.

Game three, on Friday, October 11, was the first time I had ever seen a position player dominate a game. Pitchers can dominate a game, obviously, but for position players, it's very tough to do because the player has to be in a situation to do that; he can't dominate defensively unless somebody hits the ball his way, and he can't dominate offensively unless things are set up for him to do so. Things were in place for George Brett that Friday night and he responded, both offensively and defensively.

Brett played, in my opinion, the greatest game of his career. He single-handedly won that game for Kansas City. Baseball is set up, obviously, in such a way that a player only bats so many times. If he is the number 3 hitter in the lineup, as George was, and the number 7, 8, and 9 hitters are coming up, he has no chance to do anything; he's on the bench and has to watch. The guys in the bottom of the lineup came through for the Royals and gave George a chance. He took it from there, and turned the whole thing around.

By the time he was finished, Brett had gone four-for-four with two home runs, a double, and the game-winning single in the bottom of the eighth inning. The Royals won the game 6-5. It turned the momentum of the series completely around.

When I think about George and his career, the excellence, the hard work, and the ability to come through in the clutch; all these things come to my mind immediately. He got the most out of his ability whereas a lot of guys with incredible ability, don't even tap half of it.

Unfortunately, someone failed to tell the Blue Jays that they were in Kansas City and the momentum had shifted toward the home team. Leading 1-0 after eight innings in game four, the hosts graciously allowed Toronto to score three runs and win the game 3-1, which also, incidentally, was the series count.

Once the Royals went down three games to one, I didn't think they'd win. I really thought they were dead. Toronto was a good team. It was either Frank White or Brett who reiterated that the pressure was off and they could just play loose and breathe easy.

Danny Jackson came out in the sixth game for the Royals, in Toronto, and really shut the Blue Jays down. The Jays had two chances to win at home and couldn't get it done either time. They really tightened up and the Royals played like they were the underdog without a care in the world. We could see that Toronto had tightened up, and the Royals were loose, free and easy, and managed to win.

Ironically, that season the playoff format was changed from a best-of-five series to a best-of-seven. Had it been under the old format, the Royals would have lost in four games; Toronto would have won it, 3-1.

To show how things were lined up correctly for the Royals, during a late season game in Kansas City, the Royals needed a win on a Sunday afternoon. First baseman Steve "Bye-Bye" Balboni hit a drive down the left field line that kept hooking, obviously fouled. But suddenly the wind started to bring the ball back, and brought it back around the foul pole. It literally looked like somebody took a hand and moved that ball into fair territory. Sometimes especially during day games, there's a strange phenomenon that happens in the left field corner in Kauffman Stadium. The ball can be way foul and drift sharply back into fair territory. Then you look at the flags, and they could be blowing in an altogether different direction. That doesn't happen all the time, but it does happen, and it sure did that day with Balboni. He thought he was going to be back up there with an 0-2 count, which for Balboni wasn't always a good thing (especially in 1985, when he became the team's single-season strikeout leader with 166; surpassing the old record, also his, of 139 — incidentally, he also set a single-season home run mark for the Royals in 1985 with 36). Things like that happened for the Royals in 1985 to give us the sense that maybe it was their year.

THE I-70 SERIES (I KNOW, YOU'RE SICK OF THAT, BUT IT IS WHAT IT WAS)

Broadcasting the 1985 World Series between the Royals and the Cards was probably the ultimate for me because I grew up a Cardinal fan. Obviously, if the Royals had played the Dodgers, the other 1985 National League playoff team, that tie wouldn't have been there. So the series may have worked out perfectly because of the cross-state rivalries. We knew the fans would be fizzed up. The Royals playing the Cardinals was a perfect scenario.

The Cardinals were the best team in baseball that year. They were the only team in baseball to won over 100 games in 1985 (they won 102).

Then, in a strange on-field accident, a tarp rolled over Vince Coleman's leg and it changed the entire St. Louis lineup. He was at the top of the lineup and everybody filled in perfectly after him. When Vince was hurt and Whitey, who was managing St. Louis at the time, had to pull him out of the lineup, everybody else changed. That injury completely changed the make-up of the Cardinals because it changed their entire batting order. In turn, they didn't hit a lick in the Series.

Coleman, the 1985 National League Rookie of the Year, had been their catalyst all season, and without him St. Louis couldn't manufacture any runs; they couldn't get anything going offensively. It was a dead, dull offensive Series for them and the Royals pitchers threw very well against them. That turned the thing around. Terry Pendleton, who spent his final big league season in Kansas City in 1998, was on that 1985 St. Louis team. Last season he and I were talking about the Series and he said it was like the Cardinals were a completely different team because everybody was hitting in a different position.

St. Louis had been so good on the bases all season that Whitey had them running here and there; they could drive teams nuts. We didn't really see much of that in the World Series. The only power threat they had was Jack Clark and the Royals negated him; so if the Cardinals don't have their running game and Clark's bat is quiet then they aren't going to do much offensively. They didn't. Yet, if umpire Don Denkinger doesn't make that call at first base in game six, which eventually helped the Royals win that game, it is quite likely that the Cardinals would have won the World Series. What are the odds of a tarp going that slowly, running over Vince Coleman? What are the odds of a major league umpire blowing a call that obvious in that situation? They're astronomical! Coleman being injured and the Denkinger call in the sixth game probably were the two key items for the demise of the Cardinals.

When the Cardinals took the commanding lead in the series in St. Louis, their fans let us know about it. Signs were up congratulating the Cardinals. Fans were driving around the stadium, honking their horns, celebrating. The mentality of the Royals changed, just like it did in Toronto. "We don't want you to win it here, and we're not going to let you. If you want to honk your horns, you're going to have to drive all the way to Kansas City to do it."

The Cards got 20 hits and scored just two runs in the final three games of the series. But, in game six, they had a 1-0 lead going into the bottom of the ninth, and brought in their ace closer Todd Worrell. From that point on, they just unraveled. It wasn't so much a case of self-destruction as it was the Cardinals just coming unhinged.

It all started when Kansas City's Jorge Orta was called safe at first by Denkinger. Orta bounced a slow roller toward first. First baseman Clark made a play on it, and flipped to Worrell, covering the bag. When Worrell stretched for the bag and the ball, it appeared for a split second that he may have been pulled off. Orta definitely hadn't beaten the throw. Denkinger called him safe. We saw the replay and, on the air, let everyone know that Orta was out, that the Royals were fortunate, and that Denkinger blew the call. I let the listeners know that I couldn't understand how a major league umpire could miss a call like that; I could understand a close one, but Orta was out by a step. He was out.

To Royals fans, it didn't matter, he was *called* safe. On the next play, their first baseman, Clark, dropped a foul pop-up next to the Kansas City dugout. Then a pitch got by former Royal catcher Darrell Porter. The Cardinals had a perfect streak of 88 games during the regular season of winning games in which they led going into the ninth inning; the Royals broke that string with the 2-1 victory.

Personally, I thought the Royals would win the seventh game, but I didn't expect an anti-climactic blowout. The game was over by the third inning. We had an offense going, and Bret Saberhagen was shutting the Cards down. The Saberhagens had delivered their first son the night before, but it obviously didn't affect Bret's pitching. I didn't think it was as exciting as the way he pitched. He was a dominant pitcher. The way he was throwing, it was one of those situations in which we sat there and thought how much we wanted to get through the last six innings, quickly.

After a fairly boring game, the Royals finally won, 11-0, and captured their first-ever World Championship. The scene was one of controlled bedlam. Saberhagen, after posting two wins and an ERA of 0.50, was named the World Series Most Valuable Player. In the category of "somewhat dubious honors" for the 1985 Series, the Royals became the first team in baseball history to lose their first two games at home, and then come back to win the title.

The week after the World Series ended, I was on a talk show in St. Louis, and I knew what was coming. Sure enough, the second guy who called said, "Can you honestly sit there in Kansas City and see all the Royals games and tell me that you think the Royals are better than the Cardinals?"

I said, "Well, let me put it to you this way. The Cardinals were the best team in baseball this year, for six months. Over 162 games they won 102. Nobody else won 100, so the Cardinals were the best team in baseball in 1985. However, in seven games in October, the Royals out-hit the Cardinals, out-pitched the Cardinals, out-defended the Cardinals and out-played the Cardinals. So, the Royals, for those seven games were better than the Cardinals. Would you agree with both statements?"

After a long pause he said, "Well, since you put it that way, I can see your point."

So, it kind of put the whole in tight focus. It just goes to show that, in a short series, goofy things can happen. We like to see both teams have their full complement of players, we don't want to see anybody hurt - especially a key guy, so that the fans can get the real deal - but things didn't work out that way.

Fred White

As the Royals opened the 1980s, it was apparent that it could be a special decade for the organization. After all, they were still trying to get past the Yankees and advance to the World Series. Finally, after three unsuccessful attempts, the Royals basically man-handled the Yankees in 1980. The defining moment came in the third game in the best-of-five series, when George Brett faced Rich "Goose" Gossage in the seventh inning. Two runners, Willie Wilson and U.L. Washington were on base with the Royals trailing New York, 2-1.

Someone must have been watching out for the Royals, because both Wilson and Washington were lucky to reach. Wilson, a switch-hitter batting right handed, sliced a pitch down the right field line that somehow stayed inside the foul line. Then Washington beat out an infield single. There were two outs at the time, and he busted his butt to first base! George almost never came to the plate in that situation. People also forget that in the bottom of the previous inning the Yankees had scored twice to take the lead.

It seems like Brett facing Gossage in the seventh inning was meant to be. I was lucky enough to be on the air when it happened.

As George came to the plate, I told myself to "make sure it's fair." I was telling myself he's going to pull a Rich Gossage fast ball for a home run and he might pull it foul. Brett had had such an incredible season as he chased the .400 batting average that it wasn't in my mind to debate whether he was going to do it or not; there was no doubt about it. I was just making sure I realized that he could pull it too far.

Sure enough, on the first pitch, George mashed it! As I looked at the high fly ball, it was headed fair; I thought, "that's it."

It happened so fast. There's the pitch, there's the swing and, when he made contact with the ball, it was as though he knocked every breath of air out of Yankee Stadium. That place went dead silent, which was rare. George said later that the stadium was so quiet that he could hear his feet on the ground going around the bases.

I didn't hear the call until the following February. I thought I was very calm because I honestly thought (and I'm somewhat embarrassed to say this) that he was going to do it...I expected it. So I had told myself to be calm. Then when I heard the call, I was anything but calm!

The game was far from over, however. In the eighth inning, the Yankees loaded the bases off Dan Quisenberry with one out and Yankee catcher Rick Cerone coming to the plate. Cerone hit a screaming line drive to Washington, who doubled off Reggie Jackson at second. Inning over and momentum back to the Royals.

They beat the Yankees and after all they'd gone through playing the Yankees in earlier championship series, that was the team we wanted the Royals in there against, and we wanted them to beat those Yankees.

OH YEAH...THE WORLD SERIES

As the Royals went into the World Series in 1980, it was their first one, and it inspired in them something of a sense of awe. They didn't know how to act, and it wasn't until later that they realized they were ill-prepared in more ways than one. The thing I remember about going to the World Series was the players saying, when it was over, that the scouting report on the Phillies made them all sound like Superman but they weren't. Unfortunately the team didn't realize it until they were down two games to none.

The Royals had a better team than the Phillies that year but all the pressure for Kansas City was in the playoffs with the Yankees. The World Series was more a celebration for beating the Yankees. Had the Royals been to a World Series before, they probably would have won it easily in 1980. But, they hadn't been there, the Phillies had, and Philadelphia won the Series, 4 games to 2.

Denny Matthews

Growing up, I was the oldest of the four Matthews boys in the Illinois twin cities of Normal and Bloomington, to George (Matty) and Eileen. When I was a few months old during World War II, Dad served Uncle Sam in the Navy. Mom is a wonderful lady and did a great job raising us, especially while Dad was away. (Bottom) I had thought about styling my hair like that for opening day of the 1999 season. For some reason I couldn't get that flip just right.

Dad was an outstanding second baseman for four seasons at Illinois State University. During his senior season he was co-captain and was named to the United States College All-American squad. He has the distinction of being ISU's first All-American baseball player.

Mike Matthews (on the right), my youngest brother, helps me with a Royals spring training broadcast in Florida in March of 1998.

Whitey Herzog (left) and Charley Brannan in 1978. Charley, a friend of mine from Bloomington, went to St. Louis with me in 1968 to record my audition tapes to send to the expansion Royals.

With George Brett in 1977 and 1992. I don't think we changed much in 15 years, OK, with the exception of the hair.

With the help of Illinois Wesleyan's dean of students, who was a good friend of Green Bay's defensive backfield coach, in 1964 I was allowed to work out with the Packers at Lambeau Field. Back then it was possible to just walk onto the field without being stopped (security is a little tighter there now). The day gave me an opportunity to pose with some Packer legends, such as receiver Max McGee.

Doug Rader had a solid career in the major leagues. Early in our college years at Illinois Wesleyan he was my middle infield partner. He played shortstop, I played second base. He signed with Houston after our sophomore year.

John "Duke" Wathan is the only Royal to play, coach, manage, broadcast and scout. We've had a lot of great times together including 1989 while we were taping the manager's show.

In 1981, the Royals happened to be the Yankees' opponent after their annual oldtimer's game. Hall of Famer Mickey Mantle still looked like a natural in New York pinstripes.

Dick Howser (middle) was one of the Royals' greatest managers. He led the team to its first World Championship in 1985 before being stricken with a brain tumor which took his life during the 1987 season. Fred (left) and I enjoyed spending time with Dick as we are here in 1984 in Snoqualmie Falls, Washington.

(1952) Baseball has always been a passion for me, especially when I was bigger and better than my brothers. (left to right) One of my brothers Doug, Robbie Huminik, another brother Steve, John Butler, young Dennis (me), Tom Barger and Joe Barger.

In my younger days, manager Whitey Herzog let me play in a few exhibition games. Here I am batting in one of those games at Omaha in 1977. Former Royal Tom Poquette watches from on-deck. John Mayberry (No. 7) refuses to watch from the dugout.

The original voice of the Kansas City Royals was legendary announcer Buddy Blattner. Bud was a great influence, mentor and friend to me.

Is that Boston Bruin Hall of Famer Bobby Orr? No, that's me during a hockey workout at Foxhill Ice Arena in Overland Park.

Even though I didn't play football in high school, Illinois Wesleyan coach Don "Swede" Larson gave me a chance to play in college. Here I am (number 10) dealing out some abuse to a Wheaton College defender – or is it vice versa?

Fred White

Away from the field, some of the best times I had with the Royals were spent on the golf course. This is from one of those off-season trips to my favorite course in Pinehurst, North Carolina. (Standing, from left to right) Steve Balboni, Jerry Don Gleaton, Jamie Quirk, Dan Quisenberry, Kelly Miller, Charlie Liebrandt, Bobby Watson, me and Dave Broderick. (Kneeling, from left to right) Pat McGowan, Buddy Black, George Brett and Bret Saberhagen.

Can you guess who the fishermen in the family are? On our annual spring training fishing trips off Sanibel Island. Barb with Captain Pat Lovetro watching; Joe with a friend of ours, Don Stollery; and me with, well...bait.

One of my best friends through the years has been George Brett. Whether it was taping a pregame show, or hanging out in the Stadium Club, there is always a good time to be had with George. Behind the microphone I was lucky with George because I was on the air for several of his big moments, including his 3,000th hit. George went on an incredible ride and took a lot of us with him.

While Dick Howser was managing the Royals, Barb and I became good friends with the Howsers and a couple of their friends, Trevor and Claire Grubbs (left). Even after the passing of Dick to cancer, Barb and I enjoy doing things with the Grubbs, such as skiing in Beaver Creek, Colorado.

I had one of the best childhoods imaginable, mainly due to my parents, Eddie and Mary.

My son Joe was able to take a break from shagging balls at an early batting practice at Kauffman Stadium to pose for a shot with his dad.

I have two wonderful kids from my first marriage, John (top photo, far right) and Stacy (bottom photo). John and I are seen here with Kansas State University President Jon Wefald, who sent a letter to Royals general manager Herk Robinson after I was fired, telling him that they made a mistake letting me go.

Please don't adjust your book, that is a black mark on my nose. A couple days before this picture was taken, I was blowing out a marshmallow at a cookout, and burned the end of my nose.

This is a motley crew if I've ever seen one! Former Royal great Hal McRae with college basketball commentator Dick Vitale, and former Detroit Tiger head coach Sparky Anderson. Vitale and I have worked college basketball games together, while he and Sparky have been friends since Dick was coaching in Detroit.

One of broadcasting's true legends, Ernie Harwell. Even though Ernie went to Detroit after growing up in the South, Tiger fans have always loved him and his Southern accent.

At our annual Royals for Rainbows golf tournament in Wichita, Kansas, that I hosted for 17 years. (From left to right) Me, ESPN college basketball analyst and good friend Larry Conley, Hank Bauer, Dick Howser, tournament co-director and friend Lee Elrick, George Brett and Yankee great Yogi Berra.

One of my favorite guys in the world, my brother Jack, at one of my favorite places in the world, Stroud's Restaurant in Kansas City.

Before I started with the Royals in 1973, I was sports director at WIBW-TV in Topeka, Kansas.

It's always fun to see people's reactions in the background while Gary Thompson (left) and I broadcast a K-State game in Ahearn Fieldhouse for the *Big 8 Game of the Week*.

One of my favorite ladies is my sister Marilyn. Our family had a lot of fun growing up.

No, Barb and I usually don't drink like this around the house.

Legendary basketball coach John Wooden at a Kansas-Kansas State game in the 1970s at Ahearn Fieldhouse in Manhattan during a *Big 8 Game of the Week*.

Christmas is a special time in the White household.

The vantage point from our booth in Kauffman Stadium.

1983: THE ROYALS FIRST BLACK EYE

After the 1983 season, four Kansas City Royals players involved in a drug scandal pleaded guilty to drug possession charges: Willie Aikens, Vida Blue, Jerry Martin and Willie Wilson. The organization reacted to it very quickly, and, after each served short prison sentences, the only one to come back to the Royals in 1984 was Wilson. The other three were gone in a hurry.

That was probably the club's first black eye since their inception, but again, the organization reacted so quickly and so strongly that the hype was over in a hurry, too. The problem was an embarrassment, that's all it was. I don't think any of those guys were drug addicts. Of course, they were all people who could be rehabilitated very quickly and get back to meaningful lives, and the organization, especially Mr. Kauffman, was determined to help them do that.

Since the prison sentences were handed down during the off-season, a couple months before spring training, we didn't really have to talk about it, or face it, on the air. The only thing we dealt with was when Wilson was coming back in May of 1984. Our job description says play-by-play, so the job is not like being on a talk show or making a speech where somebody asks our opinion of something and we feel compelled to give it. Our job is to describe the plays and the baseball game. At the moment the game is going on and the pitch is being thrown, those outside things really don't have much to do with that moment. We were not editorialists during the game; we got there once in a while, drifted into things like that, but basically our job was to describe the baseball game as it was being played. I remember going to Chicago to play the White Sox, and they had a sign up that said "K.C., Please don't snort the foul line." Well, the guys that were on the field at that time for the Royals had nothing to do with any of that stuff. Again, when we come on the air to do a ballgame, we're on the air to do a ballgame and the game is all that matters. People make big mistakes when they start getting into all the other stuff and want to pontificate and talk about things that really have nothing to do with that particular game. My philosophy on it is this...if you ask me right now, and this has been true since the day I started working with the Royals, how old each Royals player is and how much money he makes, I bet I couldn't get 25% of them, certainly not right on and probably not close. I don't care how old a guy is or how much money he makes. Those are personal things that don't affect the broadcast, and I'm not about to get personal on a baseball broadcast. A guy had a fight with his wife today? I don't care. In my opinion, the drug issue was a personal thing. Baseball related things like realignment, the strike zone, those sorts of things, have a place in a baseball broadcast. Personal matters don't.

For one thing, the only place 25 baseball players differ from 25 people in any other field, whether it be bankers, accountants, or attorneys, for example, is that they make a lot more money at a younger age. Other than that, if there are 25 CPAs at a convention somewhere, they are probably going to do all the things that 25 baseball players would do. The only difference is that the CPAs may be a little older and have a little more judgment. But, when this much money is thrown at these guys, this young, they ought to go out and have some fun, and they probably do. It's the old adage of what you see or hear here, leave here. Not that the players do that much wrong, but people always want to know "what's he really like?" Well, he's a lot like you...he's a human being with a family. He cares about them. He's doing the best he can do.

JAMIE QUIRK DOES BLEED ROYAL BLUE

After a difficult off-season heading into the 1984 campaign, a couple of young pitching prospects were brought up from the minors. Bret Saberhagen and Mark Gubicza each showed a lot of promise. The position players were there; the core players were still there. It was obvious that the Royals needed more pitching. They had gone through recycled veterans the year before, and it just wasn't working. The front office made the decision in spring training to go with the young arms - Saberhagen and Gubicza - and develop them. It paid off pretty quickly.

The Royals went through the majority of the 1984 season hanging around the top of the A.L. West. By late in the season the race was coming down to the Royals and the Minnesota Twins for the division crown. Our good friend Jamie Quirk, who hadn't been with the Royals in a little over a season at this point, was being sent to the Cleveland Indians. On his way to Cleveland he stopped by Paul Splittorff's retirement party. As a parting shot he announced to the crowd there, "Don't worry about it, I'll help win one for you."

The Royals won at home the next day, and later we were on the airplane and somebody had the radio on the Cleveland game because they were hosting the Twins. In his only at-bat in a Cleveland uniform, Jamie hit his longest home run ever to beat Minnesota. He hit it in the upper deck. I can still hear legendary Twins announcer Herb Carneal, "Oh no...uh oh...oh no!" Before Jamie hit it, I turned to George and said, "You don't suppose he's going to do that do you?"

George replied, "Why else would he be there? Of course he's going to do it." And he did. That was Jamie's one at-bat with the Cleveland Indians. That was his career as an Indian. Quirk's homer helped guarantee that the Royals would meet the Detroit Tigers in the 1984 American League playoffs.

Unfortunately it was not a long series for Kansas City fans, as the Tigers swept the Royals in three games. I have to admit it was expected. That was an ordained year for Detroit. They just had too much for the Royals.

1985: THIS YEAR WAS DEFINITELY NOT FOR THE BIRDS

The 1985 season was truly a magical one for the Royals and Kansas City. I especially enjoyed the World Series because it gave me a chance to be in St. Louis and broadcast games for the Royals against my lifelong favorite Cardinals. My biggest memory of going into Busch Stadium for game three of the World Series is that it was just fun.

I had a lot of family down from central Illinois and it was almost like going back to the Cub/Cardinal rivalries of my youth. It was fun to banter with the Cardinal fans in my family over which team was going to do what.

The Cardinal folks brought Gussie Busch out on the wagon to the tune of "Here comes the king, here comes the big number one," with the Clydesdales pulling him and the dogs. I remember thinking, "This is a lot of fun, this is just a whole lot of fun and its the way it ought to be." I will always remember getting together with family and friends from home, and watching these competitive games with the Royals winning. Before any of that happened, however, they had to get through the end of the 1985 regular season.

One of the most exciting, and most overlooked, things of that year was a series with the California Angels in Kansas City in early October. The Angels came to town for the last time that season with a one-game lead on the Royals, which made it a do-or-die series. I think people forget the Royals had gone through Seattle and Minnesota previous to playing the Angels, and had been swept in both places.

When we were in Minnesota, the weather was miserable; dark and rainy everyday. By that time I had developed a very close friendship with Dick Howser and I probably had a little more emotion invested in losing those games. But everyday the Royals would lose to the Twins and come back to the hotel and somebody would announce that the Angels had lost again, too. Good, we're still only one back.

The Angels came to town, and in the first inning of the first game, with two runners on, George Brett hit a ball down the right field line off Ron Romanick. The rightfielder dove for it, and missed it, and George rounded the bases for an inside-the-park home run. In a heartbeat, the Royals were up by three runs. The Royals went on to beat the Angels in that series, got the lead in the division, and won the West.

This was another of those series where we thought the Royals were going to break out. They did that all season; look horrible for a few games, then look magnificent for the next few. They could diddle along and lose five or six games in a hurry, then all of a sudden, a certain team gets in front of them, their eyes light up, and they start playing like crazy. That Angels series was like that. California had a pretty good team, but they weren't as good as the Royals and the Royals knew it. (The Angels probably knew it, too.) Incidentally, two days after Brett hit that inside-the-park home run against the Angels, on October 4, he hit another one against the Oakland A's.

The 1985 Toronto Blue Jays may have been like the Royals were in 1980 against the Phillies. It was their first time in the playoffs and the Royals were an established team. The Blue Jays probably had some doubts in their collective mind about where they were that year, but they got off to a good start in the playoffs. Once the Royals started putting the pressure on them, that whole mentality changed.

On October 11, down two games to the Blue Jays, George pulled the team through by going four-for-four, including two home runs, a double, and a single. The single came in the eighth inning and put the Royals ahead. I'll tell you how I remember that...my mother died and I didn't see that game. I had gone to Illinois for the funeral and our plane was delayed in St. Louis. Before Barb and I left St. Louis, the Royals were ahead early.

When we landed in Kansas City, and turned the radio on in the car, George was coming to the plate and Denny was asking, "How much more can George do — what can you expect?" Bang, he gets another hit and scored what turned out to be the winning run. That was the first playoff game that Dick Howser had ever won. He only managed the Yankees one year, 1980, which is when the Royals swept them. As Royals manager in 1984, he watched the team be swept by the Tigers. In the mini-playoffs in 1981, the Royals lost their only two games to Oakland. I turned to Barb and said, "Well, he finally won a playoff game and got that monkey off his back."

Sadly, I missed two great moments in 1985. When my mother was dying toward the end of the season, the Royals were getting set for the series with the Angels. I had mentioned to Denny that I could catch a late flight to St. Louis if I skipped out after the seventh inning. He didn't mind, so I did that, then drove to Champaign to see my mom. That was the night Bret Saberhagen struck out Reggie Jackson to end the ballgame. I listened to the game on the way to the airport and remember hearing the strikeout. It was wonderful.

Then I missed that entire playoff game with the Blue Jays when George went four-for-four. The thing that I could contrast was having left the team when they were down two games to none, and then the feeling of the ballpark when I walked in after they won that first one. The new attitude bore no trace of pressure.

Toronto came back the next night and beat the Royals 3-1 to take a three games to one lead in the series. When the Blue Jays were one game away from clinching (and they had three chances to do it), my thought was that the Royals were going to play hard, make it hard for Toronto to win it, and they were going to make them earn it. It was probably unrealistic to think they were going to come back and win the series.

But the Royals came back and won game five, 2-0 to send the series back to Canada. Things began to change once the Royals got that second win under their belts. There's a thing that happens in sports sometimes, when you can feel that even though you're ahead of the other guy, you feel like you are chasing him, like he's winning. That may have been what was happening to the Blue Jays.

In the World Series, when Dane Iorg drove in the run to win it for us in the sixth game, I was looking in the Cardinal dugout, and there wasn't much doubt that the Royals were going to win the seventh game. The Cardinals were sitting there with their heads down. It's a thing where they didn't want to say to themselves, "Hey, the Royals are going to win tomorrow night." But many people had that feeling. St. Louis had that feeling and the Blue Jays felt that way.

From the Toronto point of view, when the series opened up there, the headline in one of the Canadian papers read, "WE DID IT!" After the sixth game, with the series tied at three games, the headline in that same paper was "OH, OH!" The morning after the seventh game, when the Royals had won the game and the series, the headline was, "THEY BLEW IT!" Those headlines were great.

The Royals weren't finished with their seemingly patented come-from-behind series wins, as they quickly went down 2-0 in the World Series with the Cardinals playing in Kansas City. Time to go to St. Louis for three games. Here's an oddity about that, though. Had that series been arranged differently, and the first two games had instead been played in St. Louis and the Royals lost them, I'm not sure the Royals would have won a game. The Cardinals won the first two in Kansas City and as our plane was descending into St. Louis for the third game, there was a huge sign on the tower at Lambert Airport that read, "Welcome to St. Louis, Home of the 1985 World Champion Cardinals."

Our guys were kind of looking at that sign and saying, "Oh, Yeah? Bullshit!" The Royals won the third game 6-1, but lost the next night, 3-0, to put the Cards ahead in the series three games to one. Their fans were circling the hotel honking horns and celebrating like the World Series was over, and our guys kept looking at that thing saying, "Bullshit. To prove it to you, we'll win another game and then another."

Athletes are competitive enough that those motivational things do play into it. After the three games against the Blue Jays in Kansas City, the Blue Jays had to roll the champagne out of the stadium...Toronto had their champagne in the clubhouse to celebrate! When they didn't win, they rolled it out of the stadium's front door! The fans stood out there and gave it an ovation when it passed by. That's the one thing about athletes, they don't want to see opponents celebrate, especially on their home field. The Cardinal fans really helped the Royals win that 1985 World Series.

Bob Gibson and Mike Shannon were hosting a Cardinal talk show in the booth next to us, and we could hear them talking about sweeping the Royals and how the Cardinals were going to get the series over with. "This will be the day of the celebration," one caller exclaimed. (Yeah it was, but not for them!) They all came with that attitude which really got our guys' attention. The sign at Lambert Field started the Royals momentum and then their fans really boosted it along. The Royals were a pretty good team and they weren't about to just roll over and die.

When St. Louis went up 3-1 in the series, somebody asked George, "What do you think?" He said, "I think we've got them right where we want them. This is when we get good." Toronto revisited. And the truth was, the Royals were playing the heck out of the Cardinals.

Despite positive attitudes, the Royals needed to make a change to spark things. Dick changed the lineup. It looked strange, but it worked. Lonnie Smith was leading off instead of the normal leadoff hitter, Willie Wilson, who went to the number two spot. When that move was made, things began to change. Frank White hit cleanup. That was not a classic top of the order for the Royals.

Looking at the Royals batting order over the second half of that season, it was not a classic batting order by any stretch of the imagination. Going back to Frank's rookie year, we would never have envisioned him as a clean up hitter in a World Series. But he did it, and he did it very well. The Royals were sick and tired of hearing about the Cardinals and they felt, "Hey, we're a good baseball team, let's cut the BS here. They are a nice team, but so are we." By that time, there was constant talk by National League fans saying how their league was better than the American League. The Royals were convinced that wasn't true. The Royals finally thought, "We're going to do something about it. These guys aren't doing much — let's beat them."

It wasn't like the Cardinals were jumping out there beating the Royals 7-0 on the nights they won. They won with bloop hits, 3-1, 4-2. Oddly enough, the guy who won a couple of ballgames for them was Tito Landrum, the guy who replaced Vince Coleman, who was run over (somehow) by the tarp. Landrum had a couple bloop hits. Brian Harper had a big bloop to centerfield. The irony of the whole thing was that when the Royals got the hit that turned the series around in the sixth game, it was a bloop hit.

The Royals were down 1-0 in the bottom of the ninth inning of game six, when pinch-hitter Jorge Orta bounced an infield single to first. Okay, it was a close play at first base that umpire Don Denkinger ruled safe. On the air I said that to the naked eye he may have been right. But, when I saw the replay, I thought, "Uh-oh...he missed the call."

When pitcher Todd Worrell was reaching for the bag after receiving the toss from Jack Clark, it almost looked like he was trying to get his foot back on the bag when he probably was really doing it for emphasis, to show that he was on the bag before Orta. The question wasn't whether or not Orta beat the throw, it was a matter of whether or not Worrell came off the bag. Then the Cardinals really unraveled.

The game was pretty much over after that. Clark dropped the pop-up in foul territory, a passed ball got by catcher Darrell Porter and the Cardinals just fell apart. The Royals bunted into the force at third, but the Cardinals couldn't make anything happen after that. All during the Series, the Royals couldn't get a big hit and the Cardinals were winning their games with a little bloop double here or a squib single there. Ironically, the hit that turned it around for the Royals was a bloop single; Iorg's single to right to score the tying and winning run in the form of Onix Concepcion and Jim Sundberg. Sundberg scoring might have been the most electric moment I've ever seen in a baseball stadium anywhere. Looking down at Kauffman Stadium after Iorg hit the single, I thought, "My God, look at this. People aren't going anywhere!" When I finally left the stadium that night, walking across the parking lot, I was amazed because it was still full of people celebrating.

I got up the next morning and went running through my neighborhood. Throughout the neighborhood there are little statues. Well, someone had gotten up early that Sunday morning and had put blue ribbon and Royals caps on all the statues in the area. It was a beautiful October day, with temperatures around 70-degrees, so there were quite a few people outside working in their yards. I didn't even know people in my neighborhood knew who I was, but as I went running down the street, they would yell at me, "Tell the players good luck tonight. Tell them thanks." When that Sunday game arrived, the people in Kansas City thought it was the ultimate; the Royals had done all they needed to do...they took the Series to a seventh game. That was just an amazing, amazing weekend in Kansas City.

Most people can remember every detail about the sixth game, but the finale is a blur. Well, maybe to everyone except pitcher Bret Saberhagen. The Royals sent their young ace to the mound for the final game, against John Tudor. Saberhagen had won game three in St. Louis and had an earned run average under 1.00.

Saberhagen was having a blast; he thought all of this was supposed to be happening. By the way, the night before the seventh game, the Saberhagens had their first baby. Bret appeared to be an unruffled new daddy when he went to the mound, not to mention the fact that he had great veteran leadership behind him. When he looked to third, there was George. Glance back at second and there's Frank. Behind the plate he had Sundberg. Those guys were ready to keep Bret on track if they needed to, but they didn't need to.

After getting Saberhagen through the first two innings unharmed, the Royals were ready to unload on Tudor. In the bottom of the second with a runner on, Kansas City's Darryl Motley blasted a drive to left...foul ball. Broken bat. On the next pitch, with a new bat, Motley drilled another Tudor offering to left, only this one was fair. Just like that, the Royals took a 2-0 lead. Seven innings and nine runs later, the Royals won 11-0.

One reason teams win championships is presence of mind. Motley, playing in right, caught the final out of the game. If you look at the picture or the video tape of that final play, pay attention to the infield as Bret Saberhagen and George Brett were waiting for Darryl to catch it. George is saying to Bret, "Not yet, not yet," but while he's saying that, he's maneuvering him around so when the picture was taken, it said, "Brett Saberhagen" from the backs of their uniforms. How do you think of things like that? Talk about knowing who you are and where you are and what's going on!

When the Royals won it, my brother, who is a Cubs' fan, was whirling my wife Barb around in the air. The celebration in the stadium was just amazing! I didn't think it was ever going to stop.

If 1985 wasn't supposed to be the Royals year, what are the odds of Royals shortstop Buddy Biancalana outplaying Ozzie Smith? He did it in the Series. That went back to Toronto when Buddy got a big double in a game against the Blue Jays and also drew a walk. He was surprisingly sensational.

I was on a Royals caravan the next year, down in Central Missouri. A guy stood up and said, "I've got $100 that says the Cardinals were better than the Royals."

I reminded him, "I've got a (World Series) ring that says they weren't. You might want to put your $100 back in your pocket." The Cardinals were a sensational team that year, but the fact was, the Royals really did outplay them over seven games. It was too bad that the one call was the focal point of the whole thing.

MR. WHITE, YOU HAVE A CALL FROM THE WHITE HOUSE

After the season, a large group of us were in Wichita for our annual Royals for Rainbows Golf Tournament. I got a call while we were down there. "The White House just called and wanted to know when they can have the Royals." Well, put Ronald on the phone and let's talk about this. What's your schedule like, Ron? Here's mine. Obviously it wasn't really my decision; what they really wanted to know was when the tournament was going to be over so the team could go to the White House. We all left the golf tournament the next day and went to Washington.

Our day at the White House was beautiful. To me, it was really a great experience just to sit in the Rose Garden on that nice a day. The Rose Garden, by the way, is very small; I couldn't get over how small it was. For some reason, when I see it on TV, I think it's a large area. It wasn't. As we were sitting there, my wife Barb, who is from Russell, Kansas, was sitting next to me, and Bob Dole, who is also from Russell, was sitting in front of us. He turned around and started talking to Barb. It was just a wonderful time.

It was amazing to take in the whole scene. There were photographers all around. There were some Secret Service guys on the roof. If it hadn't been such a beautiful October day, it might not have had such an impact on me. But I remember sitting there thinking, "This is really kind of amazing, really kind of nice. Just a nice finish to the season."

Maybe the funniest moment, to me, was when the Secret Service lost Dick Howser. His mother had recently had a heart attack, and he was in George Bush's office calling to check on her. I was thinking, "Gee, the Secret Service just lost Dick Howser in the White House. How good are they?" It was funny because then vice-president Bush was in there with his first baseman's glove out showing it to Dick.

We left the White House and they took us to the Capitol to have lunch in the Senate Conference Room, where the Watergate Hearings were held. As we were walking up the steps to the Capitol, the Marine Band was playing "Kansas City."

My favorite moment was when we walked through the Rotunda. People were hanging over the rails applauding.

Everything happened so fast after the World Series. Now, it might be six months after a team wins a title, or even more, before they get to go to the White House, but in 1985 it happened quickly.

That was a long day, but it's one I will never forget. The fact is, we got on the plane, flew to Washington, had lunch, and came home. Barb and I had left Joe, our son, in Wichita. So when we got off the plane in Kansas City, we drove back to Wichita and spent some time with her family, picked Joe up and went home. On the drive home I couldn't help but think, "You know, for a kid from Homer, Illinois, this has been a heck of a week."

10 From Pinstripes to Royalty

Fred White

One of the things I really enjoyed about working as a broadcaster with the Royals was getting to know the managers. In general, just sitting around and visiting with them about why they like to do certain things, and what players they believe can do certain things, was informative and fun. I wouldn't attach any name to this, because they all have pretty much done the same thing, but they tell us what they think a player is capable of doing and why they will do certain things in certain situations with particular players; how much faith they have in a guy to get a certain job done. Those are the kinds of manager inside stories that you look for as a broadcaster.

I pretty much enjoyed working with all of the managers with whom I came in contact. They all brought something different to the dance. I have had different degrees of relationships with them, however. I would consider Whitey Herzog and Dick Howser good friends, for instance.

A CLOSE FRIEND

Dick and I were very close, and spent a lot of time together. During the strike in 1981 we did some minor league games together for ESPN. He had previously been with the New York Yankees, but had been fired, so he wasn't working when we got to know each other in 1981. When he came to manage the Royals, we spent more and more time together and became very good friends.

Jim Frey had been managing the Royals since 1980 but after the strike in 1981 he was fired. I can see how an outsider might have been surprised when Jim was fired, considering that the team had been in the World Series the previous year. But, as insiders, we saw things begin to unravel in September of that 1980 season.

In 1980 the Royals got off to such an incredible lead early, so much so, that no teams were going to catch them. But they didn't play very well coming down the stretch, and didn't get off to a good start in the World Series against the Phillies. The next season wasn't going very well before the strike. Then the strike hit and the Royals pretty much had their minds made up that after the strike, they were going to have to make a change to salvage the season.

Whenever a manager is fired, the first thing everyone looks at, obviously, is his performance. When an executive is considering a managerial change, he looks around and says, "Okay, who's out there to hire?"

In Jim's case, Dick Howser was out there. He had been in our ballpark scouting, and I don't know if this had anything to do with it or not, but when we were doing minor league games for ESPN, he was pretty visible to baseball people three or four nights a week. I'm sure a lot of clubs were sitting there saying, "If we make a change, we are calling this guy." As is usually the case when a club goes after a new manager, the timing was perfect to get Howser. If there is a strong candidate available, a team is more inclined to make the change. If they look around and see that nobody good is available, then they are probably going to stick with their guy. I really think that plays into it heavily. The Royals happened to be the team to go after Dick.

After the strike was settled Dick was named the new manager of the Royals. The team finished better in the second half, 20-13, than they did in the first, 30-40, but the way the season was completed made the postseason more complicated. Major League Baseball decided to take each division leader from the first half of the season, and have them play the division leader from the post-strike half of the season, in a mini-playoff to determine who would go to the League Championship Series. It just didn't make any sense at all.

The Cincinnati Reds had the best record in baseball and were not in the playoffs that year. There was more of a sense of let's get it over with and start a new season next year. It was a very convoluted year; we didn't even try to make sense out of it. Despite the fact that the Royals finished better in the second half, and played the Oakland A's in that mini-playoff, I don't think it was very indicative of what kind of manager we had in Dick Howser.

In Howser's first full season with the Royals, 1982, the team won 90 games. It was clear from that beginning that he was going to be a good manager and that the Royals were still a good team, despite their disappointing finish in 1981. That was the principle thing about the 1982 Royals - that they were still a good team.

Dick and I did a lot of things together when he was managing, but we kind of drew the line. Away from the stadium, he would leave the game behind. People would be stunned to know how little we talked about baseball. There was a certain amount of that, but then we put it away and played golf. We talked about country music, and almost everything else under the sun except the game. Dick was a guy who wanted to get away from baseball and go do things.

Dick and Nancy, Barb and I, and two more great friends, Trevor and Claire Grubbs from St. Petersburg, spent a lot of quality time together during and after the season. One of our great trips was on the Grubbs' boat. The six of us took their boat from St. Pete to Captiva Island for a week and just had a wonderful time. There have also been ski trips and fishing trips, and enough good memories to fill a book. Trevor was Dick's great friend, and had been since their college days at Florida State.

Thankfully, to this day, the Grubbs remain great friends of ours. If one could have seen Trevor and Dick throughout Dick's illness, one would understand the true definition of a friend. I've never met a better one, and Barb and I treasure the Grubbs' friendship to this day. Dick is gone, but he left us a great gift in Trevor and Claire.

In 1985, under Dick, the Royals were on top of the baseball world after they defeated the St. Louis Cardinals for their first-ever World Championship. Dick continued to manage the team into the 1986 season, and because the Royals were in the previous World Series, he managed the American League team in Houston in the All-Star game. Three days later, on July 18, Dick Howser was diagnosed with a malignant brain tumor. As was the case with everyone in the organization, I couldn't believe it. From that point on games, championships, and salaries were all inconsequential.

It was fairly apparent right away that he might not be able to manage again. But the Royals did not replace him immediately. There were other managers available, good managers, but the Royals did the right thing and didn't fill his spot with a permanent replacement. Dick came back for a few games in 1987, but it was just too much. On June 17, 1987, Dick Howser passed away at the age of 51. He was the first Royal to have his number retired, when the team had the ceremony and retired his number 10. I shall always remember Dick Howser and miss him.

FROM FIELD FOE TO FINE FRIEND

The other manager I developed a good friendship with was Whitey Herzog, when he was with the Royals from 1975-1979. He was a gregarious, outgoing, personable fellow who wanted all the guys around. He would invite 20 people to his hotel suite for a drink after the game to sit around and talk baseball. Everyone would go out and play golf together, go to dinner together, just do things together.

Whitey is a really bright guy with a terrific sense of humor, and he loves to tell stories. He is a guy who can't quit managing and coaching, regardless of where he is. One time, my wife and I, and Denny and his date, were at the Herzog's house, down in their basement playing bumper pool. Whitey was coaching the girls against us, and he was coaching them as hard as he managed any game in the World Series. He really wanted them to win and he was coaching as hard as he could coach. He was like that all the time.

I've played golf with him and gone hunting with him. He's also fun to go to dinner with. The energy level always goes up when Whitey is around. He is a very energetic guy and everything seems to go at a more energetic pace when he is around. He is a very wise man; a very intelligent guy.

When Whitey joined the Royals in 1975 he was not a complete stranger to me. In fact, he was the first opposing manager to come into Kauffman

Stadium (then Royals Stadium), when he came in 1973 with the Texas Rangers. My knowing him previously helped, but not to a great degree, because we never really know them until we watch them operate every day. When players from other teams join the Royals, invariably, after a period of time, I think, "Gee, I didn't realize that about this guy. I thought he was a better player than that." There's a pretty good truism about baseball that when you first see a guy you see the things he can do and then when you watch him everyday you realize what he can't do. The opposite is true, too: if you watch a guy every day you sometimes think, "Gee, I didn't know he could do that. I didn't know he was that good. I didn't realize he was that hard-nosed." Same with the managers.

About the most we can realize about an opposing manager is a little bit about what his personality is like and how he likes to play the game. Does he like to hit and run, does he like to do these things? Often that's not a true indicator of how he manages, because his style is often dictated by the guys he has at that time on his club. If he comes to our team and we have different kinds of players, we might see him playing a different game.

An example of that would be college basketball coach Tom Penders. I broadcast his games at Fordham when they led the nation in defense. I did his games at Rhode Island when they averaged about 90 points a game, and I did his games when he was at Texas and they were just loosey, goosey, run and shoot, trapping defenses. So I've seen Tom Penders coach three different kinds of teams, three different styles, and coach them very successfully, simply because of the kind of players he had.

The same thing is true in baseball. Give me a team that can run and I'll play a running game. Give me a team that can't run and I'm going to try and score in different ways. So what a manager likes to do and what he's able to do are sometimes two different things.

THE STORY TELLER

After the 1979 season, in which the Royals failed to advance to the playoffs for a fourth straight year, Whitey was fired. After that happened, bringing in Jim Frey was a good experiment. With him we got a lifetime baseball guy who hadn't worked as a manager; but he had been a coach in the Baltimore organization. At that time the Oriole club was producing a lot of managers under Earl Weaver. When he was with the Orioles, Jim Frey was well-liked and had spent a few years under Earl.

Jim had a great understanding of the fundamentals of the game and of how the game was to be played. If the Royals were going to fire Whitey, it was a logical thing to get Jim. It was a logical place to think, "Well, here's Jim Frey; he's like these other guys who came out of the Baltimore organization. He hasn't had the opportunity, so let's give him a try."

I played golf and spent some time with Jim Frey. He was a very humorous guy to be around, a great story-teller. He may be the best story teller of all the Royals managers ever.

Because of his baseball experience and his knowledge of the game, Jim Frey was a good choice. Apparently something happened in his ability to manage players and a problem developed, but I really never knew exactly what that was. Even though the experiment didn't work, it was a logical place to go and a logical place to look at the time they did.

DUKE, MAC AND MUSER

I really enjoyed all of the managers for different reasons. John Wathan, for instance, was a friend before he became a manager. John was a throwback. He loved to go to dinner with groups of people and sit around and talk about the game, but he was like most managers in that there was information that was only for the guys in uniform. That is how it should be.

Hal McRae, I thought, was a good manager and became a better manager all the time. Mac got his opportunity at the wrong time. When he came in to Kansas City to manage in 1991 the Royals were going downhill; it was Mac's first managing job, and he needed some time to really figure out how to get done what he wanted to do. Once he started, the team began playing well under him, and I thought he was improving as a manager.

I would go back to Whitey in describing Mac's personality. Hal has a very vocal, outgoing personality. Mac is open and honest and will say what he thinks, and if you don't like it, you don't like it. Mac is never going to tell you something just because he thinks what you want to hear. Obviously his style was volatile and not always politically correct. I've always regarded Mac as a friend, and have always enjoyed being around him. He had been improving as the team's manager, but obviously the Royals felt they had to make a change, and they made it.

Tony Muser is another wonderful story-teller, very intense, very open and honest, and says why he does things and what he believes in. Tony is like Mac in that he could not be given a million dollars to tell someone a lie, so one really gets the honesty and truth in him. Tony likes to talk about the game of baseball and why he does things. He is a baseball guy through and through.

AFFECTING THE BROADCASTS, AFFECTING OUR HEARTS

Generally there aren't a lot of external circumstances to make broadcasting difficult. Three that did, however, were based on personal relationships within the Royals. The first was Dick Howser's illness, especially his last days when he knew he was dying. It was pretty hard to put that out of my mind. Joe Burke's illness cast a pall over things. Then Mr. Kauffman's last few months before he passed away. These are people who meant so much to the Royals; they are like family members. We don't put those things out of our mind when we're broadcasting. All three instances were very difficult.

Sensing that a manager might be in trouble can make things a little more difficult for a broadcaster. Especially when we develop friendships with them; it's tough to watch particular managers operate every day and think that the guy is fighting for his job. Another example is watching players who are reaching the end of their careers, fighting like the dickens to give what they've got left and not just to hang on to a job, but to contribute to the team, knowing how much pride they had in the game, how much they wanted it, and how much it meant to them. Those things sometimes have been a little bit difficult to swallow in the radio booth.

My last two years with the Royals, in all honesty - trying to figure out whether we were going to be back or not to broadcast - were very difficult. It was tough to put that out of my mind. In 1997, through a set of circumstances, Denny and I went to November before our contracts were renewed. (Then we all know what happened after the 1998 season.) It was frustrating the last couple of years, coming down to the end of the season, uncertain of what was ahead. They would say, "We'll see." That's not the answer we wanted to hear. They never told us that we might not be back, but when they said nothing at all, then we couldn't help but become frustrated with the whole thing. Those two years were difficult at the end of the season in that regard, and somewhat distracting mentally from the late-season broadcasts.

THE PHILOSOPHIES OF A GOOD MANAGER

One of the first things you notice about a good manager is his ability to handle people and different kinds of people. Managers have to deal with several different types of people, all day, every day.

All managers have different philosophies of how to handle players, but none of them ever gave me a piece of real inside information. In general we talk about philosophies. Do they hit and run with this guy or not, and why? How do they want this guy handled? The line should be drawn for what a broadcaster needs to know, doesn't need to know, and what he doesn't want to know. As for front office maneuverings, I don't care about those and I really don't need to know about them.

For instance, with a couple of pitchers the Royals have had recently, Tony Muser has told the catcher to just sit in the middle of the plate. Don't work the corners with him, don't put that pitcher in a position where he thinks he has to make a million dollar pitch. Sit in the middle and trust his stuff to move enough to get a corner with you. Little things like that, just little insights as we go along.

"I hit and run with this guy because, or I don't hit and run with this guy because, or I believe this guy would be able to do this." Skills they think a guy does or doesn't possess. Those are the kinds of things we really look for and talk to managers about. And also their evaluation of guys on other teams. That's always helpful, too.

There's a certain way managers talk to players and there's a way they talk to people outside of baseball. There's a really tight inner circle, then there's a little more of an inner circle, and then there are several circles that they go through. All of the managers have a pretty good sense of what they can say to this group, and what they can't say to this other group. They don't talk to friends, people away from the game, like they talk to the guy in uniform, and they probably shouldn't. I've always believed that there are some things that go on in a clubhouse that should stay in the clubhouse.

That's always been my philosophy and we always got along well with it. If we went back through every one of the managers, what we would find out is that they are all good, decent guys who worked their butts off and tried as best they could to do the job they were given. It's just interesting to watch how all the different guys approached it.

THE KEY TO A SUCCESSFUL MANAGER

In order for things to work out smoothly for a manager, he needs to have a good working relationship with the general manager. I think most of the Royals' managers have worked well with the G.M.s. I started with the Royals during Cedric Tallis' last season. Joe Burke took over in 1974, followed by John Schuerholz and Herk Robinson.

Joe Burke came to Kansas City in 1973 as the business guy. Cedric was still the general manager at that time. The next year, Cedric left and Joe became the general manager for seven years before he took over as the club's President. Joe came in from the Texas Rangers; and before that, the Washington Senators.

Joe was wonderful man. He was everybody's father. He was a very reasonable man, had a ton of common sense, had a great sense of humor and had a great way of handling situations. Joe could be very blunt and very forthright when he felt he needed to be. A lot of times he would manage situations by simply teasing a little bit and letting people know that they had done the wrong thing but he wasn't mad at them. He was a very dignified man with a very common touch. Everyone who knew Joe Burke felt that they really knew him, and that they could trust him to the nth degree. If Joe said something, that was it; it could be booked.

I also think very highly of John Schuerholz, and truly regard John as a friend. He is a very honest and forthright guy. John is talented with a great eye for players, and he's willing to make a move. He can be aggressive...of course now he's playing with Ted Turner's money in Atlanta, which makes it a little bit easier, but he always was like that. I remember the trade he made for Lonnie Smith. As soon as he made the trade he was outside the press room in Kauffman Stadium saying, "I think we may have just won a divisional title here." (We won more than just the divisional title when Smith was picked up in 1985.) John is a very positive, dynamic guy, which has helped make him a terrific speaker and motivator. He is very much a leader and the kind of person one would put in charge of a project to know that it was going to be done; he would throw himself into it.

THE OPPOSING MANAGERS

Whitey Herzog

As an opposing manager, Whitey was a dynamic, forceful, brilliant baseball guy with a total 100% belief in himself and his philosophies. He also had a belief that he could get guys to believe in themselves enough to play better than they could, and it worked. He liked to play an aggressive all-out style of baseball and he did it by getting players to believe they could really do this if they would just try; as opposed to Billy Martin, who might do it by intimidating a player. Whitey got players sometimes to play beyond their abilities.

He had a very infectious personality that really affected everybody around him. He got everybody to have fun. If you ask me a word association with Whitey, I'd say we are all laughing, everything's going 90 miles an hour and we are winning. That was kind of what he brought to the game and the way he was as the Royals manager, or as an opposing one for that matter.

It was interesting watching Whitey's Cardinal teams in the World Series in the 1980s, because those teams played like his Royals teams had played in the 70s. They had tons of speed, went hard all the time, creating wins, making it happen. At that time, Busch Stadium in St. Louis also had artificial turf, so Whitey could build teams similar to those he had in Kansas City. Teams could never relax around a Whitey-managed team because he was going to be forcing the action and making something happen all the time. He was a great manager.

Bob Lemon

Bob Lemon was great. I wasn't around when he managed the Royals, but I've been around him when he managed other teams, and in social situations. A laid back and extremely knowledgeable baseball guy who did it with a totally different style than someone like Billy Martin. Bob Lemon's thought was: we all know how to play this game, so let's play it...just go out there and play the game right and we'll do fine. Bob was a guy who got everybody around him to believe in him, and he let those guys believe in themselves. He let them know that he believed in them.

I don't know anybody who was ever around Lem who didn't really like the guy — just really and truly love the guy. If Lem walked into a hotel in a major league city right now, everybody who had ever known him there would be down in the lobby and Lem would say, "Let's go up to the room, have a drink and talk." That was Lem.

There were a lot of late night sessions with Lem; he didn't particularly like to see evenings end. He, again, was a throwback to the old days when he wanted to gather 20 guys around after the game and tell stories. They were wonderful, marvelous stories coming from a guy who was great to be around. Obviously, looking at his record as a manager, he was a winner in that regard, too. He had a different way of managing people, but his way worked well.

Billy Martin

Billy Martin turned into a knuckles down, gouge them in the eyes, let's go at it hard, and there aren't any rules, kind of a guy. I was around him in both extremes. I saw his kindness and how nice he was when he didn't have a drink and didn't have a uniform; and I've seen him get mean after a few drinks, and I've seen him in a uniform do anything that he had to do to win a baseball game. Even being against him on the other side of the field, we still grudgingly admired him.

As with Whitey, the energy level went up when we were playing against a Billy Martin-managed team, because we'd better be watching everything that's going on since he was liable to try something tricky at any time. He would do anything he could to win a ballgame, but we knew from the moment the game started until it was over that Billy Martin was driving hard and his opponents had better be driving hard if they wanted to win against him.

John McNamara

Johnny Mac was fun to be around. He was a guy who was willing to sit down and talk. A true baseball guy, he had a great respect for the game and the people who play it. Everybody in the game who knew him seemed to admire and like John. He would come up to the press room after the game and sit down and talk for an hour about the game and the people in it. I always enjoyed being around him. He was just a really easy, good guy to be around.

One of his most-remembered teams was his 1986 Boston Red Sox which went to the World Series against the New York Mets. That was the series that made Boston first baseman Bill Buckner famous, or infamous, and helped Red Sox fans to remember the "Curse of the Bambino."

Earl Weaver

Earl Weaver was fun. He was at the top of the Baltimore pyramid, a very strong pyramid, for a long time. There was an Oriole way of doing things, which meant Earl Weaver's Oriole teams did not make mistakes. They executed the fundamentals of the game, they made the right plays on defense, they executed on offense. He was an interesting, dynamic individual. He fought with his players all the time. Earl was a guy who made everybody stand back and wonder, "What's he going to do now?" But, we have to admire the way his teams played.

The Baltimore Orioles played baseball the way baseball should be played. They played the kind of baseball I admired — solid in every phase of the game. Of course, Earl was fun to watch. He'd explode toward an umpire, throw his hat, kick dirt and get mad.

He was always kind to me. We did a lot of pregame shows together and he was always fun to sit down and talk to. He'd get on my case a little bit and let me get on his, and it was a good time.

The Best of the Rest

Ralph Houk, I thought, was a great manager. He was one who always got his teams to play about as well as they could play. I never thought Cito Gaston got the credit he deserved in Toronto. His Blue Jays won back-to-back World Series and everybody tried to find reasons why he shouldn't be managing the team, but he kept winning. Darrell Johnson was a guy I always really enjoyed being around. He was another manager who would sit down and talk for hours about the game of baseball and the people in it. He managed the Red Sox for a long time and then he scouted for a number of years. Hank Bauer was not a manager when I was in the game, but he was a scout and another guy I really enjoyed talking to about the game of baseball.

There are just an awful lot of guys out there. It was fun to look at them and compare their styles and say, okay, now he's different than this other guy but he's doing it this way and it's working for him. Their abilities to adapt and change have always been remarkable.

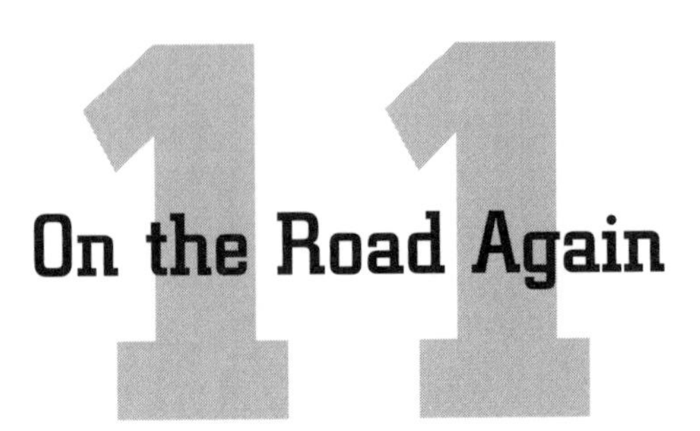

On the Road Again

Fred White

I'm not a very good tourist. Our former producer/engineer, Ed Shepherd, was the best tourist of all the guys who ever traveled with us. Don Free is probably second best. Donnie will get out and see things. In Boston, I've done the Freedom Trail a few times and I have gone whale-watching.

In school growing up, we heard and read about all of these great places, historic places, around the country, places like the Freedom Trail and the Statue of Liberty; but for someone from a small town in Illinois, these places always seemed so far away. At the same time, I always had a great curiosity to see them.

The first thing I did when I got to the old Yankee Stadium was put my briefcase down and march out to the monuments. On our first trip to New York I went to see the Empire State Building and all those things I had heard about. In Boston, I wanted to see the Old North Church and all those things I had read about as a kid. I wanted to ride a trolley car in San Francisco.

I'm not a great tourist, but I'm good enough that the things we're supposed to see in these cities, landmarks and such, I've made a point of visiting. In Baltimore, I've been to the place where Betsy Ross sewed the first American flag; and the place where Frances Scott Key wrote "The Star-Spangled Banner," at Fort McHenry.

There are things that every American should see, and I'm lucky enough to have been able to see some of them. I've done better since my son Joe became old enough to travel. My first two kids didn't live with me; I was divorced and so they didn't get to go on the trips with us. But Joe's been on a lot of trips.

I am married to a woman who is a great tourist, has a great curiosity and knows a lot about the world. She is the one who really got me out to see things and then when Joe came along, I wanted him to see them too. The historic landmarks, the Statue of Liberty and all those things - I've seen, and I think every American should go see them, as well.

MY FAVORITE MAJOR LEAGUE CITIES (BESIDES KANSAS CITY)

Boston, Toronto, Seattle and Baltimore were my favorite cities to visit while I was with the Royals. Part of the reason I like some of these cities is because it give me a chance to hang out with those team's broadcasters.

Broadcasting is very much a fraternity. Like any fraternity, broadcasters are closer to some members than to others. There are some I consider friends and some I don't do more than say, "Hi," to. For instance, when we were in Toronto, I might go out and have drinks with their announcer, Tom Cheek, after a game. I have a lot of respect for what some of them do, and their knowledge of their team. I liked to try to spend a little bit of time talking to them about their guys and what's going on with their team. They wanted to know the same about us. Other announcers were great sources of information. Most of them are pretty good guys and guys enjoyable to be around.

Baltimore used to be my least favorite city; the Inner Harbor hadn't been built, I didn't know anyone, and we stayed at the old Lord Baltimore Hotel, surrounded by rat-infested warehouses. The downtown area was run down and no one wanted to go there. Eventually, though, downtown Baltimore began to change. The Inner Harbor was built and so was Oriole Park at Camden Yards. Baltimore became a great place to visit.

On the other side of the coin, I didn't like going to Detroit or Oakland. Those are the only two that I really don't like. Things changed in 1998 with the Oakland trip because we stayed in San Francisco, which at least has some things to do. There was absolutely nothing to do in Oakland. We stayed at a hotel by the airport. We may as well have been with Andy and Barn in Mayberry - there is nothing there. There is not much in Detroit, either. Other than that, I could find something good in the other places.

"IF YOU ARE BORED, YOU JUST INSULTED YOURSELF"

If we let it, life on the road can get boring. I just don't let it. There are people with whom I really enjoy spending time. First of all, doing Royals games, I spent a lot of time with Paul Splittorff. I usually came down and had breakfast with Split in the mornings, and sometimes Royals TV play-by-play announcer Bob Davis would join us. Split and I used to love to go over to the park early and sit around and talk with Tony Muser and the coaches. That day started with me about 3:00 in the afternoon.

I have a lot of good friends on the road, like Bobby Watson in Baltimore. He has been a friend of mine for over 20 years. I enjoyed going to Baltimore and seeing Bobby and his family. Sometimes we would play golf, or sometimes we would go to lunch or dinner. I've made a lot of friends like that down through the years.

I like to read on road trips. When I have projects to work on, such as the Royals for Rainbows Golf Tournament, I'll take those materials on the road with me. But, I can always find something to do. If there's something on TV that I really want to see, I'll spend 30 minutes or an hour watching it but I'm not a guy who sits there with a channel changer looking for something to watch on television. I've always got a book with me and I enjoy reading.

Someone once told me when I was a kid, "If you are bored, you just insulted yourself." I've always believed that. Hey, you've got a mind, you can find something to do.

In Baltimore, for example, the Babe Ruth Museum is on the can't-miss list of attractions. Also, during the 1998 season, a friend of mine and I went to the Orioles Hall of Fame luncheon.

Life on the road can be tedious. Planning activities ahead can be helpful. In any case, though, it's like the old adage - "Life is what you make it."

MY MOST MEMORABLE TRIPS

The first trips to the playoffs in New York, and to the World Series, are my most memorable road trips. Those were really fun because we all had our families with us and the Royals took the front office people; it was really one big family there, watching something meaningful happen. "Hey, these are our guys, they got us here, and we're all going to have fun." It was wonderful that the Royals let us all enjoy that. We all took our families on road trips where the games meant something big. The playoffs and World Series are always electric every night at the ballpark, so those are the ones I remember the most.

Don't get me wrong, though, there were a lot of other fun trips. Dick Howser and I played a lot of golf and had a lot of good times on the road. We had a lot of great dinners with a lot of different guys down through the years. Then in the years when I had relatives living in Boston, my mom would come and visit her sister when we were going to be in town playing the Red Sox. Those times were always memorable.

THE GONG SHOW

Road trips have always been a time when players like to play jokes on each other to kill time, but a lot of those happened in the clubhouse and we weren't in on those, or didn't see them. But I do know we had some guys with great senses of humor, especially back in the 1970s and 1980s. Those Royals were winning and they were having great times. They played awfully hard on the field, then got on one another awfully hard in the clubhouse, in planes and on road trips.

I've had some great times with guys down through the years and some funny things have happened. It is strange because a lot of times when I would be speaking at a banquet or to a large group, they'd ask me for some stories of funny things that happened with the Royals. I'll sit there and think about it, but I always have trouble coming up with one. I know we laughed a lot; in fact, we laughed all the time. More than gags or incidents, I remember characters. Guys like George, Marty Pattin, Steve Mingori, were on one another having good times all the time. They laughed at one another and laughed with one another.

There have been so many things happen down through the years from practical jokers like Bret Saberhagen and Jim Colborn. Those guys were always doing fun things. I can still see Bret Saberhagen, on his pitching days, marching around wearing a coon skin cap, which became his thing. One year when *The Gong Show* was popular on TV, the Royals had their own version of *The Gong Show*. If one of the guys screwed up, they got the gong that day. Not getting that gong became a source of pride. There have been a lot of things that wouldn't seem so funny to outsiders, but could be very, very funny to us. There have been some great characters who played for the Royals down through the years.

PLANES, TRAINS AND AUTOMOBILES

In my 25 years with the Royals, there were some interesting flights. We had a bomb threat one time coming back from Oakland that forced us to land in Salt Lake City. It turned out to be a false alarm, but it was an attention-grabber.

We came home one night in a storm. We had to land in St. Louis. Hugh Forrest was our long-time pilot with TWA and he brought us home on that trip at maybe 2,000 feet. We were so close to the ground, we could literally see the interstate. Hugh could fly a plane faster than anybody and get us safely to our destination. That was an interesting trip because we were in a small plane and we came home under the clouds. We could plainly see that he was bringing us right down Interstate-70.

Those were two trips that really stand out in my mind. Luckily we never had any in which we felt like we weren't going to make it, but we had some that made us sit up and pay attention to what was happening. But the guys flying those airplanes were always pretty damn good. My thought has always been that they don't want to die either, so they are going to be fighting their rear end off up there to get us home. They always did.

PERSONALLY SPEAKING

I happen to be married to a woman who is very bright and very strong. Where long road trips have made it tough on some marriages, they have drawn us closer together down through the years. I was divorced once. I was working all the time and gone a lot, which was difficult with small kids, Stacy and John.

The strain of my schedule was too much. I'm sure most people who have ever been divorced, with children, are like me, and realize how much they missed by not being with their kids every day. It's the one thing in my life I would like to do over, to have spent a lot more time with Stacy and John. It has, however, made me treasure the experience of watching Joe grow up, and the times I do spend with all of them.

The only negative about broadcasting, and traveling with the job, is that

I've missed seeing my kids do things. That's the only regret that I have in the whole thing; I wish I could have been around them more.

As far as my marriage to Barb is concerned, my traveling has made us closer. I was already with the Royals when we met, so she knew the type of schedule I would have, but it worked because she is a woman who likes her time alone. She's a voracious reader, a good student and very dedicated to family. She comes from a very close-knit family and she is dedicated to them. She's very independent, can operate on her own and doesn't need me there.

In fact at our house, she's the one who fixes everything. I can't fix anything, except some meals every now and again. On our first date, I hated the seat-belt buzzer in my car and didn't know how to make it stop. When I mentioned it to her, she unhooked it for me, and made the buzzer stop. She unhooked the seat-belt buzzer and hooked me.

The fact that we are apart a lot makes the times we are together better. We obviously like the same things. We like to do things together. In that regard, there's a tradeoff there...I've missed a lot of things the kids have done, but I think it has made Barb and me a lot closer. Just spending more time with her has made me appreciate her a lot more. I hope in some ways it has made me a broader person. It has made me understand the world a little bit better. We have been married for 24 years now, and I feel lucky to have found her.

Traveling made me realize how much my friends meant to me. Broadcasters sacrifice some of that, but I've gone a lot of places, have experienced a lot of things, and have done a lot of things that a lot of people would like to have had the opportunity to do. It balances itself fairly well. Regardless of one's profession, when you travel a lot, you'll never be able to balance missing things that your kids do.

On the other hand, when I am with the kids, and get to see them do things, it makes life so much better. The times I have spent with my kids have meant more to me than the average guy. That could be said about everybody involved in sports. I read an article about a hockey player who was retiring. He said that all of a sudden his kids got to this age where it was critical for him to be with them; and he decided he was going to be with them. He was retiring to devote his time to his children. That happens a lot in this business.

I couldn't tell you that traveling has had an adverse effect on me personally. Overall, it has been a very positive thing. Travel, again, is what you make of it and I have enough faith in my family and friends to think that they are still going to be there when I get home. Barb always takes care of things. It's worked out well for us.

DAD, ARE WE THERE YET?

This business has been great because Barb and Joe have actually been able to go on a lot of trips with me. During the basketball season, I've done the Maui Classic on television, and they've gone to Hawaii with me to do that. They went to Champaign, Illinois with me last year to see a basketball game, with my dad and his family. The Royals were good about the family traveling; they would let families take two trips a year. We've always taken advantage of that.

Barb is a great tourist and loves to get out and see things. She always surprises me by knowing about places we go. She has a great sense of history. She loves to travel. She's been overseas to Israel, Egypt, England and France. Before she went on these trips, she knew something before she got there about every place she was going.

I've gotten to watch Joe go out on the field to shag for batting practice, and do things like that. Joe has been on the field at places like Yankee Stadium, Wrigley Field, Kauffman Stadium and others, and I think he understands that it is a very special experience. It's a lot of fun to see their reactions when we get to do things like that.

THE FOOD CRITIC

One of the things I enjoy about traveling is the chance it gives me to go to some great restaurants around the country. I love to go out for lunch or dinner. One of the reasons to enjoy a city is to sample the foods and restaurants and see what they are like. The salmon in Seattle, the chowder in Boston, the crabs in Baltimore. I usually had at least one or two favorites in most of the cities. Seattle and San Francisco have so many different choices that those are almost can't-miss cities.

My favorite of all is Strouds in Kansas City. We go there about once a week and have for a long, long time. Some of my other favorite stops when we were on the road are...

Anaheim isn't really known for its food but there is a place there called Mr. Stox, which is about the only one I've been to that would be considered pretty good.

In Baltimore, just about any that serve crab around the Inner Harbor are very good. Ocean Pride is a restaurant out in the Baltimore suburbs where I like to eat, but the Inner Harbor provides both great scenery and seafood.

Boston is just loaded with places, like Grill 23. There's one right on the water called the Sail Loft, which is great for lunch. Eli's is my favorite restaurant in Chicago, which is a short walk from the hotel where we stayed. They have terrific food there.

My two favorite places in Cleveland are Johnny's Uptown and Sammy's in the Flats. There's a Morton's Steak House close to the hotel, but my two favorites are Johnny's and Sammy's.

Downtown Detroit has a London Chop House which is a terrific restaurant. Ponchartrain Cellars was a really good restaurant there. It was not a part of the hotel but it was across the street from the Ponchartrain Hotel. Now the team stays in the Detroit suburb of Dearborn. The only place out there is the Big Fish, a pretty good seafood restaurant. I went there once in awhile.

Milwaukee is a great restaurant city, but they closed my favorite, Sally's. A place called the Grenadier is a really good European-style restaurant. There's also a lunch joint called Elsa's, which has great sandwiches and iced tea. Ratzch's is a German restaurant. In the hotel there is the English Room - very good. But Sally's and the Grenadier were my favorites.

In Minnesota, Murray's Steak House is an old traditional steak house downtown. They have great garlic bread. I love to go there for lunch or dinner. There are a lot of other good places them, too, but Murray's would be my favorite.

In New York City, our two favorite restaurants are Bravo Gianni's and Cafe Des Artiste. New York is another place with a load of great restaurants. San Francisco has a ton of them.

The Pink Door down in Post Alley, in Seattle has a garden that overlooks Elliott Bay, and you can sit in the garden and have lunch. Cutters down by the water is really good. So is Place Pigalle, which is down in the Market. In 1998 I went to McCormick's Steak House for the first time, and it was very good. Seattle is a terrific restaurant city.

Bern's in Tampa is a terrific restaurant. I love to go there. There's also some little shack on the water that has great grouper sandwiches. To me, that's very much a part of the experience.

There haven't been a lot of original places I've eaten in Arlington, Texas. About the only place I go (we're in kind of a remote area in Texas) is Joe's Crab Shack. It was across the parking lot from the hotel, so I'd walk over there and have lunch. We play so many night games in Texas that we really never found out where to go to dinner down there. The Black-Eyed Pea is another chain, but it's a place I love to go to lunch down there.

In Toronto, there is a place called George Bigliardi's that I really like. I have been there enough times that George himself has become a friend, so I'll go over sometimes and just sit and have a drink with him after a ballgame.

Almost everywhere we go, whether it was for baseball or basketball, I have a favorite place I like to go. To me, going to dinner or lunch with friends makes a great part of a road trip. We sit down, have some laughs, have a great meal and usually come away with something pretty good from it. If the family's with me, that makes it even better, because we can go to lunch or dinner and let them enjoy some of these places, too. That's a very big part of traveling.

RESHAPING THE LEAGUE, REVIVING RIVALRIES

As it is presently constituted, I don't care much for interleague play. Continuing with the American League Central division playing against the National League Central division will eventually get old I think. For instance, the last couple years, the Royals have played the Houston Astros. Those games have been fairly exciting because they are still unique. But if they played every year, the Astros would become just another baseball team that the Royals play. In reality, and especially if the Astros are not very good year-in and year-out, they would soon become as familiar as anybody else coming to town. The Cardinals, on the other hand, would always be a rivalry because they are our cross-state rival.

Denny has said that MLB should blow the whole plan up and realign everything...that's the thing to do. For the American League Central to always play the National League Central and never play the East or West doesn't make much sense to me. The Royals and the Astros, the Royals and the Pirates, the Royals and the Reds - those match-ups are not going to mean very much, for very long.

The other thing Major League Baseball needs to develop a rivalry is to have something at stake. The Royals have maybe had two and a half rivals. The A's and the Yankees were the two Royal rivals in the 1970s, because we were fighting each other for something important, whether it was the West with the A's, or the American League with the Yankees. Then the Texas Rangers issued a challenge for a little while, and the White Sox, for a year, issued a similar challenge, so there were those partial rivalries. For a couple of years the Royals and the Rangers were at it pretty hard, and a couple of years the Royals and White Sox were at it pretty hard. The outcome had some meaning in the division race.

If baseball realigned into four 8-team divisions and only the winner were going to the playoffs, there would to be some rivalries going to those, especially up at those top spots in the standings where they play them like they used to — three times at home, three times on road. For instance, in June of the 1998 season the Anaheim Angels and the Royals had an ugly brawl in Kansas City. Usually a brawl helps fuel a rivalry, but in this case the two teams didn't play each other again until August. They were playing in different divisions and since nothing was at stake, that's not going to develop into a rivalry.

The Cardinals and the Cubs have always been rivals even though the Cubs usually aren't any good. The essence of that rivalry is found in central Illinois, where the fans are evenly divided between the two clubs in all the conversation, the arguing and the fighting. The Cub fans make an argument even when they usually have no argument at all, simply because it is the thing to do. The Cardinals were clearly superior year after year, yet the Cub fans very stubbornly held their ground and argued, and fought, and went to the ballgames, and yelled and screamed.

The Dodgers-Giants rivalry would not be as good as it is today if it hadn't begun in New York City when the teams were just down the street from each other. The philosophies of Los Angeles and San Francisco are different (I don't think those people are really prone to intense rivalries), but the cities don't care for each other.

Denny's plan basically has teams divided into geographic rivals, like the Royals and Cubs, four divisions, and then those teams would also play against the teams from one of the other divisions each season. That way, there would be a lot of games with your own division, and fans could see the other divisions every three years.

I'm not sure I wouldn't be even more conservative than that. I would like to see four 8-team divisions, with a pure in-division only schedule, playing only the eight teams in each division, like they used to do it in the eight team leagues. Basically, play the teams in your own division all summer, then have the playoffs with the leaders from each of the divisions.

In the years when there were two divisions in each league, everybody was saying, "Oh the Royals are winning the West, but that's not a good division; the power's in the East." Well, it might have been, but going head-to-head with the Yankees year in and year out, the Royals proved they were New York's equal. The common argument then was that Kansas City was winning in an easy division, that they didn't have to do much to win in the West. Maybe, but they won that division over a 162-game schedule. When there are four, 8-team divisions, there is always going to be one division that's going to be stronger. That's true in any sport. It's the way it is.

I understand what Denny is saying, and there is merit to that, but I'm not so sure I would take it that far. The danger happens when we think one team is a big draw and would get fans into the park every three years, but by the time Kansas City's turn rolls around in three years, is that same team going to be the big draw, or will it be another team in one of the other divisions? I see where he's going with it and there's merit to it, but I'd like to see MLB (maybe it's because of my age) go back to the old way where teams would play maybe 154 games in their division with eight teams and only one team would advance to postseason. Then the games would really mean something. There would be pennant drives and stretch drives. That would be even more pure than the other idea. I wouldn't be opposed to that at all. They probably would not do that, but it'd be fun.

But, you see, Montreal rolling into town every three years doesn't mean anything to me. I'd rather see us play a team in our 8-team division that many more times in that year. There would be pennant races, stretch drives and rivalries. Like the last great race between the Braves and the Giants a few years back, when they both won 100 games and it went down to the end of the year. If there had been a wildcard, those games wouldn't have meant nearly as much.

There's nothing in sports like a baseball pennant race in September, going head-to-head, with every game meaning something. Major League Baseball has destroyed that with the wildcard spot, awarded to the team with the best second-place record in each league. To me, it was the greatest thing in sports to see teams coming down the stretch, having to win games to advance to the playoffs, to watch them do that day after day, see the intensity of their games and see how long they could hold on and keep going. Fans would go home exhausted one night, get up the next day and come to the park refreshed to start all over again. I don't think any sport has every equaled what baseball had when it had that, but the wildcard has taken that away.

WRIGLEYVILLE

During the interleague games in 1997 we went to Chicago to play the Cubs at Wrigley Field. That was the first time I had ever done a game there, and actually, it was the first time I had been there since I started working with the Royals. Going back to Wrigley to do a game was a little like going to church, to be honest.

All I could think of was my Uncle Bill driving us up there and taking me to my first game, and how good that experience was. He was a bachelor uncle and he took my brother and me, and my cousins to ballgame after ballgame, whether it be high school, University of Illinois, the Cubs or the Cardinals. Uncle Bill was always there to take us and he kind of helped raise us and nurture us.

Going back to that stadium was very sentimental and I got kind of teared up thinking about him and all had done for us as kids. He would have loved knowing I was in Wrigley Field doing a game. I was lucky because he lived long enough that I took him to games I broadcast, and my brother and I took him to NCAA Final Fours. He went to major league games when we would be in Chicago to see the White Sox play.

I've also been fortunate because I was able to take my parents to the World Series and the playoffs. In that sense, it all paid off. But, going to Wrigley for the first time was just a million memories for me, and really, really sentimental and more special because Barb and Joe were with me.

It was a similar experience going to St. Louis with the Royals in 1985 to do the World Series. My other uncle, who was a Cardinal fan, got to come to that. My brother and my family got to come down to St. Louis, so that meant a lot to me. I've always related everything that I've done back to my family, back to when I was growing up and how much they all loved sports. I was the youngest in the family, kind of the runt, and my family just encouraged us all the time. Whatever we wanted to do, they encouraged us to go do it.

They've all gotten a kick out of what I've done for a living. My family and Barb's family have enjoyed it. It's special to see them having a good time. Sharing these experiences with family has been the most special thing that's happened to me down through the years.

12 Is the Season Finished Yet?

Denny Matthews

There have been some interesting road trips in the past 30 years, but one that comes to mind almost immediately was in the mid-1980s when we were coming back to Kansas City from Seattle one night. It had to be our worst flight ever - it was just unbelievable! There was a line of thunderstorms going across the country, west to east. Of course, Seattle is north of Kansas City, so we went parallel with the storm as far as we could, but we eventually had to turn south. This storm was so huge that there was no way to get under it, over it, or around it, so we had to go through it. Bret Saberhagen's wife, Janeane was on that trip. She was pregnant, she was sick. It was easily the most turbulent, most frightening ride we've ever had. Planes that go bump in the night are no fun - and for around a half-hour, at that!

THE SECRET LIFE OF WALTER MITTY

The combination of being a Major League Baseball announcer and a former collegiate athlete may have afforded me some opportunities, especially in my early days, that I may not have had, otherwise. I've had sort of a Walter Mitty-type life, like the main character in James Thurber's book, *The Secret Life of Walter Mitty*.

For example, when Len Dawson was playing quarterback for the Chiefs, I used to go and workout with him before he reported to training camp. Prior to camp, none of his receivers were around the Kansas City area, and he knew that I had played. He'd get me to come out and run pass patterns with him a couple of times a week, two or three weeks before camp started. I don't know how much it helped Len, but it was fun for me.

On the baseball field, and this isn't common knowledge, I played in six or seven exhibition games for the Royals in the mid-to-late-1970s, while Whitey Herzog was managing the team. During spring training, I used to take some ground balls to stay in shape, and Whitey thought I would be a good replacement for his starters in games against teams like Omaha, the Naval Academy, and a couple major league teams. In nine plate appearances I got one hit, walked twice and struck out once. I also stole a base and scored a run. Jerry Terrell hit a sacrifice fly which brought me in.

Whitey put me in right field, left field and at third base. Even though I played second base in college, I never got a chance to play there in those exhibition games. I'm not complaining, though. When we played the Naval Academy, they didn't know all of our guys obviously, and they thought I was one of the regular players. When one of the Royals told a Naval Academy player that I was the broadcaster, he and his teammates couldn't believe it.

In the early 1990s I skated with the Boston Bruins when they were in St. Louis to play the Blues. There have been a lot of fun things I've been able to do that I wouldn't normally have been able to do if I wasn't in the position that I am. To me, playing is the fun thing...playing baseball, playing football, playing hockey...just playing. So if you have the opportunity to go out and play, do it.

ICE CAPADES

Hockey is a true love for me. It has been all of my life. I still play in a league during the off-season with a bunch of guys. I think baseball players could learn something from hockey players. In the 1998 season the Royals and Angels had an ugly brawl in Kansas City. Watching it was pretty embarrassing, not because they were fighting, but because of how they were fighting. Brawls are always bad but that one was especially ugly. If baseball players are going to fight, they should take lessons from hockey players and do it right, or not even bother. In a baseball brawl, there is usually one guy running and one guy chasing him; and that's kind of embarrassing. In hockey, it's a consensual thing. The two players are going to go at it, while everybody else stands back and watches. They get it out of their system, and everybody gets back to business.

Earlier in the book, Fred mentioned my story about George Brett wanting to play hockey with our group. George and one of his brothers, Bobby, got involved in hockey by buying a minor league team in Spokane, Washington. George likes sports of all kinds but he became especially intrigued by hockey. He went to the Kansas City Blades hockey games from time to time and he knew that I had played.

Once in a while, in the morning, on a weekday during the off-season, I'd get the ice over at Iceland South for an hour and a half and some of the guys would come out. Darrell Porter came out one time. Jim Eisenreich was a very good player and played with us. George told me one time, "When you get the ice next week or next month, can you call me? I want to come out and just get four or five guys to skate around and mess around. I'd like to do that." I told him I would.

He got some skates and a stick, and out he came one morning with gloves and those skates and stick. That's all we had, we were just fussing around, we didn't need the all the pads. George would skate around but he couldn't stop, so he'd bang into the boards. He said, "Look how I stop." BOOM! And he would go into the boards. I thought, "Gosh, the last thing we need is for George to break his wrist or something doing that."

After he did this for a year or two he got to where he could skate okay. One day we were out there and he said, "I want to race you for $5."

I told him, "George, I've been playing hockey for 30 years. There's no way you're going to beat me."

"I understand that," he replied, "but that's the way I'm going to learn how to skate better." So we raced around the rink. That's his mind-set about being competitive. He knew he wouldn't beat me but he wanted to race because he figured it would make him a better skater. He did become better. He goes out and plays, he tells me, with the guys on their Junior A-Team and just loves it.

That's the kid in him, coming out and playing hockey. He wanted to do the best he could because he just likes playing. He's a kid, he likes to play things. He says, "Look at me now."

I could've just imagined if he would have broken a bone playing hockey. That's the last thing we would have needed. I could picture it now, someone would ask him how he broke it. "Well, playing hockey."

"How did you get on the ice?"

"Well, Denny got the ice out at Iceland South." Oh, great — swell.

PLAY AND BE YOURSELF

The best advice I could give someone who wants to break into the sports broadcasting business now is to play, so he or she will have a feel for the game. It doesn't matter at what level they're playing, or how good they are; just play. Then go out and practice broadcasting. Tape a high school or college game; again, the level doesn't matter.

Do it the way you want to do it. Fit your personality into your broadcast. Find a pace and delivery that are comfortable. Be yourself; don't try to imitate me, or Fred, or Harry Caray, just do it under your own parameters with your personality. To me, those are the most important things to consider when trying to break into broadcasting.

There are always going to be things in your personal life that detract from broadcasting a game, but that's true of everybody in every occupation. There are always going to be things that can be distracting and tug at your attention. But, you have to compartmentalize, and put yourself in a little vacuum for 2 or 3 hours and go at it, because that's what you are there for and you really can't do anything about anything else anyway. You have got to train yourself to just attack the game and do it and then deal with the other stuff afterwards.

I agree with Fred when he talks about how something in the organization, such as Dick Howser being sick, can detract from our focus, and those other things are extraneous and peripheral things. Obviously some things are more impacting than others, but again, we are there just to broadcast games, and we have to do that regardless.

Everyone has to function at jobs with a lot of distractions and things going on around them in their everyday and personal lives, and we have to do the same thing in the booth.

Just remember the game will be the game. Baseball is pretty much the same as it always has been and probably always will be.

BASEBALL WILL ALWAYS BE AN OLD-TIME RADIO SPORT

Baseball is a great radio game, regardless of the pace. If there is a slow-paced game, it's a lot worse on TV than it is on radio. It's not good for anybody, but it's worse on television. Baseball is a game that is better in the mind, sometimes, than it is at the park or on TV. Maybe people used their minds and imaginations more in years past, because everything wasn't there for them, wasn't so easy.

People in the "old days" would huddle around their radios for World Series games. Or if there was a pennant race going, since there was no TV, families would sit there and listen. Radio was their only connection.

Back in the 1940s and 1950s the best job in broadcasting was the broadcaster for a Major League Baseball team. That was the best job...it made the most money, had the most exposure and baseball was king. Broadcasters were at the top of their profession if they were a broadcaster for a Major League Baseball team. That has changed. That is no longer true because of all the network jobs, and all the TV opportunities. A radio baseball broadcaster now is not the best job...it's not the best paid, it's not the most attractive. So that has changed dramatically over the years. It was great, though, 50 years ago. Announcers in the 1930s, 40s, and 50s, really had an impact, plus they were characters.

At the time I was breaking in to the business in the late 1960s and into the 1970s, things became homogenized. The characters were getting up in years and were beginning to fade out. The thing I saw when I began was that there was a lot of talk about the owners almost telling the broadcasters what to say, and putting the clamps on them, saying they didn't need to be a Bob Prince or a Harry Caray.

Today there really aren't any characters. Caray was the last of the characters. Today we have a lot of screamers, which to me, is brutal. People have told me that I don't get that excited. Well, I do, but I'm not getting paid to scream. I'm getting paid to tell the listener what happened. If I'm screaming, then the listener doesn't know what's going on; I'm just screaming and no one can understand that. I'll say what happens, and if the listener wants to scream, he or she can scream. That's the way that should work.

THE TREND: FORMER ATHLETES IN THE BOOTH

Having former athletes in the booth works out in some cases and in some cases it doesn't. When an ex-athlete jumps into the booth for a game, everybody says, "Wow, that was pretty good." Well, it was pretty good because they're hearing things that they've never heard before. Everybody who would come into a booth - player, former executive, fan - and give their thoughts on a game would be "pretty good" because they were different, unique. The key, or the trick, for an ex-athlete, or any broadcaster really, is to try to keep it fresh.

If an ex-second baseman sat down for a game, he would have his own unique perspective. Now keep that going, keep it fresh, and keep it interesting for 20 or 30 years. If he can do that, then fine, he's in there. But if he keeps saying the same thing over and over, it's going to become pretty dry and dull eventually. So that's the challenge that these ex-athletes will find as they venture into the booth. An ex-player coming into the booth, without any experience, would be like me, in my younger days, going down and playing a game for the Royals. Well, I did that for six or seven exhibition games. I was fine for a game, because it was unique, and new, and novel, and I wasn't supposed to be any good. Anything I did positively was a plus. Yeah, he's pretty good, but it's just for that one game. The same thing can apply for doing a broadcast.

A lot of times when a young player comes up and plays 30 or 40 games, people say he looks pretty good. OK, now let's see how he does over the course of a 162-game season. That's the test. The same is true for broadcasting.

MAKING THE GAME FUN AND COMPETITIVE

During rain delays, for the most part, we just sit and watch the tarp collect puddles. There is usually a call-in show, or a scoreboard show, that we throw the broadcast to, and then just wait for the game to resume. During one of those rain delays, I started to work on a realignment plan for baseball. David Glass, Royals Chairman of the Board and I were standing around in the press box shooting the breeze. He is a lifelong Cardinals fan, like I am.

I told him it would be neat if we could get the Cardinals and Cubs into Kansas City two or three times a year, and that I had been thinking about different realignment plans to see how it would benefit the Royals as well as all of baseball. That's how things got started...on a rainy night at the ballpark.

A couple of years after that, in 1997, the Cardinals were in Kansas City, but just for three games. It was a blockbuster series. Then in 1998, the Cubs were in Kansas City for the first-time ever, for easily our best weekend series attendance-wise, and excitement-wise, of the season. So, the highlight of the Royals home schedule in 1997 was the series with the Cardinals, and the highlight on the home schedule in 1998 was the series with the Cubs.

I'm a strong advocate of realignment. I don't see any reason why the Royals and Cardinals shouldn't play on a regular basis, or why the Cubs and White Sox shouldn't play on a regular basis, when it means something; but not the way it has been done for the last couple of seasons. There could be some great rivalries out there: the Angels and Giants, Dodgers and Angels, Yankees and Mets, Astros and Rangers (who haven't played during the current interleague system because the Rangers are in the A.L. West, and the Astros are in the N.L. Central — A.L. West teams only play N.L. West teams and N.L. Central teams have only played A.L. Central teams). People want to see it.

The attendance figures, for the most part, have been excellent in the first two years of interleague play. There are match-ups that don't mean anything, just because they don't mean anything, like the Rangers and Giants. Either geographically or historically they are not going to spark anybody's imagination. However, when the Cubs were at Kauffman Stadium in 1998, it was eminently more compelling and interesting than when the Angels rolled into town for a weekend. Why would anybody in Kansas City care anything about the Angels right now? There's no reason, no connection, nothing. But there are a lot of midwestern people who move around and relocate because of job requirements.

The Cubs, obviously, are a big item in the Midwest, as are the Royals and Cardinals. We always drew quite a few people from Milwaukee when the Brewers would visit Kauffman Stadium in the summertime. When the Twins come to town, the number of people from Minnesota in attendance is amazing. When Kirby Puckett would get a hit, there would be a lot of racket. It was truly amazing. When a team is playing another team from their shared geographical area of interest, they're not only drawing their own fans, but they're drawing fans from the other team's fan base.

There were a lot of people from Kansas City in St. Louis when the Royals played there in the summer of 1998. To me it's just so logical. I'm traditional and conservative, and so is Fred, but strictly American League and National League - which 20 years ago meant a lot with history and tradition on both sides - means nothing now. That's all gone by the boards with free agency, players switching leagues, expansion teams...who knows who's playing in what divisions now? So, American League, National League, to me, doesn't mean squat.

Interleague play is just a harbinger of the realignment. If teams realign they get everybody in their natural geographical divisions or alignments. Then they start playing each other a lot, and it doesn't matter who. That's what happened to the Royals and the Yankees in the 1970s and 80s. They played each other a lot and then things began to take shape; the rivalries, feelings and emotions. We don't have any chance now for that to happen because we don't play anybody enough, including the teams in our own division.

If we played the Cubs on a regular basis, obviously there's more interest where we are in the Cubs than in the Angels. After it got going with the Cubs and Royals, then things would begin to take shape and you'd get some movement toward a legitimate rivalry. The way things are set up now, interleague play is mostly helter-skelter.

The interleague series which have drawn people, just underline the fact that people do want to see the two Ohio teams play each other, for example. A lot of Cleveland people went down to see the Indians play in Cincinnati.

People are going to do that in the summer. People want to go somewhere. They can't get tickets in Cleveland so, hey, the Indians are in Cincinnati over the 20th of July weekend - let's go. So Cincinnati, which has been having attendance problems, boom, their attendance skyrockets that weekend. The way the fans have reacted to the rivalries during the interleague games, proves geographic realignment is beyond a question of success; based on the numbers from the interleague games, especially in 1998, there aren't many people who would debate that it was a success.

There are so many reasons to realign geographically. If they do realign and get those teams playing each other a lot, we're going to see some really, really good things. They are going to re-establish those old rivalries and create new ones, attendance is going to be better, baseball will be better, it will be a good deal. To hell with the National League and American League; they don't mean anything anymore.

Say there are two teams in an aligned division, a fourth place and sixth place team. For the sake of argument, we'll say those two teams are the Royals and Cardinals. Well, the fourth and sixth place teams are not going to win the division, but there would still be the territorial bragging rights to fight over. Believe me, there are Cardinal fans in Kansas City and there are Royals fans in St. Louis. They're going to be arguing about which team's best. From a marketing standpoint, they're talking about your team, which is what we want. That's an interest we're trying to create. You want people arguing and fighting about which team is best.

When the Cardinals and Royals played in 1998, neither team was in a division race, but people still wanted to go see them play. People were still talking about the series. How many people were talking about the Angels and the Royals prior to that series in Kansas City? Probably close to zero. How many were talking about it afterwards? Probably close to zero. Clearly, there is no interest, no excitement has been created.

If you don't think the territorial rivalries have any impact, all you have to do is go back and read about the Yankees, the Dodgers and the Giants when all three of those teams were in New York. Look at the history and bad feelings behind those teams. The Giants and Dodgers had a great rivalry because they were in the same league. The Yankees were a nemesis only because they played the Giants and Dodgers a lot in the World Series. But there was always that turmoil in New York. Who's the best? Well, the Dodgers and Giants could settle that argument during the year by playing each other. There was always something to talk about - they were just natural adversaries.

If we're talking about the Seattle Mariners and the Florida Marlins, what's there to compare or talk about? One team's in Florida and the other is in Seattle. Seattle and the Dodgers have a chance because they are both on the West Coast, and they are both fun to watch. The Dodgers played in Seattle for a weekend in 1998. There were a lot of Dodger fans at the game. Regional games like those help a team draw from a lot of different families.

HERE'S THE PLAN...

With my plan, there are four eight-team divisions designated, say, as follows: East, Southeast, Midwest and West. It is set up in such a way that each team has 16 games per season with every other team in its division. In addition, each team in, say, the Midwest division, would play all eight teams (home and away) six times in, say, the East division in year one of the implementation of the plan. In year two, the Midwest would play the Southeast, and in year three, the West.

Then, in year four, the rotation of interdivision play would start again. So, in Kansas City, aside from the teams in our division and the rivalries going there, we would see every player on every team over the course of three years.

The other divisions would of course have a different intra and interdivision setup from the hypothesis presented above. But a 160-game schedule for all. Division champs only make the playoffs. Best winning record of a champion plays the worst record of the four champions, with the middle two squaring off in the other playoff series in a best-of-seven, or 1-4, 2-3 seeding situation.

Winners play in the World Series. That's it. It is simple, yet has a sort of three-year symmetry to it. Beautiful!

Before interleague play came along we saw only half of the teams and half the players. Philadelphia would never see Ken Griffey. St. Louis would never see Frank Thomas. But, now they would have a chance every third year. So we'd have the Atlanta Braves coming to Kansas City once every three years. The Atlanta Braves are a team that a lot of people follow because of their exposure on TV. Hey, Atlanta's coming to town. They've never been here. They are going to be here for three games. There would probably be close to sell outs for all of the games.

That helps the team's attendance and interest. If the Atlanta Braves were coming to Kansas City this summer, there would be big crowds. I'd be stunned if there weren't.

There wouldn't be any worry about wild cards. The wild cards would be those games in September where teams either win or they don't.

That is part of the reason why the NCAA Basketball Tournament is so much fun to watch, because teams know that if they lose, they're out. There is an immediacy to winning. There is a sudden death thing that makes it "you win or you're gone." In baseball, a team doesn't even have to win its division to reach the playoffs.

The exciting thing about a baseball pennant race is that it is happening everyday. We know that something is going to happen, and somebody's going to win and somebody's going to lose. During the middle of the 1998 season there really weren't any good pennant races. The most compelling thing about the season was watching Mark McGwire and Sammy Sosa in the home run race. That was fun to watch, but the drama of the pennant race wasn't there.

Under this system the chances of having the two best teams in the World Series are greatly enhanced. Currently, the chances of seeing the two best teams are not as good because there are so many teams involved in the playoffs. In a short series, best of five or best of seven, often the best team is not going to prevail. The best team will prevail over a 162 game schedule, more than likely. Seven games is a crap shoot.

The real bizarre thing about the wild card, originally, was that it was predetermined what division would be playing where in the playoffs. So, in 1997, the Braves had the best record in the National League, but they were on the road to start the playoffs. That was changed in 1998; the team with the best record had the home field advantage.

When there is a formula (geographic alignment) that virtually guarantees the two best teams will play in the World Series, that to me, enhances the World Series. It certainly does not detract from it. A wildcard team and a second place team in the World Series, to me, would be a kick in the butt for the World Series and very uninteresting. It would be one that I probably wouldn't even care to watch.

In 1997 the Marlins were the wildcard team from the National League, and they went on to win the World Series. To me, that spoiled it. Granted they may have had a better record than one of the division winners, but they didn't win their division, so how can we say they were the best team in baseball? If the Royals were a wildcard team and won the World Series, would I think they were the best team in baseball? Probably not.

Baseball has never (until lately) rewarded mediocrity. Now they are because they think they can get a few extra bucks out of it. The thought seems to be that wildcards in the playoffs, more teams in the playoffs, generates more excitement. It's like the higher offensive output in the big leagues now; pull the fences in, squash the strike zone, and create more excitement...yeah, right. A 16-10 score in a 4 hour and 20 minute game is real exciting.

Baseball needs to make a lot of changes in format. The fans just are not connecting with it anymore. We, as broadcasters, aren't connecting...I had to struggle to remember who won the World Series in 1997...oh yeah, the wildcard Florida Marlins.

PROPOSING THE PLAN

David Glass was on baseball's realignment committee, so he took that plan and presented it at all the owner's meetings. According to David, there have been close to 150 different plans for realignment, and they always come back to mine because it's the most solid in every respect. It won't evolve into that exact plan, because there will be a couple teams, maybe by early 2000, that move.

The mathematics of it, with 160 games and 32 teams, is perfect. There are so many plusses to it that it's almost inevitable. Interleague play has underlined the likelihood that it could work.

There are a lot of people out there who voice concern about National League versus American League. Again, I'm as conservative and as traditional as anybody in baseball, but to me, American League and National League doesn't mean fiddly-dingo anymore. Guys are moving around from team to team so much that nobody can keep track of them. There was a time when if players were traded, they were traded within their own league. To have a guy play American League then National League, years ago, was very unusual. Now it's commonplace; some guys jump from league to league every two or three years. Nobody can even keep track of who's playing for whom anymore.

The National League, 20 or 30 years ago, was easily the superior league, but that has changed. To me, it doesn't mean anything anymore. The American League-National League, and All-Star game don't mean anything. So the people who are traditionalists say, "Well, we need that distinction between the two leagues." I have to ask, "Why? For what?"

IS THIS ROAD TRIP OVER YET?!

Life on the road during the major league season is not as glamorous as it may appear. In fact, it can get pretty monotonous, and obviously the longer we are away from home the worse it gets. Short road trips aren't too bad, but long trips involving three, four or five cities, really start to drag! It's not as though these trips are vacations; we are traveling for business and there is always a ballgame hanging above our heads. We can do a little bit of sightseeing, but that's very limited.

People don't always realize that it is just as bad for broadcasters as it is for players. When we count days off, it may be a little worse for broadcasters. Players get days off here and there, but broadcasters who work every game, managers, and coaches don't have any days off.

Don't get me wrong, not all road trips have been bad. In fact, for me there were different phases in traveling with the team. The first phase, naturally enough, was when I first started, and it was fun because I was getting to go to cities and places I had never been before. Especially the cities in the East, like Boston and New York; they were fun trips. It was educational and exciting, seeing sites I had never seen before, and going to ballparks where I had never been. That was phase one.

Phase two would have been going out with the players in the early to mid-70s when I was their contemporary. I had very little in common with the managers and coaches back then because they were all older. I was the same age as, or younger than, the players. For the first 10-15 years it was going out with the players mostly.

I guess I'm currently in phase three, where, after 30 years, I've seen all I need to see in the different cities, and I'm older than the players, so phases one and two are out. The savior on the road for me over the last few years has been golf. The different managers have had different philosophies on whether or not players can bring their clubs, but being non-uniformed personnel, I'm free to bring my clubs. And having the opportunity to play some of the most famous golf courses in the country has really been fun. That's kind of maintained my sanity on the road.

In 1998, for example, I was able to play at Congressional Country Club just a month after the U.S. Open was there. On a trip to Baltimore, a group of us played the Robert Trent Jones Course in Manassas, Lake Manassas, Virginia, where the President's Cup was played two years ago. I had watched both of those tournaments on TV so I remembered a lot of the holes and the way the clubhouses looked.

I hacked around a little bit on golf courses 20 years ago, but I've only been playing seriously for two years. I wanted to play those courses 10 years ago, but I thought they weren't the spot for someone like me. Not that I'm any good now, but at least I can get around without embarrassing myself.

On road trips now, if we are gone on a nine-day trip, we might try to play two or three times. When I'm at home during the season, playing golf is really sporadic because there are so many "chores" to do. For instance, when we get back from a ten-day trip, I have to do things like get a haircut, do yard work, run errands, go through mail and papers, do laundry and return phone calls. A lot of times we have a day off after a long road trip, but that day off is spent catching up after being gone for ten days. So it's harder to play golf at home than it is on the road.

YOU CALL THIS A "BREAK?"

Speaking for myself, the All-Star break is the worst thing that happens in a baseball season because it's the biggest tease in the world. Sometimes we get three days off, sometimes we only get two because of travel. So basically we only have the equivalent of a weekend off. That is the fastest three days in the calendar year. I'm being half facetious because it's nice and it does provide some relief, but it's not long. We're right back in the cauldron quicker than we realize that we were on a three-day vacation. By the time the break hits each July, we could use about a week, but we only get the three days. Granted, any break we have in our schedule is wonderful; a day off is like finding gold.

Generally during this time, I just go home. Three days isn't really long enough to go anywhere. If we had five or six days it would make a lot more sense but by this time of the season we've been traveling for 15 weeks, and we are going to still be traveling for another 15 before its over, so it makes more sense not to go anywhere.

About the only All-Star game I have really enjoyed was the one in Royals Stadium in 1973. We had tickets, so pretty much all of my family was here from Illinois. What I remember is the five days prior to the All-Star Game, because the weather was just absolutely horrible — it rained and rained, day and night. Officials were concerned because, even though the stadium had the artificial turf, it didn't drain that well and they had to get out and squeegee it. (In hockey terms, I would say they kind of zambonied it off.) But the grounds crew, and other workers, did a wonderful job of getting the field and stadium in shape in spite of some terrific odds against them. The big scoreboard, which was a marvel at the time, had been hit by lightning two or three days earlier and they didn't get that completely fixed until about 45 minutes before the game started. There was a bit of panic around that game.

Around 4:00 on the afternoon of the game, the clouds miraculously rolled away and it was a gorgeous night.

One thing the All-Star break does is prepare us for the toughest part of the season. The part of the year where we start to get a little antsy, and are ready for the season to be finished...the dog days.

There's a six-week lull period, covering the final two weeks of July and the entire month of August, when we're ready to get the season over with. That comes, we've been grinding it away for four months, it's the middle of summer, it's hot, we've had a game every night for four months, and we don't see the finish line. That's where it really starts to grind on us. Now we're going through the cities for the second time of the season, so we've already done everything there is to do in those places.

So the "dog days" are the worst part of the season. I don't think it's just for the broadcasters either; I think that goes for everyone from the writers to the players.

Then, at the first of September, things begin to cool off, there's a little hint of fall in the air, and we can start to see the finish line. That helps us get the final kick for the remainder of the season.

BROADCASTING TO COOPERSTOWN

I've said publicly that I will broadcast all of the games in 1999, but thereafter I'd like to work out a schedule where I just do some of the games. Obviously that's my idea and it would have to work out with the plans of other people. That's my desire, and if it doesn't work out with the Royals, then I would explore the possibility of doing a 40 to 60 game TV package, or a substitute radio package for some other club.

I've talked to a lot of other teams in the past, and have had other job offers. Maybe I'll "retire" after 2000 and if I miss broadcasting, then I'll try to come back somewhere the next year. If I don't miss it, then "retire" for two years. If I still don't miss it, then "retire" for four. If I don't miss it, then stay retired. I don't know.

I really do not want to do every game, as I've done for 30 years, after the 1999 season, which is my 31st season. The thing somebody pointed out to me during the 1998 campaign in Cleveland was that if I do the games in the year 2000, I will have broadcast exclusively for the same team, without interruption, in five different decades. There are fewer than 10 people in history who have done that, and all of those guys are in the broadcaster's wing of the Baseball Hall of Fame. That's something that gets my attention!

The last couple of years people back in my hometown have mentioned the Hall of Fame to me. I thought about it five or six years ago and thought that if I hung around long enough maybe induction is a possibility. There aren't any stats per se, that get a broadcaster into the Hall. Some guys have campaigned for it, others haven't; they just got in by what they did or because of how long they were around. The Hall of Fame is certainly something to consider in this business at the stage where I am now.

To help insure my staying, in January of 1999, I signed a two-year contract to stay with the Royals through the 2000 season. My real motivation behind signing - was to be assured that I could do the games through the year 2000. Dave Van Horne of Montreal began broadcasting Expos games in their first season in 1969. So even though there have been only a few broadcasters who have accomplished the feat of working exclusively with one team in each of five decades, it is likely that two more will reach that plateau in 2000.

I'm still going to explore the possibility of cutting my travel schedule down in 2000. I'm pretty damn sure I won't be doing all of the games in 2001, so the Royals are eventually going to have to get another, younger, guy to take my place. They could cut my salary back and use that to pay the new guy, which means the payroll output would be the same, but instead of two broadcasters, they would have three. That way when the team is on the road, those two guys could do the broadcasts to gain experience and give me a break, then when the team is home, I could do the broadcasts to give them a break. There are quite a few teams that have done this, so it's not like we would be re-inventing the wheel; we would just be helping it roll more smoothly.

AHHH...WINTER BREAK

When the season is over, I think just about everyone in this business feels as though they need to get away for a few months. Many broadcasters have wives they need to spend time with. Since I'm a life-long bachelor, family life isn't a concern for me. Baseball hasn't necessarily helped me stay single, but it hasn't hurt. If an announcer has a relationship with someone, they had better have a good understanding. A wife or a girlfriend would have to be pretty understanding and patient about it, because we are only going to be there half of the time during the season. Unless they understand and go for that, it's not going to work. I have had some great relationships, so if I had wanted to get married, I could have, I suppose. I have just never asked anybody. That is how it works, right?

If a broadcaster has things he enjoys doing other than calling games, then it's easy to get away after the season, and it's healthy. It clears the air. It recharges the batteries. It brings us back in the spring with renewed enthusiasm and vigor. If you stay with one project week after week after week, through human nature, you kind of get tired of it.

Once the off-season hits, I do a myriad of things; some I like to do, and some I have to do. The have-to-dos would be home projects that get put off because of a lack of time during the summer, both indoors and outdoors. I try to do the outdoor things during October when the weather's still decent, then turn my attention to the inside projects.

I play hockey with a group on Thursday nights. I have a big Lionel model train set in the basement which occupies a lot of my time. Then there is the normal stuff, like reading and listening to music. I like to watch television, especially hockey and college football. As I mentioned, I've become a pretty avid golfer the last couple of years, so I play golf when the weather allows in the off-season.

Since there are games virtually every night during the season, we really don't have a chance to visit different restaurants in town. When there is a day game or a day off during the season, I don't want to go out to dinner, because I've been going out. So the off-season gives us a chance to enjoy the good restaurants in Kansas City. We have a chance to go see movies at night.

In October, it's back home to Illinois. And I go back there around Christmas, each time for four or five days.

Basically during the off-season we are squeezing 12 months of the year into six months. When you stop to think about it - and this isn't a complaint, it's just a fact - once we start the season, we don't have any weekends off, and we don't have any holidays off; so we are doing a game every day or every night for 26 weeks. That doesn't count spring training, when we're away from home for four weeks.

When we get back from that preseason trip, we've got a month's worth of catching up to do, like mail, errands, newspapers, laundry and phone calls. So when the everyday grind of the season starts, we're already a month behind. After we're caught up from spring training, which may be the middle of May, then we're still leaving, coming back, and trying to catch up. We never really get ahead, we just try to stay even, because as soon as we're even, the team leaves again. It's a vicious circle. The off-season is our only chance to get even and maybe even a little ahead.

During the season I get up in the morning at 8:30 or 9 and have until about 3:30 in the afternoon to do the "catch ups." Because I own a house, I'm never at a loss for things to do or fix.

I have never gotten up on a day during the off-season and said, "Man, what am I going to do today?" There is always something to do...that's never, ever a problem.

Fred White

For me, usually the last day of the season was the time of year when I was ready for it to be over. Until the last day, there was always another day to look forward to. The last day of the season, we think, "Well, this is it for awhile. Let's go ahead and finish it up so we can get on with other things." I have never been in a position where I was counting days until the end. There was always something during the season to spark my interest.

By the same token, I never felt a need to take a break and get away from everything when the season was finished. There was a time earlier in my career with the Royals when I was doing baseball, then immediately into college football, then going immediately into college basketball, then back into baseball. There was enough change, though, that I was never bored and never felt like I needed a break. The last few years my break has been a few weeks right after the baseball season, because I stopped doing football. Now my basketball schedule isn't that rigorous; it's basically weekends and maybe once during the week, so I do get a break.

I'm not the type of person who needs long periods of time off. I can recover pretty quickly, refresh myself, and be ready to go again. I've always been like that, which is a blessing in this business. I've always liked to stay busy. The games interest me; the work interests me; and I've always worked with good people, so it's been enjoyable.

ROYALS FOR RAINBOWS

Each year, immediately after the baseball season finished I would put together a golf tournament, with several current and former major league players in Wichita, Kansas, called Royals For Rainbows. The money from the tournament went to a preschool in Wichita for handicapped children, called Rainbows United. I have a niece with Downs Syndrome who went to that school and I thought what they did was great, and I became interested in them. Back then, in the late 1970s and early 1980s, the school was struggling financially, so we started the tournament to try to help them out. It did very well for them over the years. Now they have three campuses. They've gone great guns with this thing down there.

We would take two buses down to Wichita on the Tuesday after the regular season ended on Sunday, and visit the school. Our guys were just great; it's a real sight to see the players with these kids in there, rolling around on the floor with them, playing with them, laughing with them. Then Tuesday afternoon the golf club was opened only to our guys, so they got out there and had a practice round, a great time. We played three different courses during the history of the tournament, Tall Grass, Crestview Country Club and Terradyne. Where we played in 1998 is where it all began: Tall Grass, a nice, Scottish-style course. On Tuesday night we had a dinner and auction. The tournament was on Wednesday, and then we came home.

I really appreciate all the players, and what they do for this, because most of them have been gone from their homes since February, yet they'll stay a few extra days after the season to do this.

We usually took around 40 guys, including the baseball players, alumni, front office and clubhouse personnel. It's a good contingent, great representation. I was always surprised that they seem to look forward to it. I'm thankful that they gave me two extra days at the end of the season.

Some of these guys, like George Brett, Paul Splittorff and Jamie Quirk, have played in every single tournament. They've just been great about it, and I get a lot of satisfaction out of it.

The 1998 tournament was our 17th year. It doesn't seem like it's been that long, but it has. That's hard work; the golf tournament is hard work. The greatest moment for me is when we're coming home on the bus, and all the guys are laughing; we've had a good time, and we made some money for the school. When I hear them laughing on the bus, I know we've had a good tournament.

BEING IN THE RIGHT PLACE AT THE RIGHT TIME

I am very lucky. I got lucky when the Royals job came along. I always was careful when I took a job that it was with a real good station, a good sports-oriented station, and I put myself in a position where I was exposed to more things and was able to do more things.

I got lucky again, and I had absolutely no control over it, when ESPN went on the air. I had just done a national back-up game for NBC. Scotty Connall and Chet Simmons left NBC to run ESPN. It just so happened that I had done one of the last games that NBC had that year, and those two guys remembered it. When ESPN went on the air, they came and got me, and gave me a ton of events to work. I was doing 30-40 events a year. They gave me some of their best basketball games, and some football games. That was probably the luckiest thing that happened to me, other than being in position for the Royals job in 1973. ESPN is in Bristol, Connecticut, I'm in the Midwest, but I just happened to do games for those guys at NBC at just the right time.

Broadcasting, whether it be in a radio or a television studio, or play-by-play on television or radio, has been a wonderful career. I wouldn't trade it for any other job in the world. Granted, I had hoped to be with the Royals for another five or six years, but it didn't work out that way. Regardless, I plan to stay in this business as long as it's fun -and that should be a little while longer.

FROM FASTBALL TO ROUND BALL

One of the opportunities that drew me to WIBW in Topeka was the fact that I was going to be working solely in sports. The main sports were football and basketball. In 1967 I started doing Kansas State basketball and football. More than 30 years later, I'm still doing college basketball. Since the time when I started with the Royals in 1973, I have done basketball during the off-season.

Some of the networks and schools I've worked for include ESPN, Creative Sports, Raycom, CBS, NBC, ABC, K-State, Memphis State, Illinois, ACC, Big 8 (now the Big 12), the Metro Conference and the Atlantic-10. A lot of different people in a lot of different places. There are very few places I haven't been to do a college basketball game.

I have really cut back on that schedule, though. There were some years when I was doing 65-70 basketball games. That got to be too much, especially with my son, Joe, in school. I just wasn't home very much, so I really cut back. Doing the Big 12 and the University of Illinois, as I've done the last couple years, is about right for me. It's what I like to do.

I've had a blast doing basketball and have been able to work with some terrific people. Larry Conley was a great partner for a long time. I've worked with all of the others, including Dick Vitale, Billy Packer and Bill Raftery. If I had to pick a couple favorites, I would say Conley and Jon Sunvold. They are both just terrific analysts. It was not uncommon for me to work with 15 different analysts in one season.

Despite what seems like it might be a hectic schedule, doing all those basketball games is really not too bad, and I can still spend plenty of time with my family. If I'm doing a Saturday game somewhere, I'll go in on Friday in time to watch the teams practice that afternoon, then have dinner with the crew on Friday night. We get up and have production meetings on Saturday morning, then go to the shoot-around. For the game, I get to the arena 2 1/2 hours before the ballgame, do whatever taping needs to be done, then do the game, have fun, and go home.

If it's a night game during the week, usually I'll go the day before to watch practice, although sometimes I just wait and go the day of the game. A lot of that depends on where the game is. For instance, if I'm doing a game in Lawrence, since it's so close to Kansas City, I'll just commute for the two days.

It's not a difficult schedule, at all, in regards to time.

THINGS ARE LOOKING BRIGHT

The future is great for young guys getting in the broadcasting business. There are so many opportunities out there with the explosion of cable television, and new major networks such as Fox. That's not to say that there won't be a huge amount of competition, but there are more opportunities than there were even 10 years ago.

When I first started doing college basketball on TV, there was one game of the week on Saturday, and that was it. It was very competitive trying to get the job to do that game. It was very important to get that Saturday game, but you knew there was only going to be one guy who was going to get the job. Now there are probably 20 games on television on Saturday. So now, just in this region, 20 guys are getting an opportunity instead of just one. Across the country there are hundreds of games on television on Saturday, and every other day.

The explosion of sports on television has given a lot of guys a lot of opportunities. It's been good for guys in our business in that regard. In fact, the overall effect of sports on television has been great for sports. There are some downsides to it, like the idea that television controls the game too much, but all in all we have to say it's wonderful for athletics.

That explosion has also brought more and more former athletes into the booth. In my opinion, if a former athlete pays his dues before broadcasting, then his getting a big-time job is great. I don't like to see a guy step off the field and directly into the booth. In case of a Paul Splittorff, for example, he went out and did what every other guy who ever was a success in radio and television did when he went to work for a small town radio station. Working hard at a small station, Split turned himself into a broadcaster.

On the other hand, if a guy gets a break as an athlete and gets put in the booth, and if he'll work at it, then that's okay, too. But I've seen a lot of them just walk into the booth like, "Here I am." They usually fail if they don't work at it; broadcasting is not as easy as they think it is. The longer athletes are away from the field, the less they know of what's happening on the field. If they won't work at maintaining that edge, they're not going to succeed in this business at all.

Pat Summerall, for example, who worked hard at the business and turned himself into a good play-by-play guy, should be admired. I don't have a problem with athletes taking advantage of being an athlete or using their celebrity status, in fact I think it's great when that can open the door for them. Again, as long as they work at it, then being a former player is wonderful. But, I resent the ones who walk in as if to say, "Here I am. I'll be a star for you today." This business just doesn't work like that. Those guys usually bury themselves and they usually ruin the broadcast.

Sitting down next to the guys like Split, or Buck Martinez, or Jon Sunvold, it doesn't take long before one realizes how seriously they're taking this. Those guys are fun to work with, and I really admire them.

Overall, I don't have a problem with former athletes in the booth. In fact, not only do I not have a problem with them, there is an important place for them...they are needed.

For anyone wanting to break into the business, athlete or not, I have some very simple advice that has helped me along in my career: work hard and when you think you're working hard, work harder. Then when you think you're working as hard as you can, work a little harder still.

Take my situation. There were a lot of other guys in the Kansas City area who I thought were really good announcers who could have gotten the opportunity I did with the Royals. There were a lot of great college announcers around the area.

I always vowed that I was never going to let anybody outwork me; I was going to work hard to prepare, and do everything possible to succeed. This business is very competitive, especially in this area of the Midwest. There aren't that many good broadcasting jobs out there, but there are a lot of good announcers wanting those jobs, so, in that regard, it's another excuse to feel lucky for the opportunity. I would like to think I had something to do with my own success by putting a certain amount of work into it, and getting whatever I deserved out of it.

Young broadcasters can't be greedy; they have to forget about holidays, time off, and those types of things. Most guys are going to have to do what most of us have done...go to a small town, take a job for a little bit of money, and get their foot in the door. College is great for an education, and that degree is important, but colleges can't teach anybody how to do play-by-play. The only way to learn how to do play-by-play is to sit down and do it. Nobody can be told to look at this play, think this, and say this, do it in an instant, do it while it's happening.

I also tell young people that a tape recorder is a radio station. They don't have to wait to have a job at a station to go do a ballgame; they can take their tape recorder to a game and do games that way. Or they can sit in front of a television with the sound turned off, and do a game.

Read a lot. Read the classics. In this business young announcers are going to be working with words for the rest of their lives, so why not read the guys who were the best in history at working with words, the greatest wordsmiths going? Listen to music and read books, because through osmosis you're going to get a different way of looking at things, or of how to work with words, or new phrases might come to mind.

Denny and I quite often would quote a line from a song or even a movie. I think the movie *Butch Cassidy and the Sundance Kid* was quoted more than anything else was during our broadcasts. Nobody is inventing new words here, we're all using words that have been around for a long time. Experience is really the only thing that is ever going to get anyone to the professional level. People just have to work hard to get that type of experience, and be unwilling to settle for less, because they're probably going to be their own worst critic.

My final advice for an aspiring announcer is to be yourself. If you go out and imitate Vin Scully, then you're only going to be a guy who imitates Vin Scully. The style you develop may end up being the best style in history, who knows? I never like to hear guys who are only imitations of another guy; show me what you've got. Quite often that's pretty good.

There are a lot of sports announcers out there who may never be well known, guys doing high school sports or small college athletics, who are very good. Bob Davis, the current radio voice of the Kansas Jayhawks and a television announcer for the Royals, is a terrific case in point. It took Bob a long, long time to get a break to do KU basketball and Royals baseball. He's a terrific announcer, but Bob Davis sat for a long time in Hays, Kansas, and not many people got to hear him and never knew what a great announcer he is. That case is multiplied hundreds, even thousands of times, across the nation.

A guy from CBS told me one time how they were having a difficult time finding basketball announcers. I told him to "meet me in Chicago on a Friday night, I'll rent a car, and we'll drive down the Illinois/Indiana border, listen to high school games, and I'll find guys who are probably better than anything you've got, but you won't have the guts to hire them." That is so true. That's why I've always been so appreciative of the breaks I've had in the business, because there are a lot of guys out there who are pretty darn good but could never catch that break. To this day I like to listen to other announcers.

We have really been blessed in this area, because Kansas State, KU and the University of Missouri have all had some terrific announcers down through the years. I could sit here when they're all three playing a game, go down the radio dial, and see that there's no place in the country where college games on radio are as good as they are right here.

PREPARATION: SURFING THE WEB

Technology is a funny thing. It's something we cuss at sometimes, and are thankful for at other times. Technology has definitely changed the way I prepare for a broadcast. It's a different kind of preparation now. Where I used to have to spend two or three hours figuring out some things, the club hands the information to the broadcasters every day now.

My baseball and basketball preparation changed in the sense that now I use the Internet, which wasn't available when I first started. I use electronic devices that I never thought I would. One time I said I'd never have a FAX machine or a cell phone or a computer, and now I've got all of them and use them regularly. So, from that standpoint, where I used to have to go back to score sheets to figure what the Royals had done against right and left-handers, what a Royal had done against a Ranger, I don't have to do that anymore since the club does it for me. That's become the norm in sports. For baseball, I gathered more color commentator-type information than I did in the beginning. Now I tend to get more on the Internet and read newspapers around the nation.

Basically, once the information is gathered, preparation is the same. I prepare by thinking about the information I've received, digesting it and getting myself keyed up for the first pitch of the night, or the tip-off. That really never has changed and probably never will.

Preparing for a basketball game is a little different than getting ready for a baseball game. I go to practices the night before the game with our crew then and we have a little dinner and talk about the game and the broadcast. The game starts and there are two hours of hellacious fun on the air. Then the game's over, and we go our own ways. Then we gather up for the next game and do it again.

I've been lucky down through the years in basketball, football and baseball because I've been blessed with terrific partners. I've worked with some of the very best analysts in the business in every sport, including the basketball guys I mentioned earlier plus guys like Paul Maguire in football. The technical people have also been wonderful.

It is the duty of the announcer to help his partner be good. If a broadcast is going to be good, the engineer, the director, the producer, the broadcast partners and the stats people all have to be good. The better each one of those people is, the better broadcast we're going to have, so I've always done everything I can to help the people I work with in hopes that it will help all of us have a good night.

THERE IS A PLACE FOR MLB ON THE RADIO

There will always be a place for baseball on radio, or at least there should be. It's changed a lot with the advent of all the games on television. For example, it used to be that if the Royals were playing an afternoon game somewhere, that would be the only game available in Kansas City, so people would listen to it in the afternoon. Now, there are a lot of games on TV, and so many other things going on radio and television. Regardless of that, at least in my lifetime, baseball will be a viable game for radio.

For a lot of people baseball is a better game on radio than it is on television. I don't know that television has changed the way baseball is done on the radio, but it has changed baseball itself a lot. Guys who play the game are so much more aware of ESPN's *Sportscenter,* and highlights, than they used to be. It used to be that when a guy hit a home run, he just ran around the bases. Now, everybody has their special way of running the bases, and their own way of greeting teammates when they get back to the dugout.

At Kauffman Stadium, I've known of guys who had an at-bat, then ran down to the clubhouse to watch it on tape. Things like that never used to happen. So TV has changed the game of baseball more than it has changed the game on radio.

One of the charms of baseball on radio is that it hasn't changed very much. A lot of people still like to listen to the radio. It's more of a timeless game on the radio, in that a person can jump into his car and drive from Kansas City to Columbia, or Manhattan, or Springfield, while the ballgame is going, and he has company for the entire ride; it's something that he can latch onto. Listeners don't have to pay rigid attention to a game on radio; they can drift in and out if they want to, but like a companion, it's always there.

There will always be a place for baseball on radio, and I don't think that will ever change. You can carry the game with you, easily, on radio. That's not possible with TV.

BACK TO THE BASICS

On occasion, I used to miss being able to just go sit and watch a game. I have three children, and at times I get to watch my youngest, Joe, play football and baseball. Those are games in the purest sense. To sit and watch a game, I would much rather see kids play than see professionals. During the off-season I will go over to Kansas or Kansas State or down to Missouri and watch a basketball game. Since my schedule with the Illini isn't terribly hectic, I am able to go watch those games. I would probably like to do more of it than I do; when I do it now, it's mostly homework because I'm going to do a basketball game with one of those teams involved. But, I do want to see them play.

I *will* miss the Royals. I do think that I had the ideal job. It was life in the toy department. I came to the Royals the same year as George Brett, Frank White and Hal McRae, so, as a baseball announcer, I grew up in the time when the Royals were kings in Kansas City. Watching those guys play together was the best. They won, we laughed, went back and did it again the next day. The Royals were just a terrific family from the top to the bottom in those days. I used to refer to it as baseball's little boutique. It was just about as ideal as it could be.

As a college basketball announcer, I grew up doing Jack Hartman-coached K-State teams and it doesn't get any prettier, or any better, than that. I grew up with the rivalry, Kansas-Kansas State and the Big Eight stuff. I've flirted with the networks and done a lot of things nationally. To me it was never any better than doing Royals baseball and Big Eight basketball, which was as good as it's ever going to get and all that I ever really wanted to do. It was nice to go out and do games for ESPN and CBS, etc., but I always felt like the Royals and Kansas State were my anchors. This was where I wanted to be and I never wanted to move to New York City or do anything like that. I'm glad that I didn't.

13 The Royals from A.O. to U.L.

Over the course of the Royals history, we have seen some great players and incredible characters. Even though it would take volumes to discuss the careers of all the players in the history of the Royals, the following are our views on some of the top players to have worn Royal blue.

At the end of the chapter we offer our All-Time Royals Team. This is the dream team that we feel could have beaten the Yankees every time we played in the late 1970s, and could even consistently compete for a World Series crown today.

Willie Aikens 1980-1983

DM: Willie Aikens was a very strong player. Very slow afoot. Excellent power. But if he wasn't hitting home runs, he was more of a liability than an asset.

He was basically a very nice, very quiet and soft-spoken person. I don't think his educational background was all that great. Willie was a follower more than a leader. That's probably why he got off the beaten path in 1983 with the drug scandal, because he didn't really make good decisions personally, and he didn't pick good friends well. I think that was his big problem.

FW: Willie was an interesting player, but he just had a lot of personal problems. He had a terrific World Series in 1980, hitting four home runs. He was a big, well-meaning guy who never wanted to hurt anybody. He just couldn't get his personal life together. As a player he was one-dimensional with power.

Kevin Appier 1989-1998*

DM: Kevin has really good natural, nasty stuff. He has a very unusual pitching motion, but most of the coaches who worked with him felt that his mechanics were fairly sound. Personally I never felt that his mechanics were that good in certain areas; certain parts were not in sync. He can be unhittable at times. He is a good competitor, maybe to the point where he is too hard on himself. Kevin tries to make every pitch perfect, to strike out everybody, rather than letting his defense help him out from time to time.

FW: Kevin Appier is unorthodox with a terrific arm. He either has not achieved what he should have, or expectations were too high. A lot of people have viewed him as a dominant pitcher, but the victory totals have never added up. There's a question mark surrounding him now as to whether he'll be able to bounce back from shoulder surgery.

Steve "Bye Bye" Balboni 1984-1988

DM: Steve Balboni was one of the nicest players the Royals have ever had. Great personality, but very quiet until you got to know him. Once you were comfortable with him you could have great conversations. He was probably the card player leader on the team in the mid-80s. Guys would get to the clubhouse at 1:00 in the afternoon for a 7:30 game, just so they could play cards, which is something I never understood because I don't play cards. I guess, in a sense, it kind of bonded the team. He was a very popular player, a very nice guy.

FW: When the Royals got Steve Balboni, manager Dick Howser said he was going to give him 500 at-bats and see what happens. He hit 36 home runs that year, 1985, and the Royals won the World Series. In the seventh game of that Series he got a huge hit, a bases loaded single that drove in two runs and took it from a 3-0 to a 5-0 ballgame. That hit really opened things up for the Royals in the game and in that inning.

He was a better defensive player than people gave him credit for being. He did a very unusual thing during the 1985 season. That year he was having trouble throwing the ball to second base when a runner was going on a ground ball, then all of a sudden he cured that himself and became a pretty good thrower. To the other players, he was one of the focal points on that team.

He was one of the most popular players on the team. The other guys loved him. A big, tough guy. The trainers told me that Balboni may have been the toughest player they had ever been around from the standpoint of being able to withstand pain and just keep going. He just went out and did his job. Even today, when the players take their annual fall golf trip, he's a very big part of it.

Buddy Biancalana 1982-1987

DM: Buddy was a very solid shortstop. (The Royals could use him now.) He was a switch-hitter who learned to be a better offensive player. He could run fairly well, had a good throwing arm, excellent defensive skills. He had his 15 minutes of fame from the 1985 World Series, including *The David Letterman Show.*

He was kind of the opposite of Balboni in personality, because he was very outgoing. He had a wonderful World Series in 1985, which is really what got him his moment of glory.

FW: Buddy Biancalana outplayed Ozzie Smith in the 1985 World Series. He was a key guy in that Series. During the playoffs he had a big double in the gap in right-center field that drove in a couple of runs in Toronto. He played very well throughout the postseason that year.

It was interesting in 1985 because Angel Salazar had been playing shortstop, and I remember that when Dick Howser put Buddy in during the season the ballclub seemed to get more life and more bounce. Obviously if you win a World Series, your shortstop is a key guy for you, and Buddy was.

George Brett 1973-1993 Royals Hall of Fame

DM: George worked so hard with Charley Lau to make himself a good hitter and get the most out of his ability. Mentally as tough as anybody I've ever known in baseball and because of that, he was so good in the clutch and in pressure situations.

Always a kick to be around off the field in whatever you did. He likes hockey and he asked me if he could come work out with me and some friends one winter. He'd come out and do that. He'd try anything. He's just a fun guy. It seems like there's nothing he's ever done that wasn't fun for him.

FW: George is the all-time player. I really think that if you took a vote of guys who played with George, on who was the best teammate they ever had, George would win easily. Clubhouse boys say that George Brett was the best tipper ever in the history of the club. George took care of so many people in so many ways.

He's obviously the best player the Royals have ever had. An obvious Hall-of-Famer, who played the game to the hilt. I don't think George Brett ever stepped on the baseball field and walked off without knowing that he had given it his best shot that night.

George would do anything to win a ballgame, paid the price so many times with his body that — in looking back through the days, how many big plays did he make for this team? The spotlight seemed to find him and he always seemed to respond. I think George Brett has fun everyday.

Ken Brett 1980-1981

DM: Ken, like his younger brother, was a good guy who was fun to be around. Even though he was a pitcher, he was also a great hitter. One time as an opponent during spring training, he hit a home run against the Royals in Fort Myers, Florida. As he was rounding the bases, he started taunting George. Spring training games are usually pretty dry, but that was funny. It was kind of neat having brothers play on the same team.

Steve Busby 1972-1976, 1978-1980 Royals Hall of Fame

DM: You can't help but wonder what Steve Busby would have accomplished had he not hurt his arm. He was a fierce competitor, a pretty dominant pitcher, really. Hard nosed. He would go after the other team. He competed hard. He threw two no-hitters early in his career, one in 1973 and the other in 1974.

Away from the field, the first time I ever played golf was with him. He is a good golfer, and took me out with him one time, and he sort of taught me some of the rudiments. He was a fun, likable guy.

FW: Steve Busby was the Royals' Tom Seaver. I think Buzz might have been the first Royals pitcher who went to the mound and made the guys think we're better than the opponents are today. It was a shame that he got hurt when he did. He would have had a Hall-of-Fame career if he had stayed healthy, I'm sure of that.

He was a very forceful personality, who walked out there with an attitude. The Royals were getting better and they had the guys to win. Paul Splittorff was a winner but Buzz was the one who came in, and made people think he could win any game. I always liken him to a Tom Seaver and what Seaver meant to the Mets when he came along. Busby meant that much to the Royals. He still is extremely competitive and always will be; the good ones are.

David Cone 1986, 1993-1994

DM: David had a good personality, and was very cooperative. We could kind of sense the pressure of his pitching in his hometown early in his career, but we always saw the potential there of a really good pitcher. I think it would've been neat if he could've played his whole career in Kansas City. I'm sure he does too, but the economics of baseball do not allow things like that to happen much anymore.

FW: David Cone is an impressive and very intelligent guy. He is a throwback to the old days in baseball, a guy who loves to sit around after the game and talk about that day's game and how he can improve. He cares a great deal about the game, his family, and the people he grew up with.

David Cone, to me, is just a real factor in baseball. Besides his great ability as a pitcher, he is a guy who has his head totally in the game all the time. He is a terrific guy to have on a team, very much a leader. It's a shame he couldn't have spent his entire career in Kansas City. He came up through the Royals system, left, came back, and left again. For some reason, I like to think that he would have been a lifetime Royal, even though he didn't spend that many years here.

When he was here, he treated people very well and seemed to have a great sense of the responsibilities he had to the game.

Al Cowens 1974-1979

DM: Al Cowens was very quiet. He was also very underrated because he wasn't an out-going personality. He was the best throwing outfielder we've ever had. As a baserunner he was very good, with great instincts for the game. In his own very quiet way, he just played the game well. I have compared him, in a sense, to former Oakland A's outfielder Joe Rudi, who was underrated because of all the "stars" the A's had. Cowens was somewhat like that for the Royals because he was quiet and didn't do things in a spectacular way.

Some guys make easy plays look great, but Al made great plays look easy, so he didn't get a lot of the ink and a lot of the publicity. He didn't want that. He was very happy to let all the other guys get the ink and the publicity. He just wanted to go out and play his game, which he did and did very effectively.

FW: Al Cowens, a terrific right fielder, is one of the most underrated players in the history of the Royals. He was raised in a tough section of Los Angeles, and had been shot in the stomach when he was a kid. He was very quiet, very unassuming.

Cowens probably had the best throwing arm that the Royals have had in the outfield, in regards to strength and accuracy. He was an excellent defensive player. He could run, and he turned himself into a solid hitter. Cowens finished third in the MVP voting in 1977. He had not been a starter, but when Whitey Herzog got here in 1975 he made Cowens and Frank White starters the next year. Those are probably two moves that got the Royals on the fast track and really got them going. I'm sure Al Cowens is the best right fielder we've ever had.

Bruce Dal Canton 1971-1975

DM: Bruce Dal Canton is one of the nicest men that you'll ever meet, really a quality guy. He had the broadest shoulders of anyone I've ever seen. He fussed with the knuckleball and had a good one. He was a pro's pro. He had a great attitude, great habits, and didn't mind helping the younger guys. Bruce was the epitome of what you would want out of a professional baseball player. He didn't have great ability, but he did everything well. He was a teacher in the offseason.

FW: Bruce Dal Canton devised a knuckle ball during the middle of his career. He didn't get a lot of breaks in his career. During one stretch, he went 30 days without getting in a ballgame. I remember interviewing him on a pregame show in Baltimore and he said, "I would like the fans out there listening to know that I really do want to pitch."

He became a coach after he got out of the game. He was another guy who was liked by all the other players; he never had an enemy. Bruce may have been a little short on ability, but he did everything he could to keep himself in the game, including coming up with the knuckleball. Bruce was one of the veterans on the ballclub when I first started, and he was always nice to me and made me feel better about everything.

Johnny Damon 1995-1998*

DM: He improved a lot in 1998, and really came along as a player. I said two years ago that in 1999 he would be an 18 to 25 home run hitter per season, while other people at that time were saying that he would never hit more than 12. He hit 18 in 1998. His only detriment, really, is his arm. He's learning the game little-by-little. Now he's a better bunter, a better base runner, a better base stealer, he hits for average better, he throws better; he did everything better in 1998 than he did in 1997. He's not improving in one quantum leap, but he is improving by increments.

One of the big mistakes people made was putting him in the category with George Brett, saying he was going to be our next superstar. It's like saying, "OK, here you are Johnny, we know you haven't played AAA baseball, but now you're our star." Then all of a sudden all of those great players we had are gone, and he doesn't have any protection in the lineup. When Brett was the star, the spotlight shone on him, with shadows on everybody else, and that allowed everybody else to quietly, efficiently do their own thing.

All of a sudden here's Johnny Damon, a guy who played double-A, 20 years old, and we're telling him that he's our star. He was having trouble even finding the ballpark at that point in time. That's totally unfair. Compound that with the fact that there were no hitters in front of him or behind him in the lineup to protect him. Whew! That was grossly unfair and ridiculous. I think that hurt him a little bit as a player.

I doubt he'll ever be a "superstar," but he may be a "star." He could be a very solid big league player. He just has to keep improving. If he improves over the next two or three years as much as he did last year, I think we could probably say he's one of the star players.

Johnny is very good with kids and fans. He is outgoing but not the way that some people are. This might sound funny, but he's both quiet and outgoing. He's very friendly and has a great smile.

FW: Johnny Damon was a victim of other people's expectations. He is a super kid. He is genuinely as polite and as nice as anybody. It was very tough for him when he got tagged as the next George Brett. Those are unreal expectations. Ken Brett once said that "there's nothing as damning as unlimited potential." He said that because he was a 19-year-old kid in the big leagues who everyone thought had unlimited potential, and everybody expected more out of him than he was able to give.

On the other hand with Johnny, when you watch his career, he's such a tough-minded kid. He played in every game last year, and he's getting better. His numbers have been better each year. So Johnny is a kid who has been able to fight through other people's expectations, work hard, keep his head up, and keep improving himself. I've never seen him be cross, or surly, or anything other than a nice kid who works very hard at his craft. He is going to be a very viable big league player.

Al Fitzmorris 1969-1976

DM: Fitzy was a switch-hitter and he was the first Royal to get a hit from both sides of the plate. That is one of the great trivia questions in Royals history...who was the first Royal switch-hitter to get a hit from both sides of the plate in the same game? Pitcher Al Fitzmorris.

He was a sinker-ball pitcher who threw a lot of ground balls. He was a very solid starting pitcher. He was a fun guy to be around and go out with, as a player, at night, when we were all doing that kind of stuff. He has been on the scene ever since as a player and now a broadcaster, doing pregame and postgame commentary on the radio. He is really a good guy and a good friend. I like Fitzy.

FW: Fitzy was a great sinker-ball pitcher who had a much better career than people give him credit for. If you look through the Royals media guide, Fitzy is in the top 10 in several career categories, including victories, ERA, and shutouts. He was a good, solid pitcher who would take the ball and do his job. As a player he was very valuable.

Off the field he has a great sense of humor, a very dry sense of humor. If you listen to him on *Royals Line*, that sense of humor really comes through sometimes. Fitzy was one of those guys who always seemed to be at the center of all the fun.

Mark Gubicza 1984-1996

DM: Mark Gubicza was a great pitcher with a good sinker and hard slider that was nasty for right-handed batters. Mark was also a very hard worker. Again, like Bruce Dal Canton, Mark was the kind of guy who, if you're a manager or a general manager, you wished all of your players had the same work ethic and approach to the game. He really had a good career and he deserved it, because you like for nice people to have good things happen to them.

As I began to drift away from the players because of the age difference, a few of the players kind of bridged the gap, and Mark was one of them. Gubie and I always got along. We would do a thing each year before the NHL playoffs where we each picked three teams and had a little $5 bet to see who's team won the Stanley Cup. He is very much a hockey fan, and since he grew up in Philadelphia, he's really a big Flyers fan. Despite that, he is a great guy.

FW: Gubie was a terrific athlete, and probably could've played about any sport he wanted to. He had a great arm and was very durable until the end of his career when he got hurt and could never get it back physically. He is a fierce competitor. He and Bret Saberhagen came up together in 1984, and they were both very competitive. Gubicza was right up there as one of the all-time best defensive pitchers the Royals have had.

He was a guy who you didn't mind seeing take the ball in a big game. You knew he was going to give you all that he had that day. Usually what he had was pretty good.

He was very quiet and unassuming. He had a great sense of humor. He would sit in the clubhouse and launch barbs at guys with a great way of sticking the needle in people. If someone's ego started to get a little big, he had a great way of bringing them down. He was a terrific guy in the clubhouse.

One guy he liked to wear out was Kevin Appier; he talked to Kevin all the time. He had a great way of looking at somebody and finding something funny about what they were doing, and letting them know it. But when he got on you, he did it in such a way that you didn't resent it. He was just having fun.

Larry Gura 1976-1985 Royals Hall of Fame

DM: Gura was kind of a surprise; nobody knew much about him. He was a very hard worker. He worked on his defense, he worked on his move to first. He had a little fast ball, a little breaking ball, a little changeup, turnover changeup. He was really a pitcher. He had great idea of setting up hitters and had a good feel for pitching. He was not overpowering — really a good guy off the field. I enjoyed spending time with him. He was very quiet, not an outgoing guy, but really a nice person.

FW: Larry Gura was probably the greatest trade in Royals history and there's an interesting story behind that trade. The Royals were going to trade Fran Healy for Ron Guidry, and at the last minute, Clyde King, who was a scout with the Yankees, said don't trade Guidry, he's going to be a terrific major league pitcher. So the Yankees came back to the Royals and asked if they would take Larry Gura. The Royals made the trade. Larry Gura turned out to be a rock solid heart of the Royals rotation for so long.

He won the game in Oakland that clinched a tie in 1976, the first time the Royals ever won it. Larry Gura was one of the first health conscious guys who played the game. He was into concoctions like wheat germ and honey and things like that. He swam a lot. Very health conscious, very quiet, but again very competitive. He'd get a sly little smile on his face and say something to you once in a while. Larry Gura brought an element of style to this ballclub that really solidified the pitching rotation and is part of the best, or one of the best, trades the Royals have ever made.

Al Hrabosky 1978-1979

DM: Al Hrabosky was a character. His off the field persona was very different than his on the field persona. He does the St. Louis Cardinal games on TV now.

FW:"The Mad Hungarian" was colorful. Hrabosky invented "The Mad Hungarian" and that alter-ego was very good to him. There was a lot of flash there, that's for sure. In fact, there was probably a little more sizzle than steak when he got here, but he put people in the ballpark, and people got excited when he came in the game. He was really fun to watch.

He is a great guy. In fact, he has called and offered to play in our Royals for Rainbows golf tournament that we have at the end of every season.

Bo Jackson 1986-1990

DM: Bo was different. He had great physical skills although he never really learned how to play baseball like he could have. Once you got to know him, he was a nice guy. Strange personality. Kind of moody at times. Fast, a great runner. Even though he may have been too muscle-bound, his career was too short for that to ever really come into play.

FW: Bo Jackson had to be the greatest athlete I've ever seen; he could do incredible things. It's a shame that he didn't have a work ethic to go with his ability because he could have been a Hall-of-Fame baseball player. Bo didn't work at the game, he literally played ball. Bo would get to the park later than the other guys, put his uniform on, play the game, take his uniform off, and go home or go do whatever he was going to do. He loves his family. He loves the outdoors, including fishing and hunting.

The first home run he ever hit in Kauffman Stadium was unforgettable. It was the longest one that has ever been hit there. The video board that is beyond the left-center field wall, was not there at the time. Bo hit a home run about 10 feet below the light standard to the left of the main scoreboard, up on top of the hill where the video board is now. That was the first home run he ever hit in the major leagues. I thought that we had really seen something special there.

He made a throw one time from left field in Seattle that was incredible. He basically picked up the ball in the left field corner, wheeled and fired, and threw a strike to home plate to get Harold Reynolds. That is one of the most incredible things I've ever seen. He could do things that no other human being could do.

Danny Jackson 1983-1987

DM: Danny Jackson was very workman-like, both personality-wise and pitching-wise. He was kind of a workhorse, kind of like Dennis Leonard in that regard. Every fourth or fifth day he would take the ball and give the Royals solid innings. He had really good stuff. As a left-hander, his ball really moved all over the plate. He had a very live arm and was difficult to hit. In his quiet way, he was a very effective pitcher. I compare his demeanor to that of Al Cowens; he just went out and did his job without the glamour and hoopla. He was pretty consistent every time he went out to the mound.

FW: Danny Jackson was a guy who came up with the Royals and they expected him to be a star. He had a lot of ability and turned it on for the Royals when it counted. During the 1985 season he was a huge part of the club as we came down the stretch and into postseason play. He pitched a couple of the greatest games that have ever been pitched here in the drive to the World Series championship. He was a very vital cog on that 1985 team.

Charlie Leibrandt 1984-1989

DM: Leibrandt was what we would call a craftsman as a pitcher. He had a good idea of how to pitch and what he wanted to do. He had a real good sense of what his stuff was and what he could do with it; he didn't try to be the type of pitcher that he wasn't. Charlie was an intelligent pitcher, so he had a great sense of what he was. His style was to pitch inside, and he did that very effectively. Charlie is a nice guy, a gentleman.

FW: Charlie was a better pitcher than he appeared to be. He didn't throw hard, but he probably broke as many bats as any Royals pitcher ever, with a terrific way of getting inside on right-handed hitters. One of the Royals best pick-ups when they got him from the Reds in 1983 for Bob Tufts.

Dennis Leonard 1974-1986 Royals Hall of Fame

DM: Dennis Leonard was a workhorse, chewed up a lot of innings, got a lot of wins. Always a slow starter, then much better from the first of June on. He was hard to beat, finished a lot of games, finished a lot of innings.

Real quiet away from the field. He was with his family a lot. We didn't see a lot of him off the field. We'd have a couple of beers with him and he'd get a little louder and open up a little more. Really a good guy, nice guy. I see him on occasion; he's still around Kansas City.

FW: If the Royals wanted a win, they just gave Dennis Leonard the ball. Dennis was not only talented but he was a ferocious competitor. In 1977 he had 21 complete games. In 1978, he had 20 complete games. The 21 games is something that probably won't be done again, the way the game is structured today. If Dennis Leonard were a football player, you would say when he smelled the goal line it was over. Dennis Leonard would get a game to the seventh inning and it seemed like he had an extra fuel tank strapped on, because he could close the game like nobody else we have ever had.

He pitched the most memorable game, in Detroit when Mark Fydrich was a rookie sensation. He beat Fydrich 2-1 or 1-0 before a packed house up there. You could tell from the way he came out in the first inning that he was thinking, "All right, you've got the Bird (Fydrich), you've got 50-some thousand people, but by God, we are going to beat you." And he did. He was as ferociously competitive and as good as anybody I have ever seen.

Dennis didn't care about things like the politics of the club, but he loved his kids, loved to hunt and fish, and now he loves to coach kids baseball and things like that. Just a great human being. He was probably the most dependable pitcher the Royals have ever had.

Mark Littell 1973, 1975-1977

DM: Mark Littell had the nickname of "country" because he was somewhat naive, and young. When he first came up he was a country-bumpkin-type of player, but he was very smart. Even though he was a little different in his own way, he was a very nice guy, and took the nickname good-naturedly. He was the closest thing we had to a stopper in 1976. He was the one who gave up the home run to Chris Chambliss in the ALCS in 1976, but that was the only one he gave up that year. He threw well as a fastball, hard curveball pitcher. He could be a little erratic at times, in regard to control. He was well-liked by his teammates.

FW: Mark Littell went through the entire 1976 season without giving up a home run, until the one to Chris Chambliss in the 9th inning of the fifth game of the playoffs. It happened after a long delay. The Yankee fans had been throwing stuff onto the field and there was a delay of at least 10 minutes.

He had a great arm, and was kind of a country boy.

Mike Macfarlane 1987-1994, 1996-1997

DM: Macfarlane was a spark plug-type of player. He was a nice guy, very friendly to everybody. Optimistic. Hard-worker. When Mac was getting started, Bob Boone helped him a great deal, and Mac never forgot that. Then, when he was in a position to do so, he helped some of the younger guys when they came up to the Royals, and returned the favor. That's the type of guy he was. Even with guys who were competing against him for the job, he was free with advice and always willing to help out. That says a lot about Mike. He was a great person to have in the clubhouse.

FW: Mike is tough, really, really tough. Mac played hurt at times when he probably shouldn't have, but felt an obligation to be in the lineup and do the best he could. He fought hard to get to the big leagues and fought hard to stay there. He is probably as tough a player as the Royals have ever had. He is also very competitive.

Buck Martinez 1969-1971, 1973-1977

DM: Buck was involved in one of the fiercest collisions ever, with Bob Allison of the Minnesota Twins around 1970. It was an unbelievable collision in one of his first big league games. Everybody thought he was dead when Allison ran over him at the plate, but he hung in there and gave people an early insight into his make-up. When he got up and bounced back at it, I couldn't help but think, "Hmmm, this guy is going to be a player."

FW: Buck got as much out of himself as any player I ever saw. He was very intelligent, and a complete team player. He was the kind of guy you would want on your side in anything.

John Mayberry 1972-1977 Royals Hall of Fame

DM: John Mayberry is one of the funniest people I've ever met. A great first baseman. He had the softest hands; he saved so many errors from Brett and Patek and even from some of the second basemen. John was the Royals first bona fide power hitter and easily one of the nicest people I've ever known.

FW: Big John. The team personality. The guy everybody looked to on the team to hit the long ball and say the right thing. A guy who was a big-time needler. John, back in the days when buses had a bench seat in the back, would sit in the middle of the bench seat and was on everybody more than anyone else. Funny, needle, get on you, and had a big booming laugh, a great personality.

When John got in the batter's box, he was a menace to the other team and they knew it. He was a force in every game he ever played in. At one time, more than anyone in the Royals lineup, he was the guy the other dugout feared. They would figure that they needed to get out of the inning before he came up to the plate. John put his own stamp on everything.

Brian McRae 1990-1994

DM: Brian had a good, solid work ethic which obviously came from his dad, Hal. Brian worked hard to improve. He was fearless defensively; he covered a lot of ground and challenged the walls numerous times. A good contact switch-hitter who hustled a lot. Good with the media. He usually had a good outlook on things.

He had been in Kauffman Stadium since he was two- or three-years-old, along with Paul Splittorff's kid and John Wathan's kids. All of the kids would come out there, so it was a great advantage for them. They weren't in awe of the major league scene, because they had been around it since their earliest memories. Who knows...there may have been all the pressure of the world on him, but he just never let on about it.

FW: Brian McRae found himself after the Royals changed his position. He was an infielder in the minor leagues for four or five years, but it wasn't working, so they put him in centerfield. He immediately blossomed. Then he established himself as a big league outfielder, and a good player.

I think there was some additional pressure on him because he was Hal's son. He would probably say there wasn't, but I think there was. He was an interesting kid. From the time he was very little, he was on the field with his dad at the stadium. Early on he hit you with his ability to go out and catch a ball. He couldn't have been more than 10 years old at the time. All the kids were out there running around, but he stood out.

Hal McRae 1973-1987 Royals Hall of Fame

DM: Hal really had hitting problems when he came from the National League to the American League. It took him four or five months to adjust to the new league. Once he and Charley Lau went to work, Mac just shot the lights out. He brought a lot of aggressiveness from the National League to the Royals. He gave the team that spark and I think he lit a fire under Brett. Just unbelievably aggressive on the bases, stretched singles into doubles and doubles into triples, aggressive in all aspects of the game. Off the field, very quiet and introspective, smart. As I said, I liked to talk hitting with Mac and Lau more than anybody, which started when Hal was still a player.

FW: Hal was tough, good, and had a terrific appreciation of what guys have to do to play this game well. When Mac first came here from the National League, he was really struggling, to the point where he tried to tear his uniform top off one night in Texas in the dugout. That was when he went to Charley Lau and said, "I need help. Let's go to work." No one could outwork him, or out-hustle him. He'd fight at the drop of the hat if he thought it would help win a ballgame. I'm sure that the guys on the other teams hated him and everybody on our team loved him because of how hard he played the game. He played with a ferocity and dedication that was really something to behold.

He did an incredible thing. He led a very good baseball team from the DH spot and I would tell you that that's impossible to do. Mac was a guy whom everybody else on the team looked up to because of his toughness and his ability to fight a pitcher and get a hit. When he got on base he would do anything to win a ballgame. His teammates thought he was going to put his body and his mind on the line for his team, and he did every night.

Steve Mingori 1973-1979

DM: Steve Mingori is one of my favorite guys of all-time. He is a good friend. He is not imposing physically, but he had great stuff. As a left-hander, he had incredible movement on his pitches. He didn't overpower anybody, but he had a really good screwball with really good control. He was an excellent competitor, and a very effective pitcher.

I don't remember the exact circumstances, but one of my favorite stories came from a time when Whitey had run out of starters, and he had to start Mingo. Well, Mingo had always been a relief pitcher, so he had never been on the mound when the game started. When they played the National Anthem, Mingo was facing the wrong way.

He is one of the funniest guys the Royals have ever had on the team. At one time there were so many guys on the team who were funny...guys like Mingo, Marty Pattin and Doug Bird. It was a great collection of guys who fed off each other in regards to humor. Mingo was right at the top. Someone could fire a zinger at him and boy, he would come right back at them so quickly that they didn't have time to even think about another one. He was good. Then again, he liked to get in the middle of it and mix it up with the guys.

FW: Steve Mingori is another guy who got a ton out of his ability. The thing I remember most about him is a game when he started instead of pitching in relief. Whitey Herzog started Mingori in a game against the Yankees because he was out of pitching, and needed three or four innings out of him. Well, Mingo went seven innings and the Royals won the game. Steve was valuable in a lot of different roles, in a lot of different ways.

Jeff Montgomery 1988-1998*

DM: Jeff is one of the best relief pitchers in Royals history. He worked hard to get where he is. He's another one of those players who's size was against him somewhat, and a lot of scouts looked at him and thought that a right-handed pitcher with his size would never amount to much. He worked hard on four pitches and made it. It was unusual for a relief pitcher, a closer, to have four big league quality pitches. The top closers throughout the years have been two pitch pitchers, and in rare cases, one pitch pitchers like Doug Jones, who threw a changeup, off a changeup, off a changeup. Monty was an excellent closer with four pitches, and that was pretty unusual.

Jeff is an all-around good guy. He is good in the community, good in the clubhouse, always friendly, and analytical. If we ask a good question of Monty, we'll get a good answer, which isn't always the case with some players.

FW: Monty is a guy who had to battle to get the job as the team's closer, and battle to keep it. After he finally won the job, the front office people and managers kept throwing challenges at him. They brought in several other guys who they wanted to try out as closers, like Mark Davis, but Monty kept winning the job back. Finally they decided that he was the best of all of them, and he won the job permanently.

Bob Oliver 1969-1972

DM: Bob Oliver was a big guy who was the Royals first true power threat, and runs batted in guy. He was a versatile player who could play a lot of different positions. He was very helpful, very friendly, very outgoing. Bob still holds the Royals record, along with Kevin Seitzer, with six hits in one game. That happened on Sunday afternoon, May 4, 1969, in California against the Angels. He was a super nice guy, a great player for us.

In January of 1969 he and I were among the people on the first Royals caravan, before the team had ever played a game, so I got to know him pretty well then. I always liked him. Last I heard, he was a policeman in California. Last time I talked to him at length was at the 25th anniversary reunion a few years ago.

Amos Otis 1970-1983 Royals Hall of Fame

DM: One of the things that sticks out to me about Amos Otis is his big sweeping swing. He had great ability in most categories. He was a great base runner and a great defensive player. Pretty good arm. Not to mention the fact that the glove he used had a hole in the palm.

Off the field he and I got along great. He was a different guy — a lot of people didn't know him or took him wrong. I was one of the few people he would do an interview with. People would ask me, "Can you get Amos to do an interview for me?" "No, I'm sorry I can't." "Well, he did one with you." "Well, I'm sorry, yeah he did, but I've know him two or three years."

FW: Amos was mysterious, fun, always up to something. He had a twinkle in his eye. Amos lived like he played. He always had a little something in reserve for you, could get on your case and laugh when he did it. I don't think Amos wanted people to know everything there was to know about him. He let people in as much as he wanted them in, but he was still a fun guy to hang around. A fun guy to have a little verbal joust with, a needler. Off the field, like he was on the field, smooth, stylish, classic and a little mysterious.

Probably the smoothest player I have ever seen. He and Jim Eisenreich were the two smoothest fielders I've ever seen going after a ball. I always thought Amos was a better all-around player than he ever got credit for being. A clutch performer.

One of the great memories I have of him is when the Royals first won the Western Division in 1976. He had been hit in the head by Stan Bahnsen at a game in Kansas City a couple weeks before the end of the season. In the game that clinched a tie for the division title in Oakland, Amos hit a home run off Bahnsen. I remember getting on the bus after the game when Amos got on, and the guys were all chatting A-O, A-O.

He was just a very stylish guy who got it done in the clutch. There had to be a lot of Royals pitchers who were really glad he was in the outfield. When the team needed a big play in the ballgame, we felt pretty good when Amos Otis was up there.

Freddie Patek 1971-1979 Royals Hall of Fame

DM: Freddie solidified that all important position at shortstop and gave the Royals not only a great shortstop but a terrific offensive player. As lead off man who could steal bases, he gave the Royals that element of speed they really needed. In 1976 he stole 51 bases, then he came back in 1977 and stole 53. He gave the Royals such a solid, solid player at short. He had pretty good range, a great arm and was fun to watch. He and Cookie Rojas did their little magic tricks around second base and were just a great combination for those early teams.

FW: Good little guy (5-foot-4). He was probably one of the first guys the fans fell in love with, and brought people to the ballpark. They loved to see him play. A little guy who played like a giant sometimes. Fred was a good player. He could do a lot of things that he probably didn't get credit for on the field. He had some range, a strong arm, could play the game on offense, could steal a base for you, could do a lot of things.

Here again, he was one of those early guys, when the Royals became a good team, one of the really important cogs. Looking at a guy of Fred Patek's size, a guy who fought his way to the major leagues, played on championship teams, and was an intricate part of those teams, we have to say he's got something special inside him. Patek obviously did have that something.

Marty Pattin 1974-1980

DM: Marty Pattin and I played baseball against each other through high school, college, summer college league, and American Legion ball. I would bet I had probably 50-60 at-bats against Marty Pattin when we were both amateur players. We've known each other since we were sophomores in high school.

Marty was a high fastball, right over the top, pitcher, with a good curve. He got a lot of strikeouts. Batters had to lay off the high fastball if they wanted to do anything against him at all. His game face was always firmly attached.

Marty was just a fun-loving, hard working (sometimes those two don't go together) guy whom everybody loved. His Donald Duck imitation is unmatched, the best ever. He is a good, good guy; a friend of mine since childhood. I was always a big Marty fan and supporter, and I still am. We still see each other quite a bit during the summer and sometimes in the off-season. He is one of my all-time favorites.

FW: Marty was a bulldog. Royals managers could pitch him any way they needed him, whether it meant starting him, using him in long relief or in short relief. They could use him to close. He could also do something very unusual. He went through two or three rain delays during a game in Minnesota one night, and kept coming back and pitching. He was a guy who wouldn't give in; he battled through any spot he was put in. He usually won those battles.

Lou Piniella 1969-1973

DM: Lou was the Royals first star. He was a late spring training acquisition in the first season. On April 1, 1969, the Royals traded Steve Whitaker and John Gelnar to the Seattle Pilots for Piniella. Lou had never really been given an opportunity to play as a full-time big leaguer until he joined the Royals. He made the most of it. He was in his mid-20's when he started playing in Kansas City, but he was the American League Rookie of the Year in 1969.

He was a good solid hitter; it was fun to watch him hit. He had a good idea of hitting and how to go about it. Lou was a much better defensive player than people gave him credit for. I don't ever recall Lou Piniella dropping a ball. He wasn't blessed with great speed, so there were balls that he couldn't get to, but boy, he never missed a ball. He was really a decent outfielder. A lot of times he might be thinking about his hitting while he was in the outfield. He was not, contrary to some beliefs, a liability defensively.

If someone would have said that Lou Piniella would be a successful big league manager some day, I don't think a lot of people would have believed that. Sure enough, he has been successful with the Seattle Mariners. Of all the surprises in Lou's baseball career, that would probably be the biggest. He was just so funny. We could start telling Lou Piniella stories and go until Christmas.

Tom Poquette 1973, 1976-1979, 1982

DM: Tom Poquette platooned in the outfield with Jim Wohlford when Whitey Herzog was managing. Tom and Jim were a great complement to each other. Pokie played more than Wohlford did because he was a left-handed hitter, and he was a very solid player. He wasn't gifted with great baseball skills, but he really worked hard and made the most out of what he had. While he was playing he made future plans to manage or coach. He has done those things, and done them very well. He and Wohlford really thrived in Whitey's platoon system, as they both hit close to .300. It worked out very well.

FW: Tom was a tough player, a hustler. He was very good against right-handed pitching. A game that will always stand out about Tom is when he hit the wall face first at Royals Stadium, before the padding was put on the wall. Kevin Bell of the White Sox hit a line drive down the left field line with the bases loaded and Pokie took the wall face first, and immediately we knew he was hurt. He was out like a light. Bell's hit went for an inside-the-park home run. Tom had fractured his cheek bone. When that happened, the Royals decided they needed to pad the wall.

Darrell Porter 1977-1980

DM: Darrell came to the Royals from Milwaukee before the 1977 season, for Jamie Quirk and Wohlford. He gave the Royals a really solid guy behind the plate, offensively and defensively. He was a fearless guy. A good competitor, always driving to win the game. He played hard. He was a big factor in the early championship years for the Royals. Anytime a team has a catcher who can put up the kind of offensive numbers that Darrell did, especially as a left-handed hitter, they've really got something working.

Look at the years the Royals had when Porter was catching, and you'll see how effective he was. Whitey thought enough of Darrell to later get him in St. Louis, and they won a couple more times there. I tend to think that that speaks highly of Darrell's skills and his efforts.

FW: Darrell Porter controlled the running game for the Royals. He filled a big need at the time. The team needed a front-line catcher when they got him from Milwaukee in a deal that sent Jamie Quirk to the Brewers. Darrell immediately proved that the Royals had a big league catcher behind the plate. He was a big reason they reached the playoffs all those years.

Jamie Quirk 1975-1976, 1978-1982, 1985-1988

DM: Jamie was a player who was torn between college football and pro baseball. He chose pro baseball over a chance to go and be a college quarterback at some of the nation's bigger schools. He was a shortstop when he signed with the Royals, but he ended up playing everywhere and never really had a position to call his own. In fact, his big league career was extended when Whitey asked him to go to the instructional leagues to learn how to catch, which he did. It's funny that he never really had a position as a big leaguer, yet there weren't many positions that he couldn't play.

Some might say that Jamie wasn't that good, so managers didn't have a position for him. I say that he was good enough to play them all. Who knows what that says, but that was Jamie. Offensively he had a great mind and a great feel for the game. He knew how to do all of the things to help a team win. Jamie just carved out a terrific big league career for himself, then went on to be a coach, and now he is wanting to manage on the big league level. He is also a close friend of Brett's.

After the 1974 season, Jamie, George, and I did a trip to Hawaii. It was one of those things that was promoted, "Join George Brett, Jamie Quirk and Denny Matthews on a Hawaiian tour." We took about 80 people over to Hawaii for 10 days, and had a ball, had a great time. We would do all of the touristy things on the bus, following a pretty rigid agenda they had for us during the day, then around 7:00 at night, Jamie, Denny and George would disappear and not be seen until the next morning. It was quite a deal...we had a lot of fun with that.

FW: Jamie is one of the all-time Royals. He was a number one draft choice for the Royals in 1972, drafted as a shortstop. By picking baseball, he turned down a football scholarship from Notre Dame. He battled his way to the big leagues and held on to stay. Jamie became a catcher during the middle of his career, and wound up playing 20 years in the major leagues, which is a very rare feat. It seems like Jamie got traded for everybody. If for no other reason he should go down in the history of the Royals because he got a lot of good players on our side. He was a great student of the game. He will be a major league manager one day, and he'll be a very good one.

Dan Quisenberry 1979-1988 Royals Hall of Fame

DM: Another one of my all-time favorite Royals is Dan Quisenberry. He always liked words, so we used to sit and give each other a word for the day. He would try to work his word for the day into his post game interview and I would try to work his word for the day into the broadcast. We'd sit together on the bus a lot and he had a little quirky way of looking at everything, just like I have my own little quirky way, and we would (with Jamie not around) try to out-quirk each other.

We were up in Detroit one year and I gave him the word "gelid," which means very cold or icy. Quiz got a save that night and was doing his interviews. He explained to the reporters that he had a hard time gripping the ball because of the "gelid conditions." I'm sure there were some guys trying to figure out what in the world he was talking about.

Dan got into poetry after he got out of baseball. The words; there was something about words that really captured his imagination. It was kind of interesting that we would play these word games all the years he was with the Royals. It is also somewhat humorous that no one knew we were doing that. There were so many words, we did that for years. I always felt that he probably knew more words than I did.

Sadly, we lost Quiz to cancer in 1998. The Royals family has lost one of its shining stars. On a personal level, I shall miss his wry countenance, his dry wit. We had a great relationship.

FW: Quiz probably put fans in the best comfort zone of any pitcher the Royals have ever had. No matter what the situation was, when he came into the ballgame fans had the feeling that he was going to get out of any jam the team was in. People forget that Quiz was brought in the games in the 7th and 8th innings a lot of times. He was not a one inning guy. The role hadn't evolved to the place where it is today, where guys are one inning relievers. Quiz would come into the game with the bases loaded with two guys on, boom, he'd throw his little sinker, get a ground ball, a double play, then he could go sit down.

What a sense of humor. When we were around him we had better have our brights on cause he was going to say something that would go right over our heads if we didn't. On top of that, he was a high quality, caring human being. What he did with Harvesters and what he gave to the community demonstrates that he was probably as decent a human being as ever put on the Royals uniform. A caring individual, but at the same time, he was a guy who would needle and trick people verbally.

He was a real catalyst on the club with the other guys. He would say things sometimes that other guys really didn't understand but they knew that they had just been needled. Very inventive, he probably made more good quotes than anyone who ever wore a Royals uniform. We never knew what he was going to say, but we knew it was going to be pretty good.

In 1998 he fought a hell of a battle with a brain tumor, and he fought it the way people would expect him to, with dignity and humor. He was always a very good person and he knew that. He was a very good husband, father and citizen, and I don't think there's anything in Quiz's life would have made him say, "I wish I could do that over again." There's never been a better human being to ever wear our uniform, nor a better closer. We're going to miss him.

Cookie Rojas 1970-1977 Royals Hall of Fame

DM: Like Freddie at shortstop, Cookie really solidified second base and was a crowd favorite. I don't know if it was a nickname or what it was that sparked the fans imagination about him. Cookie was a good big league player, one of those guys who could play a lot of different positions but he played mostly second base during his major league career and only second base for us. Just a real solid big league player. He gave the Royals early credibility.

FW: Cookie Rojas brought the Royals something similar to what Steve Busby brought them. He came to the team as a proven major leaguer who had been a winner and gave the Royals a very steady personality on the infield. He had a great appreciation of how to play the game, and he played it to the best of his ability. Cookie was a guy the other players looked up to and admired. He brought them a major league style when he came over from the Cardinals. When it was time for him to turn the glove over Frank White, he turned it over with dignity.

I'll never forget the night they had Cookie Rojas Night on the field. Some people probably forget that the fans in Kansas City did not want Frank White to be their second baseman; they loved Cookie, and even though Frank was a home town guy, he caught tons of flack from fans. The night they had Cookie Rojas Night was very symbolic, because he took his cap off and put it on Frank's head and in essence passed the torch in front of all the fans. From that time on, they began to accept Frank. Then to this day, people say that Frank White was easily the best second baseman the Royals have ever had. But it was a tough start for Frank because Cookie was so well respected and admired by everyone.

Bret Saberhagen 1984-1991

DM: Saberhagen came up with Mark Gubicza and Danny Jackson. He pitched remarkably beyond his years. He was an outstanding competitor with super confidence. His confidence carried over to help Gubicza and Jackson, then it carried over to the veterans of the staff, because the team knew they were going to get eight or nine solid innings every time he went to the mound. The defense loved him because he threw strikes and pitched quickly, so good plays were made behind him. He was a phenom in his own way. He obviously had great stuff, but his control is what was remarkable for his age.

Sabes had a very good idea of how to pitch. Some guys get out there and they're very mechanical, even if they have good stuff, and they can't put it together mentally. Saberhagen had the good stuff and he could put it together mentally.

FW: Wow! Bret Saberhagen and Dennis Leonard are probably the two best pitchers the Royals have ever had. Bret came to the big leagues at the age of 19 and immediately fit. He came to the big leagues with a great fastball, a great curveball, and a very good changeup, plus outstanding control.

He and Gubicza came up at the same time. They were probably a gamble because they both came from Double-A and started the season with the big league club. But they came up and immediately proved to everyone that they belonged here.

Paul Schaal 1969-1974

DM: Paul Schaal was Brett's predecessor at third base. He came to the Royals from the Angels. The year before he joined us in the expansion draft he had been hit in the ear by a pitch (this was before they had ear flaps on the helmets). From that point on, his balance was impaired, and so sometimes on pop-ups when he would have to look straight up, he'd get a little bit disoriented, and a little dizzy.

He and Freddie Patek had a deal where, on a pop-up, even in foul territory off third base, Freddie would come all the way over and run Schaal off the play if he could get there in time.

But, Paul was really a solid player for the Royals. He was very smooth defensively, with a good arm. He was not a big home run or RBI guy, but he was a good, solid hitter who could make contact. He was a solid third baseman until George came along. Paul is now a chiropractor in Kansas City, and has been for a number of years.

Kevin Seitzer 1986-1991

DM: George's successor at third was Kevin Seitzer, who was a really good hitter. He was one of those guys who was easily overlooked by scouts, but worked his way up through the minor leagues, getting better each year. He fashioned a great big league career.

Kevin had a great rookie season in 1986 as a hitting machine. We always felt like he was going to get two or three hits every game. In fact, he was one of only two players (the other was Bob Oliver, as I mentioned earlier) who had six hits in one game. Seitzer did that in 1987 against Boston. He also had two five-hit games, and numerous four-hit outings. He didn't have tremendous physical skills, but he got the very most out of the skills that he did have.

When Kevin showed that he could hit in the big leagues, and play defensively, he basically took George's spot at third, and Brett moved to first. Seitzer's progress was pretty much the catalyst for Brett moving over there.

FW: Kevin came to the Royals with a big splash. He got 200 hits during his rookie year and everyone thought he was going to be another George Brett. Seitzer was a terrific offensive player, but they had problems finding a position for him when he first got here. Finally he went to third and George moved to first.

The Royals got rid of him too soon. I really believe he would have been a great lifetime Royal had they kept him. He went on to prove himself as a very valuable major league player.

Paul Splittorff 1970-1984 Royals Hall of Fame

DM: Split has the same kind of a personality as Buzz. He was fun to be around and got a lot out of his ability. He worked hard, got an opportunity and made the most of it. He really had to work for his success, and he did. Nice guy, good personality, funny. He would kind of stir things up in the clubhouse, then back away and watch as everybody else got in trouble.

FW: Split is as good, genuine, true and dependable as any player or any person I have ever met in my life. A terrific pitcher, and looking back at the games that Split pitched, he pitched a lot of the very big games in Royals history. He is the winningest pitcher in club history with 166 victories. Paul brought a great dignity to the game by doing everything well. He did everything to give his team a chance to win. Took a lot of responsibility on himself for the game.

Paul Splittorff was probably more of a big game pitcher than people realized he was. He was very tough, very honest and very determined. If given a 100-pound weight and told to take it 100 yards down the field, some guys would find some help to get it down there, but Paul Splittorff would simply pick it up, put it on his back and begin to march, and he wouldn't quit marching until he had the 100-pound weight where it had to be.

Paul Splittorff has gone through life like that, and he approached broadcasting like that. He went out and went to work for a 1000-watt station, drove all over town interviewing high school football and basketball coaches, putting a show together and broadcasting high school games. He became a broadcaster like all the rest of us — by going out and paying his dues. He's turned himself into a terrific baseball and basketball announcer. I consider him a great friend and I always will. He's just someone very special.

Danny Tartabull 1987-1991

DM: Tartabull was very outgoing with an infectious smile. For the most part he was easy to get along with. He was always a very good home run and RBI guy who put up big numbers. If you can believe it, he played second base when he came up, and was then switched to the outfield. Danny was not that good defensively, but I'm not sure how hard he worked on his defense. He wasn't a good baserunner, either, but he could sure swing the bat. When you look at his raw numbers while he was here, he got the job done.

FW: Danny Tartabull never found his potential. He was a guy with a lot of talent who, for whatever reason, never seemed to want to work hard enough to realize his to the fullest.

U.L. Washington 1977-1984

DM: The first thing that sticks out in my mind about U.L., as it does with a lot of fans, is the toothpick he always had in his mouth. He came out of a small town in Oklahoma before spending some time at the Royals Baseball Academy in the early 1970s. He was kind of the unsung guy, an unheralded guy, on some of the championship teams, because of all the other stars. But like at catcher, if a team doesn't have a solid player at shortstop, it isn't going to win many championships.

U.L. was on those winning Royals teams and he kept improving both offensively and defensively. One thing I remember about U.L. is how he worked to improve from year to year; that says a lot about his abilities and about the man. He was a switch-hitter with decent tools. There really wasn't one thing that would stand out about U.L., and make you say, "Wow!" He eventually wanted to, and did, get into coaching. He has done a good job in that regard.

FW:U.L. Washington was just the opposite of Danny Tartabull. U.L. was tough. He couldn't be run out of a ballgame. U.L. Washington was a good offensive and good defensive player. He was a guy who made himself into a terrific major league player. He came out of the Royals Academy like Frank White did. Both times that George Brett homered off of Rich "Goose" Gossage (the 1980 playoffs and the "pine tar game") Washington was on base. In fact, both times there were two outs in the inning and he busted his tail down the line to beat out an infield single and kept the inning alive. That typified his game...whatever it took to win a ballgame, U.L. was willing to do.

John Wathan 1976-1985

DM: John, as a player, spent several seasons in the minor leagues for the Royals. On the player evaluations that the scouts fill out at the end of the season, for Wathan they put the simple designation of "NP," which stands for "No Prospect." Well, he was undaunted by that and he continued to work his tail off, slowly through each level. That designation of "NP" kept following him around. But he loved baseball, so he kept going.

When Whitey was here, the team needed a catcher, so they brought John up from the minor leagues. Whitey fell in love with him because of all the little things that Duke could do, along with his work ethic. He's a terrific person, which comes out right away. A player will endear himself to his manager if he has those attributes, and John did. He was the type of player who, even after he made it to the big leagues, continued to improve. He realized that getting to the big leagues was not the deal, it was staying in the big leagues. He worked his fanny off at every facet of the game. He holds the record for most stolen bases in a season by a catcher with 36. John's physical attributes don't make people think about a base stealing threat, but he worked at that part of his game. He was just a hard working guy.

John didn't have a lot of power, but he was a great contact hitter and a very good bunter who could play a lot of different positions. He was kind of a manager's dream, which is why he had a fairly long and productive career. We could also tell that he might make a good manager one day. He's done that. During the 1996 season he joined Fred and me in the booth. In fact, he's the only guy who has been a player, coach, manager, broadcaster and now a scout for the Royals — who is going to beat that record?

FW: The first time I ever met John Wathan was in Ft. Myers during spring training when he told me, "They'll have to tear this uniform off of me someday." That typified his career before he ever got going. He was a catcher who could really run. He could do everything. He played first base and the outfield, was a good offensive guy, could run the bases well, and was as good a student of the game as the Royals have ever had.

The Royals front office probably rushed John to become a manager, but he still responded by doing a good job. During one season under Wathan, 1989, the team won 92 games, which is more than they had won since 1980 and more than they have won in one season since. He was fired during the 1991 season. He should always be involved with the Royals in some way.

Frank White 1973-1990 Royals Hall of Fame

DM: Obviously, Frank was one of the best second basemen ever to play baseball. He had great range, a good arm, masterful on pop ups, made himself a good hitter, very well spoken off the field, nice to everybody, good to the fans. In return, the fans loved him. He had good rapport with them, good rapport with the press and just did all the right things on and off the field.

FW: Class, smooth, maybe the best second baseman to ever play the game. We watched him play and marveled at the things he could do defensively. Tough enough that he batted cleanup in the World Series when the Royals won it in 1985. He made himself into a good offensive player. Defensively, I don't think anybody has ever had the range that Frank White had.

The only guy we could ever compare him to probably would be Bill Mazeroski and even then that would be a difficult comparison. Frank had more range, but maybe Maz got rid of the ball quicker on the double play. Frank is either the best or one of the two best that ever played the position in the game. If a ball was headed up the middle or to the right side, Royal pitchers felt pretty good because they knew that Frank was there and Frank was probably going to get to it and make a play for them. Just an incredible talent.

Because of our common name, we have exchanged phone calls and suit cases and had a lot of laughs down through the years. I would often get a call a day for him on the road, and he got calls of mine. In 1997 when we were in Baltimore, my wife was with me, school had started, and our son, Joe, was sick. He called at six in the morning to see if he had to go to school. He got

Frank. Frank said, "Gee, I don't know Joe, you probably better call your dad." Because of the similarity of the name, I have always been close to Frank.

I remember the day Frank came to the big leagues in 1973. I was at the airport. I had gone out there to meet the team, and there was this young guy sitting there. I introduced myself, and it was Frank White; he had just been called up from Omaha. He was a shortstop and made his debut in Baltimore. My first impression of him was that he reminded me of Bambi around second base; he was so agile and he could jump and bound and run and do all these things. I looked at him and thought what an incredible athlete this guy is. They converted him to a second baseman. He actually started as a third baseman in the minor leagues.

Watching him play second base was like watching a concert or a great orchestra play. He conducted the game like an orchestra conductor at second base, the way he could do it, and he could reach notes we didn't think anybody could reach. He was great that way. Greatness is the only term to describe the way Frank White could play defense.

Willie Wilson 1976-1990

DM: Willie Wilson, who was a high school football star in New Jersey, was signed by the Royals because of his raw athletic ability. The big question on Willie was whether or not he could ever hit. There was no question about his speed and his ability to play defense. Becoming a switch-hitter really opened the door for Willie to be a great offensive player. His ability to get on base and put a tremendous amount of pressure on the other team's defense helped the Royals a ton. One scout said that "the Royals play more like a National League team than some of the National League teams, and any team in the American League." That was the running style and the pressure that players like Willie, Freddie, and Amos put on the opposing defenses. Everybody talks about how Brett and McRae always tried to take the extra base; well, Willie did it, and the rest of the guys did it. It was an infectious thing.

Willie was a beautiful runner and showed the way at 6-foot-3, with his long strides. Watching him go from first to third on a triple (133 in his career) or an inside-the-park home run (he had 13 in his career to become the Royals all-time leader), was as exciting an event as there was in baseball, with his sheer speed, trying to beat the relay throws. He was one of the keys to those great years for the Royals.

FW: Willie was a tremendous athlete. When he came to the big leagues they said that if he could just bounce the ball in the infield and beat out the throws, and hit .240, he would be a valuable player. In 1980 he led the league with 230 hits on the season. Then in 1982, he batted .332 and won a batting championship. So he obviously became a good offensive player. He got the base hit that wrapped up the American League Western Division in 1985, as he drove in the winning run for Kansas City in the 10th inning against Oakland.

He could simply go get the ball in centerfield. He was a terrific defensive player. Willie was also the best base runner the Royals have ever had in terms of stealing bases, going first to third, going first to home, things of that nature. He scored more than 100 runs twice in his career with the Royals, and is the all-time stolen base king for the Royals with 612 in his career. Willie was such a force on the bases, he could disrupt any game.

** Denotes still on Royals roster after 1998 season.*

All-Time Royals Team

	Denny	Fred
First Base	John Mayberry	John Mayberry
Second Base	Frank White	Frank White
Shortstop	Fred Patek	(tie) Fred Patek U.L. Washington
Third Base	George Brett	George Brett
Left Field	Willie Wilson	Willie Wilson
Center Field	Amos Otis	Amos Otis
Right Field	Al Cowens	Al Cowens
Designated Hitter	Hal McRae	Hal McRae
Catcher	Darrell Porter	Darrell Porter
Pitchers **(4 starters)**	Dennis Leonard Bret Saberhagen Paul Splittorff Steve Busby	Dennis Leonard Bret Saberhagen Paul Splittorff Steve Busby
(1 reliever)	(tie)Dan Quisenberry Jeff Montgomery	Dan Quisenberry

Matt Fulks, a native of Overland Park, Kansas, began broadcasting as a student at Lipscomb University in Nashville, Tennessee. His six-year stint as a play-by-play announcer (no, he wasn't in school all six years) included baseball and basketball games on the Bison Radio Network. He also spent two years during college as a weekend sports producer for Nashville's NBC affiliate, WSMV-TV.

Since graduating from Lipscomb, Matt has worked as sports director for WAKM radio in Franklin, Tennessee, and as a sports writer for *The Review-Appeal Newspaper*, where he covered high school, college, and professional sports. He is the author of *Behind the Stats: Tennessee's Coaching Legends,* and *The Sportscaster's Dozen: Off the Air with Southeastern Legends.*

Matt resides in Atlanta with his wife, Libby, their daughter, Helen, and their Doberman retriever, Alex.

01495
7 08850 11078 7